P 8 22
STRAND PRICE
5 00

D1070864

International Labor Migration

International Labor Migration

Foreign Workers and Public Policy

David Bartram
University of Reading, UK
Department of Sociology

© David Bartram 2005

All rights reserved. No reproduction, copy or transmission of this publication may be made without written permission.

No paragraph of this publication may be reproduced, copied or transmitted save with written permission or in accordance with the provisions of the Copyright, Designs and Patents Act 1988, or under the terms of any licence permitting limited copying issued by the Copyright Licensing Agency, 90 Tottenham Court Road, London W1T 4LP.

Any person who does any unauthorised act in relation to this publication may be liable to criminal prosecution and civil claims for damages.

The author has asserted his right to be identified as the author of this work in accordance with the Copyright, Designs and Patents Act 1988.

First published in 2005 by
PALGRAVE MACMILLAN
Houndmills, Basingstoke, Hampshire RG21 6XS and
175 Fifth Avenue, New York, N.Y. 10010
Companies and representatives throughout the world.

PALGRAVE MACMILLAN is the global academic imprint of the Palgrave Macmillan division of St. Martin's Press, LLC and of Palgrave Macmillan Ltd. Macmillan® is a registered trademark in the United States, United Kingdom and other countries. Palgrave is a registered trademark in the European Union and other countries.

ISBN-13: 978–1–4039–4674–4
ISBN-10: 1–4039–4674–4

This book is printed on paper suitable for recycling and made from fully managed and sustained forest sources.

A catalogue record for this book is available from the British Library.

Library of Congress Cataloging-in-Publication Data

Bartram, David, 1966–
    International labor migration : foreign workers and public policy / David Bartram.
        p. cm.
    Includes bibliographical references and index.
    ISBN 1–4039–4674–4
        1. Alien labor – Government policy. 2. Emigration and immigration – Government policy. I. Title.

HD6300.B37 2005
331.6'2—dc22   2004059169

10 9 8 7 6 5 4 3 2 1
14 13 12 11 10 09 08 07 06 05

Printed and bound in Great Britain by
Antony Rowe Ltd, Chippenham and Eastbourne.

Contents

List of Tables and Figures

Tables

Figures

Acknowledgments

As a student, I used to think that, when authors wrote lengthy passages acknowledging assistance and intellectual debts, they were essentially showing off. Having completed a book, I now know better: a project of this sort would have been impossible without the generosity of a large number of people.

My primary thanks go to Erik Olin Wright, Gay Seidman, and Alberto Palloni, who read the entire manuscript at an early stage. Other individuals read substantial portions and provided very useful feedback. Ezra Kopelowitz has been my "front line" reader, bravely slogging through initial drafts (in addition to sharing his office, his dog, and other tokens of collegiality and friendship). Mark J. Miller provided some much needed encouragement at a crucial stage. Ari Zolberg, Mark Gould, Erik Cohen, Michael Shalev, Richard Katz, Ehud Harari, Ephraim Kleiman, Ira Sharkansky, Yishai Yafe, Orly Levy, Beth Fussell, Maria Toyoda, Eytan Meyers, and Zeev Rosenhek all gave constructive critiques on various pieces of the argument. Roni Sanegor did some excellent research on the profitability of Israeli construction firms. Chikako Kashiwazaki made a key contribution by finding a crucial few pieces of data concerning the Japanese labor force. Of course I retain responsibility for any errors that remain.

Research support was provided first by a grant from the Social Science Research Council's program for Disciplines Under-represented in Near and Middle East Studies (with funds from the United States Information Agency). At a later stage, I received generous assistance from the M. David Blazouske Fund at the Hebrew University of Jerusalem's Faculty of Social Science. Assistance also came from the Vilas Foundation at the University of Wisconsin-Madison and the Nuffield Foundation. Ari Zolberg and Peter Benda arranged a very useful affiliation at the International Center for Migration, Ethnicity and Citizenship of the New School for Social Research; Rob Smith made possible a similar arrangement at Columbia University.

The third and fourth chapters draw from material previously published as articles: "Labor Migration Policy and the Governance of the Construction Industry in Israel and Japan." *Politics & Society* 32(2): 131–70, © 2004 by Sage Publications, reprinted by permission of Sage Publications; "Japan and Labor Migration: Theoretical and Methodological Implications of Negative Cases," *International Migration Review*, 34(1): 5–32, 2000; and "Foreign Workers in Israel: History and Theory," *International Migration Review*, 32(2): 303–25, 1998. My editor at Palgrave Macmillan, Briar Towers, made the publishing process remarkably straightforward and painless. Howard Sacks and George McCarthy played key roles in my early development as a scholar and continue to be important sources of support. Finally, I am grateful for the support I have received from my family, especially Sharon and Peter Bartram and Karyn Aviani.

1
Introduction

In the film *Bladerunner*, the ostensible villains are a rogue group of "replicants," substitutes for human beings who perform menial labor on another planet and are forbidden to set foot on Earth. Replicants are designed to live and work for four years and then to die, to be replaced by others. This particular group have decided to rebel against their fate and have stolen onto Earth to discover the secrets that will allow them to prevent their "early" death and to live as ordinary human beings.

The premise of the film – the existence of "replicants" who perform menial tasks and then expire – is the ultimate *Gastarbeiter* fantasy.[1] The replicants free "real" humans from unpleasant but necessary work, but they are not allowed membership in the society of human beings. They die before they can become fully aware of their condition and develop the means to challenge it. And because they are not real humans but mere "replicants," there need be no moral qualms about treating them in this fashion. If West Germany had acquired replicants instead of Turks and Italians, everything might have gone much more smoothly. Of course, in science fiction as in life, something goes awry and the replicants refuse to accept their fate passively. Nevertheless, the fantasy remains a powerful one for many in advanced capitalist countries who must reconcile citizens' aspirations for the good life with the continuing desire for inexpensive labor.

One underlying message of the film – a message that is even sharper in Phillip K. Dick's *Do Androids Dream of Electric Sheep?*, the novel that inspired the film – is that the fantasy itself is immoral. Many Western policymakers have known this for a long time, at least since the Swiss author Max Frisch declared, "We called for workers, and there came human beings" (Frisch 1967: 100; cf. Zolberg 1992). But more important than the fantasy's immorality is the fact that it simply does not work – and

1

this too is well known, after the multitude of failed efforts since 1973 to induce guestworkers to return to their "home" countries. "Temporary" worker migrations almost always result in permanent settlement in the "host" country.

Thus countries that have more recently turned to foreign labor as guestworkers have done so reluctantly, precisely because there is widespread awareness concerning the disadvantages, both moral and practical. And it is common for these countries to discover that they cannot avoid the disadvantages that have accrued in their predecessors' experience. On the other hand, a number of advanced capitalist countries have followed a different path when confronted with labor shortages, refraining from large-scale use of foreign labor – belying a widespread scholarly perception that importing labor is an inevitable part of capitalist development.

This book attempts to explain the variation in extent of use of foreign labor in capitalist countries.[2] The approach offered is new in two main respects. First, and most importantly, it makes variation the explicit focus of a study of labor migration. Existing approaches, perhaps implicitly assuming that labor migration is inevitable, try simply to explain why migration happens. That question is incomplete, however: we must ask, why it happens on a large-scale in some places but not in others. Answering the former question properly requires taking the latter seriously. Thus a key innovation here is to consider "negative cases" of immigration, i.e., countries that have *not* received significant numbers of foreign workers. Second, I relate the question of labor migration to the political economy literature on capitalist development and the state. Labor migration is very much a matter of economic and social policy for the receiving country. Explaining policy choices requires finding the proper theoretical context for framing those choices. A fruitful context for understanding state policy regarding foreign workers is the comparative political economy of development. The issue of foreign labor is not only a question of migration, of individuals changing the location of their residence and employment. It is, more importantly, a question of capitalist development, of the structure and trajectory of capitalist economies (Öncü 1990). Regarding receiving countries, this connection has seldom been explored systematically, despite its intuitive appeal.[3]

My main argument is that labor migration flows reach significant dimensions when the receiving country state does not have the ability to inhibit or constrain rent-seeking behavior on the part of private sector interests. There are alternative solutions for addressing perceived labor shortages, but those solutions require inducing employers to make choices that are often difficult and not necessarily the most profitable. Importing foreign workers is the path of least resistance, the cheap and easy solution from employers' point of view – though from other points of view importing labor is costly on many levels, especially in the long term. Receiving country governments can only frustrate this preference if they work from a position of strength vis-à-vis capital. Analyzing governments' policy choices regarding foreign workers, then, requires identifying the institutional foundations of state autonomy and strength regarding this specific policy area as well as investigating the particular historical contexts in which decisions are made.

The rest of this chapter has four main goals. First, I specify the fundamental problem the book will address. Second, I show why there is a need for a new theoretical approach to that question. Third, I lay out the basic features of the argument I develop in succeeding chapters. And fourth, I discuss the research strategy, in particular the underlying methodology and the logic behind the case comparison that comprises the bulk of the empirical analysis.

Specification of the problem

This book analyzes international labor migration flows in the post-1970 period. Taking Israel and Japan as two exemplary cases, I ask, how can we explain the existence of significant new flows in this period? The issue is not simply why some countries have many foreign workers. The question is, more productively, why are there many foreign workers in some countries and only relatively few foreign workers in other countries? Thus, empirically, why does Israel have so many foreign workers (as a percentage of its labor force), and why has Japan had so few for so long? This section elaborates on three important features of the main research question: first, its focus on the post-1970 period; second, its concern with the migrations themselves and not the process of settlement; and third, its explicit focus on variation.

Why post-1970?

The process of introducing foreign labor into Europe in the postwar period followed relatively little policy deliberation. To the extent that debate occurred, foreign worker programs were generally seen as a win-win endeavor for "hosts" and "guests" alike (Miller 1997; Papademetriou and Martin 1991); even unions were appeased without much difficulty (e.g., in Germany – see Castles 1992; Herbert 1990; Rist 1978).[4] Potential migrants were to benefit from their First-World wages, and receiving countries welcomed the extra labor power as they recovered from population losses of the war and as their growing economies generated employment demands that citizens were unwilling to satisfy. The German government in 1964 held a festive celebration in honor of the one-millionth guestworker to enter the country and presented him with a motorcycle (Bendix 1990). And at least one economist (Kindleberger 1967) wrote that the unlimited availability of labor power was the most important factor allowing for sustained rapid economic growth in the first place: countries that either had large labor reserves or imported it grew more quickly than those whose supplies of labor were limited (especially Britain and the Scandinavian countries).

The apparent success of foreign worker programs and the positive mood surrounding their initial implementation differentiated this early postwar period from the caution, pessimism, and ambiguous benefits concerning foreign labor that mark the post-1970 era. The economic recession that followed the 1973 oil crisis typically resulted in decreased demand for labor and is commonly cited as the reason many countries stopped recruitment. But at least one country (Sweden) had stopped recruiting new workers well before the economic downturn, for other reasons that remained clear even when the revival of growth made recruitment plausible once again (Hammar 1985; see also Hansen 1993). Even in Germany, there was a perception that the oil crisis was being used as a pretext for a foreign labor policy shift that was already emerging, but for different reasons (Bendix 1990). This shift was driven primarily by worries about the difficulty of integrating large numbers of immigrants. Concerns about the long-term impact of foreign workers were already being voiced in official and academic circles in Germany as early as 1966 (Bendix 1990), and it is likely that these debates were taking place in other countries as well, and not just in countries that already had many foreign workers. Thus the fact that other receiving countries stopped recruitment after the first oil shock does not diminish the possibility that they might have done so even if the recessions had not reduced demand for labor: this decision was driven by a major shift in European democratic politics, not just economics.

The original conception of guestworkers, particularly in the postwar period, relied on two related components: rotation and "economic buffers" (*konjunkturpuffer*). Rotation meant that no single worker would stay in the host country for a long time: he or she would return "home" after a specified period and, if the host country required it, would be replaced by other foreigners. The idea of a buffer drew on this notion of rotation (which in fact was frequently abandoned) and proposed that, when an economic boom ended and the host country no longer required replacement workers, the whole business would stop and the entire population of foreigners would leave. Several factors combined to frustrate these intentions (see e.g., Castles 1986; Castles *et al.* 1984; Martin and Miller 1980). First, many foreign workers had no real incentive to return to poverty and unemployment (or underemployment) in their country of origin. Second, their employers had no desire to lose experienced workers and to train replacements. Third, host country governments had begun allowing workers to send for their families, in part to avoid the perceived dangers of a concentrated population of young single male foreigners. And fourth, host country governments discovered that efforts to induce workers to leave against their will were legally complicated, very costly, and not very effective.

These factors underlay a process whereby temporary guestworkers slowly became permanent settlers in the receiving country. As noncitizens, and typically ethnically distinct, they became resident minority groups facing distinct relative disadvantages. Several things quickly became clear to policymakers and citizens alike. First, many European receiving countries were ill prepared to deal with minority groups, especially from diverse cultures in the Third World (though these European countries had not been as homogenous as some liked to think). Second, the experience had, it seemed, permanently transformed "their" societies in ways that many citizens found unpalatable. Third, there were tangible and intangible costs associated with the presence of the foreign populations, especially when the foreigners began making successful demands on Europe's already expensive welfare states. In short, it was no longer clear, at least to the "hosts," that importing labor was an optimal solution to certain economic problems. Public opposition to immigration also became an important political factor, especially once political parties began organizing constituencies around the issue (Schain 1990).

Labor migrations that have begun since roughly 1970, then – such as the entry of large numbers of workers into Israel since 1993 – are a different phenomenon from migrations that began before 1970.[5] Gerschenkron (1962) established that the explanation for "late development" had to be different from the explanations for development in countries such as the US and Britain. The same point holds for labor migration. Less developed countries do not see their future in the past of the advanced countries: the environment had changed precisely because of this history, and therefore the phenomenon of labor migration changes as well. This is an important distinction, and its significance is that my theoretical claims in this book are not meant to apply to the earlier period, e.g., to the cases of Turks in Germany or Algerians in France. Those claims may apply, but I will make no attempt to investigate whether this is the case, and I suspect it is not. Additional reasons for focusing only on the later period will become clear once we discuss the specific theoretical claims I make, later in this chapter.

Why migration?

To explain the presence of foreign labor in a receiving country at a certain time, we can identify two aspects of the problem: first, foreign workers came, and then they (i.e., many of them) stayed. The explanations for these two parts of the problem are different (Böhning 1984; Massey *et al.* 1987; Piore 1979). I focus only on the first issue.

There is widespread agreement that labor migration flows result in permanent settlement of the so-called "guests." Many countries, and certainly most advanced capitalist countries, have found it very difficult to induce foreign workers to leave once the latter have begun to settle. The legal and political constraints of democratic countries make large-scale deportation difficult (Hollifield 1992).[6] As discussed above, some foreign workers are not likely to leave, even in the event of economic recession and unemployment: instead, they are very likely to settle permanently and to facilitate the entry of their families and friends, who also will then settle permanently. Not all foreign workers stay: many guestworkers did leave Germany in the postwar period (Martin 1997). But those who stay are numerous enough to constitute a significant population of foreigners in many advanced countries. Martin exaggerates, but not outrageously, when he refers to "an iron law of labor immigration: there is nothing more permanent than temporary workers" (1994: 84). In most cases, in particular in the period before a country has significant numbers of foreign workers, the only policy question worth asking is whether to admit such workers or not: once they are present, the opportunities for effective policy intervention are sharply reduced.

The analysis of the migration itself, then, is analytically (not just temporally) prior to the analysis of the process of settlement (cf. Massey *et al.* 1998). When we want to explain the presence of foreign labor in a particular country, we must start by explaining the flow itself. We know that settlement of a significant number of such workers is almost inevitable, at least in democratic countries. The real "action," then, is in the migration, not in the settlement process. If it were possible to reverse a labor migration flow, then part of the variation in foreign worker prevalence would derive from the extent to which particular countries succeed in reducing their foreign worker populations. Given the inevitability of settlement, this variation derives almost entirely from the migration itself (again, at least in democratic countries).

Why variation?

In at least one respect, studies of international labor migration have been characterized by a significant blind spot: scholars have for the most part studied only instances where labor migration has actually occurred and have ignored instances where it has not occurred even though it could reasonably have been expected.[7] The result is that they have developed theories that are not well suited for distinguishing positive from negative cases. Paying explicit attention to variation in the field of labor migration should allow a significant advance in theorizing about its causes.

In most cases, labor migration involves low-skilled and low-wage workers. As such, foreign workers are a particular solution to problems of labor supply at the lower end of the labor market. But these problems are sometimes solved in other ways, e.g., allowing wages to rise, which can attract citizen workers, give companies incentives to increase productivity, and/or result in price increases in goods and services such that demand and production decrease. Foreign labor and citizen labor are often said to be complementary, not competitive: citizens refuse to take jobs typically held by foreigners. This statement, however, is too static and assumes that the conditions of such employment are held constant: low wages, lack of job security, and unpleasant work. It is precisely the point here that these conditions are subject to change, partly in response to government policy (including a policy of refusing to allow the hiring of foreign workers) (Martin and Taylor 2001). Governments can provide incentives for companies to modernize production and use a more skilled work force. Firms can (be encouraged to) relocate production to low-wage areas, at home or abroad, at least for tradable goods. If use of local labor leads to higher prices for particular goods and services, consumers can accustom themselves to consuming less (landscaping, valet parking, etc.), so that the demand for such labor declines. Cutting welfare entitlements can reduce or hold down reservation wages. And governments can try in other ways to mobilize inactive citizens into the labor force. There are a number of different ways in which labor shortages might be resolved; turning to foreign labor is just one solution (cf. Bourguignon *et al.*, 1977).

When we have specified the problem in this way, it becomes our task to explain how and why various countries (or perhaps economic sectors) have solved labor supply problems in different ways – noting first that importing workers has been a very common solution. What then becomes interesting are the patterns and the ways in which different countries make different choices concerning the various options.

Addressing the issue of labor migration properly thus requires an expanded framework that incorporates "negative cases," i.e., instances in which countries have mainly used other approaches to ensure that employers do not lack the necessary labor.[8] There has been much discussion in the literature about the rapid increase in international migration and the increasing inability of advanced capitalist, liberal states to control their borders. Forces of globalization are said to be breaking down barriers to the movement not just of goods and capital but of people as well. The increase in movement is impressive, but we should not forget that the vast majority of the world's population stays put and that, from the outside, the rich countries appear remarkably closed (Brubaker 1994; Freeman 1994). Migration is in some respects the exception (Zolberg 1999). It should be a basic methodological axiom that if we want to know why some countries become destinations for large populations of foreign workers, we also have to know why other countries have experienced only small influxes of such workers. I return to this point in the discussion of research strategy below.

The need for a new approach

The previous section forms the basis for the conclusion that available discussions of international migration leave gaps in our understanding of why labor migration occurs to some destinations but not to others. If the theories presumed to explain labor migration to other destinations also invoke factors that characterize countries where numbers of migrant workers are small, then clearly something is amiss with those theories. Neoclassical theory, for example, emphasizes development gaps (especially as expressed in wage differences) between sending and receiving countries as the main factor affecting decisions of income-maximizing individuals. Several wealthy countries have very few immigrants, however – a fact that neoclassical theory seems incapable of explaining. Zolberg raises the closely related question of "why *more* [migration] was *not* taking place" (1999: 72) given these premises.

A similar analysis can be applied to other schools of thought concerning the causes of migration. Japan (and probably other negative cases as well) poses a challenge to Piore's dual labor market theory of migration (1979). Japan is recognized for having a highly dualistic economy and labor market (Pempel 1978), the key factor that leads to demand for immigrant workers in this view. The point here – one suggested by a consideration of negative cases – is that while dualism might lead to employer demand for immigrant workers, there is no guarantee that that demand will actually be satisfied: employers sometimes go hungry (cf. Lim 1992; Weiner 1995). I am not prepared to support empirical statements about the issue of economic dualism in other negative cases. However, if Piore's analysis of dualism is substantially correct, then it would be surprising to encounter an advanced capitalist country that did not embody a significant economic dualism. The argument is that dualism – and in particular the development of a secondary labor market in which employers find it necessary to turn to immigrants – is a response to the inevitable swings of the business cycle: employers are unwilling to make firm commitments to some of their workers, especially when employment legislation makes it difficult to retract those commitments when recessions necessitate shedding costs. Indeed, Piore's analysis seems to rest on the notion that dualism of this sort is a universal feature of advanced capitalist societies. It is not clear why Japan, Finland, and other negative cases would be exempt from this dynamic. In methodological terms, we would want to beware of trying to explain a variable with reference to a constant.

World-systems theory raises some similar issues. The key factor leading to migration in this view is incorporation into the capitalist world-system, e.g., through the formation of ties of trade, investment, colonization, etc. between core and peripheral countries (Sassen 1988).[9] These ties have two significant consequences: they disrupt local - "survival strategies," and the ties themselves constitute "bridges" that people exploit as a way of gaining access to core countries (where demand for cheap immigrant labor arises in a way not terribly different from the process described by dual labor market theory). Thus Britain's colonial legacy creates opportunities for people to move from these (former) colonies to Britain; likewise for more recent relationships between the US and, say, South Korea.

The difficulty is of the same type we have already encountered: the explanation for migration invokes factors that also characterize countries that have few immigrants. Japan's experience is the most relevant here: as a regional (not to mention global) economic superpower, Japan has long had ties of the type described by this explanation. These ties are undoubtedly a central factor in accounting for the immigration of those people who have moved to Japan: I do not wholly dismiss the value of world-systems theory here. But the problem is that, with a world-systems understanding of migration, we would have to wonder why the level of immigration to Japan is not much higher than it is in reality. World-systems theory helps us understand why immigrants to a certain place come from some countries and not from others, but it doesn't seem to clarify why some countries have considerably more immigrants than others.

Another theoretical approach worth consideration here concerns attempts to explain features of migration policy (e.g., Hollifield 2000; Portes 1997; Zolberg 1999, 1993). This is a promising school of thought and the one most likely to benefit from consideration of negative cases. As matters stand, however, scholars concerned with policy have constructed questions in a way that obscures the existence of negative cases. Typically, the questions asked resemble the following: how do we explain the significant increase in international migration in the postwar period? In other words, why do advanced industrial countries maintain relatively open immigration policies? We can accept the premise of these questions in its own terms – there has been an increase in international migration in the postwar period – while still understanding how that premise presents an incomplete picture of the relevant reality that this increase has been uneven, occurring in some countries but not in others.[10]

The difficulty is apparent in the otherwise insightful work of Gary Freeman (1995). Freeman argues that liberal democracies maintain open immigration policies because of a central feature of interest politics: the interests that benefit from immigration (mainly employers) are small and more easily organized, while the interests that suffer from immigration (mainly labor) are diffuse and more difficult to coordinate. This interesting argument is nonetheless challenged by the need to explain why some liberal democracies do *not* maintain open immigration policies. Freeman tells us what many immigration countries have in common (liberal democracy, with opportunity structures that benefit certain kinds of interests over others), but the problem is that this feature is also shared by some countries that have few immigrants. A further difficulty concerns the fact that immigration policies change over time, while the factors highlighted by Freeman would appear not to do so.

Other migration scholars as well have offered analyses that take politics and the state seriously (e.g., Calavita 1984; Fitzgerald 1996; García y Griego 1992; Hollifield 1992; Weiner 1993). In each case, however, the lack of attention to negative cases or to the issue of variation means that it is difficult to generalize these arguments successfully. There is much to learn from, say, Fitzgerald's institutionalist approach or García y Griego's attention to the autonomy of the state. But developing these ideas requires framing the right question in a comparative empirical investigation.

It is likely that at least some of the insights of each of these theoretical approaches can be preserved by adopting an important methodological principle advocated by Ragin (1987, 2000): appreciation of "multiple and conjunctural causation." Multiple causation refers to the fact that different instances of a phenomenon might have different causes: it is not necessary to presume a unitary causal process. Thus, even if not all economic gaps between countries lead to migration flows, we need not abandon the compelling notion that such gaps play some sort of role in many migrations. Conjunctural causation denotes that certain factors can lead to an outcome only in combination with other factors – an insight that is not easily accommodated by a traditional variable-oriented approach in which variables compete with one another to explain a certain proportion of variation. Thus, as above, economic dualism might lead to migration only when combined with some other factor – say, a clientelist political regime that privileges certain kinds of private interests over others (to invoke Freeman, without assuming that such regimes characterize all liberal democracies).

The basic argument

The theoretical argument I intend to make about international labor migration flows has two main components. The first is that variation in labor migration results not from ineluctable economic and demographic forces but from political processes that mediate economic and demographic pressures which are thus central to the explanation of labor migration itself. The second is that political processes relating to labor migration are themselves subject to systematic variation, in ways not terribly different from political processes in other economic policy realms. This section discusses these arguments in turn.

Politics as a central variable

As discussed above, much of the explicitly theoretical writing on labor migration is economistic, invoking economic variables that are implicitly viewed as "natural" or "given." Most of the attention is directed towards economic phenomena such as wage disparities, reported labor shortages, investment flows, etc. The theoretical account I will offer takes issue with this type of approach. The effects of economic and demographic realities are in part contingent on political factors: when governments can control immigration to a reasonable extent, labor shortages only raise the question of labor migration when those who suffer from labor shortages have the power to get the issue onto the political agenda. One of my main arguments here is that we must understand labor migration as the outcome of a process wherein actors strive to advance their interests, in the context of structures that issued from previous struggles: that is, more simply, we must take politics seriously.

There are many highly insightful analyses of particular migration flows that do take politics seriously, and the previous paragraph does not assert that the study of labor migration as a whole is devoid of serious engagement with political economy. Frequently, scholars who relate migration and politics focus on issues of immigration control. But some analysts (e.g., Cornelius *et al.* 1994) have been so concerned about the failure of states to control immigration that they fail to ask, what is the role of the state in starting it? In any case, my contention is that existing *theories* of labor migration are economistic, even if many empirical studies are not. This is especially true of the neoclassical approach (e.g., Lee 1966; Todaro 1969), which in turn informs most of the empirical analyses that do *not* take politics seriously.

The problem could be construed – unproductively, as we will see – as a matter of not exploring the prior causes of the economic variables that, according to neoclassical theory, cause labor migration itself. For example, if labor migration results primarily from wage and employment opportunity gaps between sending and receiving countries, we might be interested in understanding how political factors help create those wage and employment opportunity gaps. But this would not affect the assertion that the development gaps themselves are the primary cause of labor migration. In other words, political factors are merely "upstream" variables that affect labor migration only indirectly.

Although political factors are indeed relevant to labor migration in this sense, I make a further and more fundamental claim, i.e., that political factors should play a direct role in a theoretical explanation of labor migration (cf. Cohen 1987). There are two parts to this claim. First, insofar as labor migration is a matter of state policy in the receiving country, politics is a crucial determining factor in the way various players respond to the economic and demographic pressures that, in the absence of government controls, would typically lead to labor migration. While most receiving country governments do not have absolute control over immigration of any kind, the control they do exercise is very significant (e.g., Miller 1994; Zolberg 1999).

Second, political factors are usefully conceived as endogenous variables because labor migration – itself a result in part of political factors – has feedback effects on the structure of a country's economy and political processes, such that earlier decisions on whether to permit (or restrict) the importation of labor help determine the economic and political variables that create pressures for more (or less) foreign labor at later points in time (cf. Castles and Kosack 1985). Importing cheap labor facilitates the survival of industries and production methods that depend on cheap (foreign) labor. It can also create and strengthen political forces that benefit from the use of foreign labor, such that those forces typically push for expanding its use. The same point holds for the decision *not* to allow large-scale labor immigration: preventing immigration can be part of a state-led initiative to induce changes that mitigate the "necessity" of foreign labor.

If political factors had only an indirect relationship to labor migration, we could pay attention to them as upstream variables that eventually affect the process that really concerns us. But this would not amount to a compelling critique of existing theories themselves. If, on the other hand, politics is central to the process of labor migration itself, then such a critique is warranted. Political processes *interact* with demographic and economic processes; analysis cannot fruitfully attend to the latter to the exclusion of the former.

Systematic variation in political processes

Knowing that political factors are important in the process of labor migration would not take us far beyond existing empirical analyses of particular migrations, analyses that already document the role of political forces in the specific histories they tell. It will be more compelling to develop a general argument identifying and explaining systematic variation in the way those processes contribute to the process of migration. This is the main ambition of the book, though it is limited in these terms to a suggestive two-case comparison. In other words, I will argue that the variation in extent of use of foreign labor is explained in significant part by the institutional and organizational structure of the receiving country's state.[11]

To begin to specify the theoretical argument here, we may recall a point made earlier, i.e., that foreign labor is not just a matter of migration but of different capitalist development trajectories. At a very broad level, development consists of accumulation and structural transformation, as a result of which its citizens become more productive workers and command more purchasing power. Large proportions of the population develop aspirations for well-paying jobs that provide a so-called "middle class" life; some even insist on jobs that involve pleasant, satisfying work. Capitalist economies, however, apparently continue to produce large numbers of low-paid, unpleasant jobs, only to find that there are fewer citizen workers willing to accept them, a choice

facilitated by expanding welfare safety nets. The resulting labor shortages are widely seen as the primary reason advanced capitalist countries
turn to foreign labor. Foreign workers take the menial, low-status, low-
paid jobs that citizens typically spurn and thus make it possible for these
"low-end" firms to survive without relocation abroad (Piore 1979).

The problem with this picture is that it is only one possible trajectory
of advanced capitalist development. Faced with an incipient labor shortage, policymakers in advanced countries have other options, besides
cheap foreign labor. If imported labor is the "low road" of advanced
capitalism, the "high road" involves minimizing the extent to which
development produces low-end jobs. We identified components of this
alternative path above: increasing worker productivity (and therefore
wages, usually), in part through government incentives to upgrade productive processes; and, for tradables, offshore (re)location of production
processes that cannot be run profitably in a high-wage environment.[12]
Of course no country has succeeded in completely eliminating low-level
work, nor does it seem possible to do so; the high road is an ideal type,
as is the low road of cheap foreign labor.[13] But the distinction is worth
making, given the large amount of variation in the extent to which
different countries have integrated foreign labor into their workforces.

The puzzle, then, is extensive use of foreign labor versus its functional
substitutes. To begin to explicate its relationship to causal factors, we
need to discuss three common features of foreign worker initiatives. All
three features bolster the conclusion that the guestworker option is
often perceived as highly problematic for the host society. The first has
to do with the fact that the "guestworker" model leads to permanent
settlement. The real point here is that the importation of guestworkers
is often "unwanted immigration" (cf. Joppke 1999). The guestworker
model has been especially common in (though not exclusive to) countries characterized by an ethno-nationalist conception of social
membership – hence the reluctance simply to permit immigration
of individuals with the presumption of eventual full membership
(cf. Zolberg 1987). Permanent settlement of guestworkers is thus perceived as a threat to the host nation's ability to preserve its "community
of character" (Walzer 1983) when that character is rooted in ethno-
nationalism (as in Israel and Japan, among many others).

The second feature is that foreign labor typically involves significant
externalities: costs associated with its use that are not borne by its
employers. The settlement of foreign workers in the receiving country
typically results in the creation of distinct minority groups. Through no
fault of their own, these communities often create or constitute – at least

from the point of view of their "hosts" – social problems that must be solved through government action and, therefore, government budgets. Settlement is unanticipated, undesired, and nevertheless inevitable, and foreign workers are typically concentrated in ghettos that embody problems common in ghettos everywhere: most notable are inferior education and social isolation, which help reproduce the disadvantaged position of the new minority group(s). Over time this stratification becomes a problem not only for the minorities themselves but for the larger society, as the immigrants and their descendants become part of "us" rather than remaining simply as "them" and as the immigrants themselves become politically active (Miller 1981). One need consider only briefly the history of American race relations to appreciate the magnitude of this sort of problem: Martin and Miller assert that "foreign workers have given rise to a European variant of what Gunnar Myrdal termed 'the American dilemma' " (Martin and Miller 1980: 328).

The third feature relates to the fact that legal foreign workers typically are given permits that tie them to a particular employer. This politically determined restriction allows employers to pay workers less than the workers could otherwise get in the open labor market (cf. Cohen 1987; Miles 1987). This lowering of wages (relative to a competitive rate) for some firms results in what is known as a quota profit for the employer: the decreased wage bill creates additional profits that depend on the number of permit workers an employer can acquire from the government, when the overall number of permits available is limited (Amir 1999). If permits are unequally distributed (say, in consequence of political connections), those who succeed in acquiring permits for foreign workers would see their production costs decline relative to those of producers relying on citizen labor. The market price of the product would not decline by as much, and the firms with access to foreign workers would enjoy increased profits. The excess profit mechanism is especially relevant to sectors, like construction, where product prices are less elastic than prices for other types of goods. If a contractor can sell a house at a demand-determined "market price" that has only a weak relation to production costs, then much of the expense saved on labor becomes extra profit for the contractor.

These extra profits deriving from employment of foreign labor are usefully conceptualized as rents.[14] They derive from access to government concessions (employment permits) to a scarce commodity (foreign labor). The same point holds concerning externalities: to the extent that the prices of certain products do not reflect the entire range of costs associated with their production, the demand for them is higher and, therefore, the profits for producers are higher as well. Taxpayers in effect subsidize these profits for producers when governments provide access to cheap foreign labor and pick up some of the costs associated with its use.[15] The additional profits can be characterized as rents. The subsidy character of these rents is reinforced when the tax burden is borne primarily by middle-class earners and employers are predominantly upper class or bourgeoisie.

So a typical foreign worker program involves, first, unwanted immigration; second, externalized costs met by governments and taxpayers; and third, extra (quota) profits that emerge from the fact that work permits (and workers) are a scarce commodity. The last two points, in particular, combine to lead us to the conclusion that foreign worker programs are an area of government policy that is fertile territory for rent-seeking.

This point is significant because it helps us connect the question of policy variation in (potential) receiving countries with questions addressed by the comparative political economy of development. The research question is then usefully put: what kind of state typically facilitates rent-seeking via implementation of foreign worker programs? And what kind of state is more likely to follow an alternative path, the high road of wage/productivity increases and offshoring of low-productivity work, such that foreign labor is not "necessary" to the same extent as in other countries?

Posing the question this way thus allows us to connect concerns about labor migration with the literature on capitalist development and the state. Evans (1995) opposes the developmental state to the "predatory" state. In the latter, state power is used primarily to extract resources from the society for the personal benefit of the rulers. There is little or no rationalized bureaucratic capacity for governance beyond keeping order (if even that), and the lack of ties to the dominant social class mean there are few constraints on the arbitrary actions of government officials. Few if any developed capitalist countries have a state of this type. A more appropriate contrast to the developmental state in the present context draws on a refinement to Evans' typology suggested by Wright (1996). When there is a high degree of embeddedness between the state and civil society but a weakly rationalized – or simply weak – bureaucracy, we may speak of a "bourgeois clientelist state." Such a state facilitates rent-seeking, but because of the ties between government officials and the dominant class, elite groups as well as government officials frequently use state power for their own self-aggrandizement.

Given the opportunities for rent-seeking associated with introducing foreign labor, my argument is that in the post-1970 period foreign worker initiatives are more likely to be adopted in a country with a bourgeois clientelist state than in a country with a developmental state. A crucial piece of the explanation of labor migration, then, is that the state in the receiving country in question does not have the capacity or the structural characteristics necessary to induce or facilitate the various structural economic changes that can minimize the demand for and use of foreign labor. Instead, the state is a vehicle for rent-seeking, either on the part of government officials or (more typically) of employers, through the importation of foreign labor. This point builds on Freeman's argument (1995) concerning clientelism in immigration policy; it differs from Freeman's discussion insofar as I find that neither clientelism nor use of foreign labor is an unvarying element of democratic advanced industrial societies. Again, an explicit focus on variation should enhance theory-building efforts.

It should now be clear why this argument applies only to the more recent period as I have defined it. Part of a state's capacity to resist rent-seeking consists of the ability to recognize that it is occurring – or, in this case, at least to recognize that foreign labor involves significant externalities. While this recognition may have occurred in various places earlier than 1970, it seems clear that most relevant policymakers in the receiving countries had a firm grasp of the associated problems by the early 1970s. As long as the dominant perception was that foreign labor programs were "win-win" for essentially everyone concerned (as discussed above), there could be no reason to expect policymakers even to attempt to adopt an alternative solution. The lesson that it would not be possible to send home the "guests" when they were no longer needed was especially damaging to this perception and reinforced the notion that the quick fix of foreign labor involved serious long-term costs. It would therefore be difficult to establish a connection before roughly 1970 between labor migration policy and a state's relationship to rent-seeking. In other words, I am not claiming that the guestworker initiative in West Germany grew out of an alleged weakness of the German state; likewise, only the temporal distinction proposed here will allow us to reconcile my theoretical claims with the fact that French immigration policy was constructed largely in the ministries and not in the Parliament (Freeman 1979).

There are several reasons why we should expect to find this connection in the more recent period, however. First, because of the externalities associated with the importation of labor, it would be surprising to find government officials – at least those who are not already pawns of private interest groups – who would embrace the idea of foreign labor because they believe it will benefit the entire society. In the post-1970 period, when we encounter a government decision to allow a new labor migration flow, we should attribute that decision to one or more of the following factors. First, government policymakers *are* already pawns of private interest groups that favor importing labor because those groups stand to benefit from it. Second, government policymakers are able to implement policies that advance their own private interests, and their own interests are advanced by a policy of importing labor. Third, policymakers really want to pursue policies that would in some sense benefit broad sectors of the country, but they function in an institutional and organizational environment that inhibits adopting and implementing such policies. (Policymakers may have other reasons for implementing guestworker programs as well – this point is discussed later in this chapter.) In all three cases what is at issue is the structure of the state. In the first two cases, structural factors facilitate the actions of private groups and policymakers, respectively, who are seeking mainly to advance their own interests. In the third case, structural factors inhibit the actions of policymakers (and perhaps other interested parties) who can be said to care about the welfare of the country as a whole. These are mainly analytical differences, and to the extent that they are substantive as well, we should expect that the different cases will coexist.

On the other hand, when we encounter an advanced capitalist country that has relatively small numbers of foreign workers, despite facing some or all of the economic and demographic pressures said to lead to labor migration elsewhere, we should expect to find explicit government-led initiatives to pursue solutions that reduce or bypass those pressures. This is not a simple matter; in fact it is no simpler than government-led structural transformation, for the simple reason that it *constitutes* structural transformation, at least within particular economic sectors. Describing the connection between state structures and low numbers of foreign workers therefore involves specifying the relationship between state structures and industrial transformation, a subject that has concerned social scientists now for some time.

Briefly, numerous scholars argue that the most important factor contributing to successful industrial transformation is a rationalized bureaucratic state employing officials who can develop long-term perspectives by virtue of being insulated from politicians and private interest groups and their short-term interests (e.g., Evans 1995; Johnson 1982; Wade 1990). Major economic policy decisions are made by high-level bureaucrats, not by politicians. Beyond simply securing the conditions for the operation of efficient markets, policymakers in the developmental state set economic goals and then manipulate or bypass markets in order to achieve those goals. In such an environment, policymakers will find it easier to induce the structural transformations necessary to minimize the reproduction and proliferation of undesirable jobs and, therefore, the "necessity" of importing cheap foreign labor. One of the main consequences of this mode of policymaking is that opportunities for rent-seeking are relatively diminished, in relation to foreign labor as well as other fields. The state pursues a more purposeful and coherent approach to economic policy and attempts to ensure that government resources are used more efficiently and "wisely," i.e., not simply as largesse for private individuals; as Amsden puts it (1989), the state must ensure that quids are given only in return for meaningful quos. Of course opportunities for capturing "unearned" rents are not eliminated, but they are constrained, relative to the opportunities that typically exist in a bourgeois clientelist state. We should expect to see government efforts to control rent-seeking behavior in particular when that behavior creates programs (e.g., foreign labor) that inhibit precisely the kind of structural changes the developmental state is typically attempting to bring about in the first place.[16] On the other hand, when the developmental state does reward rent-seeking, the opportunities for rents are usually structured such that the recipients must engage in activities that embody the desired type of economic change. As Evans writes, "All rental havens are not equal. They arise for different reasons and have different effects" (1995: 223).

A country with a bourgeois clientelist state, then, is more likely to experience labor immigration than a country with a developmental state in the post-1970 period. This argument recognizes the importance of the economic factors identified by other theories of labor migration, but it suggests that they are useful as part of a cumulative model. In this model, economic factors such as development gaps and labor shortages create demand pressures for foreign workers, but political factors determine to what extent and how those pressures are actualized (Bartram 1998).

This argument improves on existing explanations of labor migration, insofar as it can better explain variation in receiving country experiences, in particular when we incorporate negative cases into the empirical framework. In addition, as the individual country chapters will show, the political argument I develop here is more effective at explaining what happened in the cases themselves than the arguments commonly offered about those cases individually. In Israel, those arguments typically draw (at least implicitly) on neoclassical ideas and center around the idea that Israel is "finally" a developed country and therefore naturally has foreign workers, just like other developed countries; some people also invoke supposedly unique "security" concerns. To the extent that Japan is seen as a negative case[17] (most analyses concentrate instead on the growing numbers of foreign workers there, understating the significance of the fact that the numbers are relatively low), typical arguments focus on Japan's unique culture, its closure to foreigners, and its reliance on domestic reserves of labor. In both cases, the arguments offered suffer from a lack of a comparative perspective, as analysts typically fail to consider that their chosen argument cites factors that also characterize countries where the outcome is significantly different.

The general argument, then, can be stated in a series of five propositions:

1 Developed capitalist countries tend to experience significant problems of labor supply for cheap labor.
2 There are various solutions to this problem, among which importing cheap labor is only one. The alternatives include: increasing wages to expand the domestic labor supply; increase labor productivity (in part to "justify" higher wages); allowing marginal firms to close and marginal sectors either to close or relocate abroad.
3 Employers tend to prefer a guestworker solution because it constitutes a quick and easy answer to labor shortages, has the potential to be a very profitable proposition, and imposes the least costs on them.
4 Guestworker programs as a solution to cheap labor supply problems are in the long run more costly *to the society as a whole* than alternative solutions.
5 The extent to which guestworker programs are adopted in a given developed capitalist country will therefore vary according to the following conditions:
   5.1 When policymakers *perceive* Proposition 4 to be true, and when the structure of the state is such that they can block or constrain the rent-seeking behavior of private sector interests (i.e., a developmentalist state), then they will adopt a non-guestworker solution to labor supply problems. Japan is an example.
   5.2 When policymakers *perceive* Proposition 4 to be true, and when the structure of the state is such that private interests are able to impose their will on the state and prevent the implementation of policies that run counter to their interests (i.e., a bourgeois

clientelist state), then they will allow the large-scale use of guest-workers. Israel is an example.

5.3 When policymakers do *not* perceive Proposition 4 to be true, then they will generally allow large-scale use of guestworkers. West Germany is an example: the guestworker program was launched before there was evidence concerning the long-term costs.

Some of these propositions are more problematic or less obviously true than others. I take 1, 2, and 3 as unproblematic. With respect to proposition 2, while some analysts have asserted that labor migration is an inevitable component of advanced capitalist development, it should be sufficient to reject this assertion merely to highlight the existence of countries where foreign labor is not a significant factor, especially where it can be shown (as I do for Japan in Chapter 4) that such countries did in fact experience labor supply problems.

Proposition 4 is probably the most problematic. Conclusions about the costs and benefits of guestworker programs inevitably depend on judgments about what gets counted as a cost and how such items should be valued. There is no avoiding the fact that a key contextual factor underlying some of the costs is the racism of many among the receiving country's population. We might wish it were different, but our analysis should nonetheless address the reality we encounter, counting as a cost that which is experienced as a cost, e.g., the foreign worker slums that arise from unwillingness of natives to accept foreign workers as neighbors. The main point here is that the contention that guest-worker programs are highly problematic is strengthened when we take a broad view of what counts as costs and benefits. The limits of a narrowly economistic view are obvious and well known: we can consider not only the effect of foreign workers on such measures as GDP per capita but also the social and political costs. In other words, while there is disagreement about the economic impacts (concerning e.g., whether foreign labor delays or facilitates industrial rationalization), there is a consensus about the broader impacts,[18] as expressed in a piece by Philip L. Martin and Mark J. Miller:

> These programs [i.e., in Western Europe] have produced a widespread sociopolitical malaise, evident first in the integration problem that has developed to the point of altering the sociopolitical fabric of Western European democracies ... [and] has also fostered right and left-wing political extremism, which periodically erupts into violence. ... Second, the presence of a large alien population without

full rights has been detrimental to the functioning and legitimacy of Western European democracies. (Martin and Miller 1980: 327)

The fact that these impacts are more difficult to measure than economic factors has not inhibited analysts from recognizing their fundamental significance.

In the end, what matters most for an explanation of different paths are the perceptions held by policymakers and the general public concerning costs and benefits; there should be no difficulty with the notion that perceptions can matter more than reality. There are grounds for defending the contention that the costs are greater than commonly understood by economists – in large part because many of the costs are not strictly economic (social unrest, political uncertainty, erosion of homogeneity, etc.). Policymakers who, as part of making policy, *must* conclude whether the benefits outweigh the costs have some foundation for deciding that they do not; such decisions are not pure whimsy (though they can certainly include elements of pandering to xenophobia). Finally, the question of net benefits for the country as a whole is probably too blunt; what matters more as a question of distributive justice is who reaps the benefits and who pays the costs. If employers benefit and citizens/taxpayers/workers (though not necessarily consumers) lose, a government concerned with distributive issues might be troubled.

Proposition 5, of course, is the main theoretical argument to be explored via the empirical analysis of the two cases.

My argument, then, is offered as a significant advance over existing theories of international labor migration. It is, however, also worth considering the limitations (both real and apparent) of the argument. The most obvious is that it relates only to factors and processes in the receiving country. Since many analyses agree that labor migration is in fact driven mainly by what happens in the receiving country (world-systems theory and the networks literature are significant exceptions), this limitation should not be fatal. Still, there is a growing sense that there are important processes in the sending country that constitute push factors that are increasingly difficult to counter (e.g., Portes 1982). On the other hand, while such processes, usually considered under the heading of globalization, have been increasingly salient, it remains true that governments in receiving countries have significant influence over the degree to which those pressures actually produce migration flows.

Second, the argument works best in relation to legal labor migration, i.e., official foreign worker programs. A certain portion of labor migration to most countries, however, is illegal or undocumented. An argument that pays close attention to government policy is perhaps ill suited to explain a phenomenon that apparently contravenes that policy. But there are two reasons why my argument is useful in spite of this apparent limitation. First, illegal immigration exists in significant part because governments fail to make it a priority to stop it, by allocating enforcement resources and reducing the legal obstacles to enforcement and deportations. In some respects this lack of determination derives from the constraints of international law and from the increasing cost of immigration prevention given economic globalization (Hollifield 1992). But to the extent that governments show a lack of will to control immigration, it seems useful to explain this state of affairs by way of policy analysis (Zolberg 1999). And because there are rents and externalities associated with illegal as well as legal immigration, my argument concerning rent-seeking and the developmental vs bourgeois clientelist state should be useful here as well. The second reason to pursue an argument focusing on policy concerning illegal immigration is that illegal immigration typically follows legal labor migration. One way of becoming an illegal foreign worker is to enter on a permit and then leave the employer specified in the permit. In addition, communities of workers with permits usually constitute networks that provide important resources for their fellow nationals who subsequently attempt to find work illegally in the same receiving country (Massey *et al.* 1987). If undocumented labor migration begins partly as a consequence of legal foreign worker programs, then explaining the former depends in part on an effective argument concerning the latter.

Third, the argument works better concerning some economic sectors than others. There is probably little connection between state type and foreign labor in the personal service sector, e.g., maids and caretakers for the elderly, especially when these workers are employed by individuals and not by companies. In countries with many foreign workers, however, domestic service workers typically form a small proportion of the total.

Fourth, it is conceivable that officials even in a developmental state might calculate that the benefits of foreign labor outweigh the costs and begin recruiting workers. Much depends on the time frame of policymakers. Importing labor can solve employment problems quickly and most of the costs do not emerge immediately, while structural economic change is slow and requires patience. Part of the essence of the developmental state is that policymakers adopt a long-range perspective and tolerate short-term costs. But solving short-term problems, including labor shortages, may in particular cases be viewed as essential for pursuing long-term developmental goals. The argument, then, is not that the developmental state will always reject foreign labor, simply that it is *less likely* to adopt this option. The argument is probabilistic (Brubaker 1989) and recognizes that there may be more than one path to a particular complex outcome (Ragin 1987). In particular, policy-makers may have other reasons for adopting a foreign worker program: for example, throughout the 1990s Germany allowed the employment of East Europeans as a means for achieving certain foreign policy goals (Hönekopp 1997). However, even in such a case, when we cannot attribute labor migration to the absence of a developmental state, the cumulative model described above is still quite relevant: economic and demographic pressures for importing foreign workers accumulate, but political factors help determine the actual outcome.

These limitations add up to a warning not to overstate the main theoretical argument. Decisions on foreign worker policy were made in particular historical contexts and are not entirely attributable to the state logic presented here.

Research strategy

This project is primarily an exercise in comparative political economy (cf. Evans and Stephens 1988). Research in this mode is concerned with accounting for the diversity of capitalist development trajectories (Berger and Dore 1996; Crouch and Streeck 1997). Against many of the claims of neoclassical economics as well as much of the globalization literature, most comparative political economists hold that there are important differences across the range of capitalist countries: in the way economies are organized, in their growth rates, in the way products are made, etc. And a principal claim of scholars in this field is that differences are often best explained by relating them to differences in state structure concerning economic governance. One of the important arguments here is that the "technical" problems governments and capitalists face, which may be universal, do not dictate the manner in which they are solved (Katzenstein 1978; Pempel 1982). As we will see, problems such as an incipient labor shortage are resolved, if at all, in a variety of ways, depending in large part on the "policy bias" inherent in particular state structures (cf. Hall 1986).

The literature on institutionalism is especially relevant here. Variously called the "new institutionalism" (March and Olsen 1984), historical institutionalism (Steinmo *et al.* 1992), and the "institutional-political process model" (Weir *et al.* 1988), this approach explains cross-national variation in policy outcomes by relating them to differences in national institutional configurations as well as to changes in those configurations over time. This type of analysis focuses on the political struggles that are played out in diverse institutional contexts. Rather than invoking large-scale economic changes, the strength of a particular class, or ideological shifts as isolated variables, institutionalists analyze how such variables are mediated in their effects by institutions, which then leave their own imprint on policy outcomes. Institutions both enable and constrain behavior and policy and are usually not neutral in their effects: they typically introduce a bias into the policymaking process, so that some types of policies are likely to prevail over others. Often this bias results from the fact that institutions distribute power unequally to different types of actors – power to set agendas as well as to determine outcomes.

The focus on capitalist diversity has powerful implications for an effort to advance our understanding of labor migration. As noted earlier, scholars of labor migration have typically emphasized the apparent ubiquity of labor migration. It would indeed be very surprising to find a single capitalist country that had no foreign workers, even if we limit our query to cheap/unskilled foreign labor, eliminating foreign managers of multinational companies, foreign technicians, etc. But that does not mean that there is no significant variation. In fact, the range of variation in receiving countries is quite striking: in some relatively wealthy countries (Japan in particular) the proportion of foreigners in the labor force is less than 2 percent. In some western European countries, that figure exceeds 10 percent. It is puzzling that analysts can look at this range and see one essentially monolithic process at work.

This point leads us to a discussion of the use of Israel and Japan as positive and negative cases respectively. The contrast between these two cases is significant: in 1998, foreign labor constituted more than 10 percent of the Israeli labor force, while in Japan the figure was about 1.3 percent. Japan is clearly the most significant anomaly among advanced capitalist countries concerning labor migration. In spite of its "miraculous" economic growth, its wealth, and its proximity to very poor countries, the percentage of foreigners in its labor force long remained very low and until recently consisted mainly of long-term Korean and Chinese permanent residents. Japan's anomaly status has been recognized as such (see Cornelius 1994; Reubens 1981), but the explanations offered have suffered from lack of a comparative perspective. In any event, there is no difficulty in drawing on Japan as a negative case here.

The choice of Israel as a positive case, however, may appear strange: Israel is not typically considered a "normal" capitalist country. Recently, however, and against a previous tendency to treat Israel and Israeli institutions as unique (Kimmerling 1995), it has become more common to analyze Israel in comparative political economy terms (e.g., Barnett 1996; Nitzan and Bichler 1996; Shalev 1990, 1992), carefully specifying the limits as well as the advantages of the comparisons – as would be wise for any case. Many of the problems the Israeli state has faced are not so radically different from those faced in other capitalist countries, especially if we conceive of them as issues of capitalist accumulation in the face of certain socially and politically constructed imperatives. In addition, Israel is especially interesting as a "guestworker" country because its closure to non-Jews (even to its non-Jewish citizens) would seem to imply that its government would seek at all costs to avoid importing workers; its failure to do so demands explanation. Clearly Israel's experience with foreign labor is strongly related to its long history of relying on non-citizen labor from West Bank and Gazan Palestinians,[19] which itself is perhaps a product of unique circumstances. I will argue, however, that this history in no way suffices to explain the later appearance of foreign workers and that Israel would most likely have imported labor regardless of its occupation of the West Bank and Gaza. Finally, given that I will advocate a "politicized" theory of labor migration, it may seem unwise to analyze a case that is widely viewed as a highly politicized society: is it not already obvious that politics played a role in bringing foreign labor to Israel? Remember, however, that my main argument is not only about the relevance of political variables but about their *form*. I will argue that what mattered in this context was the *weakness* of the Israeli government, not its control. Politics mattered in Israel, but not only in the way that certain preconceptions might lead us to believe.

At first glance the comparison between the two countries may seem odd as well, given a cursory consideration of the very significant differences between them. If they are different in a large number of respects, how can we hope to establish that the cluster of variables relating to state structure is really what accounts for the difference in the outcome variable of foreign workers?

As it turns out, the comparison is useful not in spite of these differences but *because* of them. The most important factor that ought to complicate and inhibit the comparison is the difference between the two economies themselves. Japan, a very wealthy country, has an extremely large and diverse economy, with an output value greater than that of all of the rest of East Asia combined. Israel is much smaller and less diverse, with a per capita income that places it towards the lower end of high-income countries as defined by the OECD. Does this difference help us account for the different levels of foreign workers in the two economies? We might be tempted to answer yes, until we consider that, according to existing theory (neoclassical theory in particular), we would expect on these grounds that the outcome would be *precisely the opposite* of what it is in reality. The "development" gaps between Japan and its regional neighbors are significantly larger than those between Israel and its regional neighbors, yet Israel's labor force contains a much higher percentage of foreigners.

The point holds, somewhat less forcefully, concerning certain respects in which the countries do not differ. According to dual labor market theory, a large secondary economic sector is fertile territory for the assimilation of a foreign labor force. But both Israel and Japan are characterized by a high level of economic dualism. According to world-systems theory, strong investment, trade, military, and colonial ties typically lead to labor migration. But Israel and Japan both have such ties with many countries. Moreover, the main sending countries to Israel (with the significant exception of occupied Palestine) – Rumania and Thailand – do not have strong relationships with Israel of the type often thought to precipitate labor migration. And Japan, in spite of a long history of military conquest and occupation in East Asia – not to mention its role as regional economic superpower – has not experienced labor immigration on the scale of Israel or of the main European receiving countries.

In other words, once we consider the two countries *in terms of existing theory* concerning labor migration, we see either that the main differences lead us to expect outcomes quite different from reality, or that the countries do not differ in terms of factors that would be presumed to explain the (different) outcomes. Another important difference, however, has to do with the type of state that has long characterized each country. Odd as it may seem, then, the comparison is therefore quite promising for exploring an argument concerning how state structures help explain labor migration.

So we may note as a first step that Japan has relatively small numbers of foreign workers and, especially during its first experience with labor shortages in the 1970s, a developmental state (Dore 1986; Johnson 1982)[20] and that Israel has quite large numbers of foreign workers and a bourgeois clientelist state. These sweeping generalizations are of course in need of historical discussion: the state in each case has by no means been static or unchanging. The Israeli state during the 1950s and 1960s was in fact quite autonomous from capital (though less so from labor) and played a major role in the stimulation of economic development. More recently, however, the organization of capital has increased significantly, to the detriment of state autonomy: politicians, rather than professional bureaucrats, are the real decision makers regarding economic policy, in a way that has had very real implications for the development of foreign labor policy in the 1990s. The Japanese state has evolved as well: the autonomy and the developmentalism of the Japanese state during the 1960s and into the 1970s provided a paradigm for development scholars (e.g., Evans 1995), but here too there has been a deterioration, though not nearly to the same degree as in Israel. As of the mid-1990s, scholars such as Chalmers Johnson (1995) still contended that the bureaucracies and not the politicians had primary responsibility and authority for economic policy. Others have emphasized change rather than continuity in the Japanese state, noting political developments (such as the fall of the Liberal Democratic Party in 1993) as well as the dysfunctions of economic governance. So, as we will see in Chapter 4, the relationship between the institutional structure of the state, economic policy, and foreign labor was more complicated during the more recent period of labor shortages, beginning in the mid-1980s. Japan in the early 1970s, however, provides strong support for the argument that a developmentalist state is a key condition for pursuing alternative solutions to labor shortages.

We must then go beyond noting this correspondence and develop a theoretical understanding of why there are strong relationships among these phenomena. The discussion in the previous section goes some way towards substantiating this relationship, by specifying its components and their connections, drawing on established theory in related areas. The other main procedure for defending my overall claim is to present a convincing history of each case, where the relationships I am asserting are clearly an indispensable part of the story.

Those histories are constructed with evidence typical of most comparative historical projects. The research began with extensive reading in the secondary literature concerning the political economy of each society. In both cases, I began to form an initial impression concerning important events and junctures by reading selectively in the respective national newspapers (usually with the help of computerized indices). Government publications and statistics were useful as well. From this point, collecting evidence regarding the two countries involved different strategies. For Israel, because the relevant history is relatively recent and not yet well documented, I engaged in a very significant amount of primary source research, the heart of which consisted of dozens of interviews with government officials, employers, trade associations, and other private organizations. The relevant political economic history of Japan has received much more scholarly attention than that of Israel. I am essentially retelling a well-known history of policy and structural change, drawing out the implications for our understanding of how Japan has avoided large-scale labor immigration. Therefore the discussion of Japan relies more heavily, though not exclusively, on secondary materials. In addition, I conducted interviews in Tokyo and collected official data and records, though to a lesser extent than for Israel.

Placing these histories in comparative context, in particular in light of the above discussion, provides leverage to offer my claim about the developmental state and labor migration as a general statement, worthy at least of further investigation in other cases: International labor migration in the post-1970 period begins in part as a result of receiving country state structures that facilitate rent-seeking and inhibit positive economic development. Of course the economic and demographic factors invoked by existing theory must also be present: development gaps must attract workers from poor countries, and employers in the receiving country must "feel" a labor shortage deriving from citizens' refusal to accept jobs on the terms offered. But given that these conditions are widespread in capitalist countries, the real issue then becomes how governments respond to them. In an alternative scenario, the developmental state facilitates industrial or sectoral transformation such that economies do not produce low-wage jobs to the same extent, increasing the likelihood that citizens will satisfy employers' labor needs and reducing the extent of foreign labor.

Normative interlude

The tone of the discussion so far, in particular at the beginning of the chapter, has undoubtedly revealed an opposition to labor migration *per se*, and a few words are perhaps in order to explain and defend this position, as it will reappear throughout the book. My perspective derives not from an opposition to immigration in general, whether to Israel, Japan, the US, or anywhere else, but from a critique of guestworker programs as a particular *form* of immigration. Guestworker programs, as they almost inevitably result in settlement of the workers themselves, create oppressed and excluded minorities in the receiving country, subject to discrimination and sometimes violence on the part of citizens: almost by definition, these programs are incapable of offering workers full membership in the "host" society. All that is desired is labor power, at a discount. The workers themselves, enjoying something approximating advanced country incomes, might object to such philosophical niceties, if the implication is that they should be sent home. After all, workers choose to come even though they know they will not be accepted as citizens. The implication instead, then, should be that countries in need of labor power should accept immigrants as full members of the society, not just as workers (cf. Castles and Miller 1993).

I want in particular to dissociate myself from the critique of foreign workers as a Zionist problem. Many Israelis are concerned that adding hundreds of thousands of non-Jews to the Israeli labor force will dilute the Jewish and Zionist character of the state/country. There is a philosophical debate concerning whether a community has a right to preserve its character by limiting immigration, in the face of a potential migrant's right to try to improve his or her life-chances by moving to a richer country. Carens (1988) establishes that the former right exists but is outweighed by the material interests of the migrants (though for an opposing view see Walzer 1983 and Weiner 1996). On a more practical level, however, there may be an additional reason for opposing labor immigration to Israel to the extent that some foreign workers take jobs traditionally held by Palestinians from the West Bank and Gaza, undermining the Palestinian economy and hindering efforts for a negotiated settlement of that conflict. Still, one must weigh this concern against the interests of the foreign workers, and it is not clear to me what such a calculation would yield.

Plan of the book

In Chapter 2, I present a historical and typological survey of labor migration in the postwar period, highlighting the extent of variation in use of foreign labor in wealthy countries. Chapters 3 and 4 are the main empirical chapters. Chapter 3 analyzes Israel's experience with foreign labor, beginning with the Palestinians but focusing in particular on the large-scale flows that have developed since 1993. Chapter 4 defends the conceptualization of Japan as a negative case and explores the history of that country's methods for resolving labor shortages, placing those policies in the context of state-led economic growth and transformation. Chapter 5, the conclusion, reviews the comparison in theoretical terms and considers the problem of foreign labor with regard to two related issues: inequality and race.

2
Labor Migration in the Postwar Period

The existing theoretical literature on international labor migration has been constructed using a remarkably limited sample of empirical cases, relative to the available "population." Germany and France have received a great deal of attention as the two largest importers of foreign labor in Europe. Writers have also focused on the US, Canada, and Australia as the main alternatives to the guestworker model. There are also contributions dealing with foreign workers in a wider variety of countries, including Belgium, the Netherlands, Sweden, and Austria, but most writings concerning these countries do not attempt to make theoretical statements concerning the causes of labor migration.[1]

The main goal of this chapter is simply to establish that use of low-wage foreign labor varies extensively in wealthy capitalist countries, to a greater extent than is usually recognized in theoretical writings on the issue. Scholars of international labor migration have not sufficiently appreciated that there is a significant amount of variation to explain in advanced countries' use of foreign labor, and theoretical efforts have suffered accordingly. The first step in moving forward is simply to describe this variation. In doing so, we will consider a number of countries not usually included in theory-oriented discussions of labor migration because of the fact that they contain very limited numbers of foreign workers. Japan, Norway, Denmark, Finland, and Ireland are quite relevant here, however, because according to some theories these countries *should* play host to large foreign worker populations. The fact that there are a number of very wealthy advanced capitalist countries with very low populations of foreign workers should be of great interest to migration scholars. Even without these countries the range of variation in use of foreign labor is significant. When we include them, however, the range of variation becomes rather impressive.

This discussion depends on a specification of exactly what is meant by foreign worker. As we will see, in some receiving countries substantial numbers of foreign workers are quite different from the paradigmatic Turkish guestworker employed as unskilled labor in a German factory or as a sanitation worker. I thus argue for and present a more systematic approach to defining and measuring the presence of foreign workers in advanced capitalist countries. It would seem that the term "foreign worker" is frequently used by migration scholars in a casual way, which presumes that its meaning is obvious and unproblematic. I attempt to construct a more precise conceptual definition, one which will prove more useful for various types of research on the topic. Cross-national comparative research of this sort requires serious attention to the definition of the phenomenon to be compared. Because different countries use different types of workers under different legal, economic, and social arrangements, we must make reasoned judgments about which of these types and arrangements are sufficiently equivalent to be categorized together – and thus which ones must be excluded. The goal here is a set of "decision rules" that will enable us to carry out this categorization in a consistent manner.

Concepts: from intuition to greater precision

The premise of this analysis is that the notion of "foreign worker" is exceedingly complex. While the concept of foreign labor might seem straightforward for any individual case, the subtleties and variations become apparent when one turns to a comparative analysis of diverse cases.

To begin to elaborate principles for categorizing different types in different (or similar) ways, it will help to make explicit a general, intuitive sense of what we mean when we invoke the notion of a "foreign worker." The key point here is that scholars and others are typically interested in the foreign worker phenomenon because it constitutes a particular kind of social problem for the receiving country. (I hasten to add that the problem may not be the presence of the workers themselves but the way they are or are not accepted by the receiving country.) To anticipate, the problem is rooted in the notion that the workers are too different in too many ways from the receiving country population to be considered anything other than workers; such persons are considered not acceptable as potential full members of the society. Foreign workers – to use the term in a less precise sense – who do not constitute such a problem, perhaps because they "fit in" more easily, are from this point of view something different. To support this statement I suggest simply that, if all foreign workers were accepted by receiving countries with no difficulty or friction, there would most likely be much less scholarly interest in the phenomenon.

The paradigmatic case of foreign workers is Turkish *Gastarbeiter* in West Germany. The problem – and I choose the word deliberately – is well known: Turkish workers (and others) were brought to West Germany in the 1960s with the assumption that their presence would be temporary, as a sort of economic "buffer" – a solution for cyclical labor shortages. The prospect that they would become permanent members of German society was both unanticipated and unwelcome. Hence the problem of foreign workers in Germany – a problem that German governments and society have been attempting to address for several decades now.

There are several simple, person-in-the-street understandings of what makes someone a foreign worker, but I believe it is unwise to rely on them. The reason is that these "rules" lead to decisions that seem counter-intuitive with respect to the discussion in the previous paragraphs. The most common example: many laypersons (and perhaps scholars as well) probably believe that an employed person is a foreign worker if he or she does not hold *citizenship* in the country where employment takes place. Alternatively, some people might believe that a person is a foreign worker if he or she was *born* outside the country of employment (and thus remains a foreign worker even after naturalization). As we will see below, however, these views lead to seemingly strange results: certain types of people are categorized as foreign workers despite being part of a group that does not constitute the type of problem identified above. To foreshadow this particular argument, it probably does not make sense to think of Norwegians working in Sweden as the same type of foreign worker as Turks in Germany.

The main claim here, then, is that foreign workers, as understood in much of the research and popular literatures, are international migrants (and perhaps their offspring born in receiving countries that do not adhere to *jus solis* citizenship traditions) whose presence increases the supply of low-wage labor in the host country, under conditions of restricted political or civil rights that impair their ability to compete in the labor market. It is a truism in this context that foreign workers are viewed solely as workers and not as people. They are not viewed as full members of the receiving country's society and polity; if they *were* full members, they would not be useful as foreign workers. This incomplete membership – which often does not even amount to what Tomas

Hammar (1990) refers to as denizenship – encapsulates the "problem" as defined above: foreign workers are typically segregated into ghettos, their children receive inferior educations, they feel aggrieved about their diminished and restricted status and rights, etc. Foreign workers, then, to be included in this study as such, must be significantly *disadvantaged* by their foreignness, relative to citizens. Foreign birth and non-citizen status are typical markers that create and maintain that disadvantage, but they mean different things in different contexts, and our use of these markers must be flexible and sensitive to those contexts.

Some additional examples will illustrate the difficulties of the cruder approaches. Equating foreign workers with non-citizen workers would place American managers in Britain, professional intra-EC migrants, and illegal Moroccan busboys in France in the same category. The former two have very little in common with the latter beyond lack of citizenship: they are different in their legal and political status, their levels of education and occupational training, and their cultural resources. Moreover, their incorporation into the host country labor market has very different consequences for that market. Defining foreign workers as those born outside their country of employment would produce similar undesired effects: here we would lump together (for example) children of Canadian citizens born abroad but later returned to Canada, illegal Moroccan busboys in France, and American-born Jewish doctors practicing in Israel after receiving citizenship under the country's "Law of Return," while leaving out children of Turkish guestworkers in Germany (most of whom are not German citizens). This grouping is counterintuitive. These approaches are not subtle enough to define and distinguish a population that can be studied as a reasonably distinct social phenomenon.

Nonetheless, it is useful to start with a baseline, drawing on the first laypersons' notion above, i.e., that foreign workers are distinguished by lack of citizenship in the country of employment. The implicit argument is that citizenship status really makes a difference for life chances, wage levels, work conditions, etc., and thus such an approach is appropriate only when that condition holds. We may then consider alternative rules that derive from the fact that some such persons fit quite uneasily into the category itself on this basis.

The non-problematic categories

Guestworkers.   The preeminent form of labor migration in the postwar period is that of workers on temporary restricted contracts. Contract workers are often not permitted free mobility in the labor market: the contract and visa often tie the worker to a specific job with a specific employer, or at least to a certain region and/or occupation. Freedom of movement is also sometimes restricted: contract workers often receive a residence permit in tandem with the state-issued work permit, and residence can be restricted to the area where the job is located. Such restrictions are often lifted as a worker's tenure increases.

Illegal immigrants. It is easy to conclude that illegal immigrants, when employed (as they usually are), are foreign workers as that term is being used here. Their presence as workers is desired by employers and perhaps implicitly by others who benefit from their inexpensive labor, but they are clearly unwelcome as members of the society. The stereotype is that such workers do the most undesirable jobs for low wages – and in most cases the stereotype certainly contains more than a kernel of truth, even if by definition it is usually difficult to get good data on such workers. Are there illegal immigrants who would not be considered foreign workers as per the approach here? I can think only of a time when I myself violated the terms of my Israeli student visa by editing a manuscript for a sociologist whose native language was not English; here the exception seems to prove the rule.

Primary exclusions

The types above do not pose any real conceptual difficulties; people in those types generally fit our intuitive sense of what makes someone a guestworker. There are several types, however, that might constitute *prima facie* cases of foreign workers – but on further consideration there are convincing reasons to exclude them from this category.

Common labor markets. I contend we should exclude workers who move within a common labor market arrangement such as the European Union or the Nordic Common Labor Market. Norwegians working in Sweden, for example, probably have more in common with Swedish workers/citizens than they do with Turks in Germany or even Turks in Sweden (at least those who have not gained Swedish citizenship). The most obvious reason is that Norway itself is quite similar to Sweden in wage levels, labor rights, political development, etc. Workers from a poorer country might accept an undesirable job at a wage low by Swedish standards simply because the absolute increase in income is substantial; a Norwegian who seeks work in Sweden is unlikely to feel compelled to accept a job that is any less desirable in Sweden than it would be in Norway. Beyond that, the common labor market arrangement itself guarantees equality in labor rights, pension transferability, etc. While it would go too far to assert that Sweden and Norway are really one country, that notion makes a bit more sense in *this* context than it would if it were applied to Sweden and Turkey. Common labor markets are typically formed among countries that do not worry about being "swamped" with one another's cheap labor; new members are usually admitted when their economies have advanced to the point that membership will not stimulate a mass exodus to the richer countries, as with Portugal, Spain and Greece's accession to the EEC.[2] Indeed, there has been no great exodus of workers from those three countries since 1993. The reluctance and foot-dragging concerning proposals to allow Turkey to enter the EU illustrates the point quite nicely.

Professionals and managers. The category "foreign workers" should also not include professional and managerial workers, such as the large numbers of managers of international corporations in Britain or foreign teachers in Ireland. The fact that there is no common labor market arrangement between the US and Britain does not mean that US managerial staff of multinational corporations employed in Britain are properly conceived as foreign workers. Integration in receiving countries of professionals and managers receiving high salaries has apparently been much less problematic: in many respects such individuals remain "invisible" (Hopkinson 1992; Böhning 1991; see also Castles and Miller 1993), in part because they are less likely to create close ethnic communities (Portes and Rumbaut 1996). This fact has not prevented employers (such as software companies in the US and Germany) from trying to restrain wages for skilled employees such as software engineers by attempting to import such workers. A case might be made for emphasizing the similarities over the differences between the use of high-skill and low-skill foreign workers. But the opposite argument seems more compelling to me. A personal note is appropriate here: as an American sociologist employed by a British university, I am confident I do not face anything like the degree of exclusion encountered even by some non-white UK *citizens*, despite the fact that I have precisely the kind of visa and work permit typically held by guestworkers as described above.

Workers from wealthy countries. The ideas in the previous two paragraphs lead directly to the notion that workers from rich countries should not be considered "foreign workers" even when they are not professionals or managers and even when there is no common labor market arrangement. Even a semi-skilled worker from Germany who seeks work in Switzerland would seem to have more in common with Swiss citizens than with (to invoke another paradigmatic case) Algerians working in France. The numbers of such persons in most cases is probably not large, but the exception is necessary to deal properly with the fact that some countries – Switzerland in particular – employ many workers from other wealthy countries despite not being part of the EU or some other similar arrangement. Canadians working in the US and vice versa constitute another important example.

More troublesome issues

The attempt to create a set of rules to be applied consistently to a diverse set of cases leads inevitably to difficulties of fit. The categories above are fairly straightforward, but there are several other categories that are more challenging. Nonetheless a determination of how to treat them is precisely the point of this analysis.

Family reunification. Workers with guestworker-type permits are typically not allowed to bring their families, at least at first: host-country governments often say they want to discourage settlement, and employers probably benefit from minimization of consumption needs of their workers to the extent that this mitigates pressures for wage increases.[3] Often, however, governments' opposition breaks down (e.g., because of International Labor Office conventions guaranteeing the right of family reunification) and they permit the entry of immediate family members, especially when the original workers begin receiving extended-duration work permits. By the late 1980s, the vast majority of migrant inflows to Europe were attributable to family reunification provisions (Hopkinson 1992).

Are such persons foreign workers when employed? I would argue they are. Some governments mandate a waiting period before the family members can receive a work permit; governments do not usually view family reunification programs as a form of labor migration. But eventually the result is an increase in the number of foreign workers whose status is quite similar to that of the original migrant.

The second generation. The issue is more complicated for the children of original migrants. If children receive citizenship under *jus solis* provisions, then it would be difficult to argue that they grow up to become foreign workers – though that statement might be qualified for countries where holding citizenship does not always help individuals overcome the stigma and other disadvantages associated with immigrant status (such as Britain). But children in host countries that grant citizenship only to children of citizens or nationals (under *jus sanguinis* provisions) become foreign workers themselves despite never having lived anywhere but in the "host" country. This is an incongruous notion in some respects: such children are raised in the receiving country, educated in its schools, and speak its language with greater ease. But the segregation that pervades even those processes marks these individuals as different much as in the case of their parents. The "problematic" status of the second generation is perhaps even greater than that of their parents: the latter typically migrate with the low expectations of outsiders, but the children grow up with at least some of the aspirations and expectations of their native peers and perhaps experience greater frustration when they encounter exclusionary attitudes and structures (Portes and Rumbaut 1996).

Such workers usually find it easier (or even automatic) to get the required work and residence permits under more relaxed conditions, so their economic status is not identical to that of their parents. But their lack of citizenship and their restricted political, economic, and social rights continue to distinguish them from native workers. This status extends in some cases to the third generation, and there is no reason to believe it will not continue with future generations as well in some countries (though even Germany after the 1998 elections eased naturalization requirements for some foreigners).

Legal immigrants.   Some "immigration countries" permit or encourage immigration for reasons other than the desire to add to their labor forces. Migrants to these countries are not foreign workers in the same sense as guestworkers: from the outset these migrants are seen as potential citizens, and their status and rights are usually better as a result. Nevertheless, most countries require a waiting period before naturalization, during which immigrants are typically "permanent residents" with work permits. Their situation thus resembles that of other foreign workers to some extent. Many immigrants to these countries begin their employment experience in low-wage work, and they are usefully viewed as a type of foreign worker in these settings, where the numbers of other types are usually quite moderate. The US, Canada and Australia are the obvious examples of this type, but immigration rights have been offered by other countries as well (Britain, France, the Netherlands), especially to people from former colonial possessions. This argument is likely to evoke some doubts; Canada and Australia, in contrast to the US, have devised immigration policies designed to attract people with high levels of education and skills. Perhaps it is unwise to advocate a general rule in this context. But the issue is less problematic if we return to the exclusions discussed above: immigrants to "immigration countries" would not be considered foreign workers if they are employed at a higher level or if they come from wealthier countries.

In some countries (particularly Australia and Britain), immigrant or foreigner status continues to stick, especially to certain racial groups, even after naturalization and to offspring of immigrant citizens. In theory there is no difference in legal status or rights, but in practice discrimination (concerning jobs, housing, education, etc.) contributes to an inferior position in the labor market. We might then ask whether employed citizens of immigrant origin (especially from poor countries) should be considered foreign workers. This possibility seems especially important for the case of Britain. Here, however, receiving country citizens born locally will not be considered foreign workers: social and labor market discrimination against "minority groups" of citizens is a different (even if related) issue. The notion of a "citizen foreign worker" in relation to the native-born seems too oxymoronic. The distinction involved should not be overstated: Castles and Miller (1993), for example, make a compelling argument concerning the similarities between guest-workers in Germany and naturalized immigrants in Australia. Still, we should recognize the differences that do exist: Soysal's arguments (1994) concerning the demise of national citizenship seem exaggerated in this light.[4]

Asylum seekers and refugees. The mode of entry for asylum seekers and refugees is, at least on the surface, quite different from that of workers, as is the motivation for their acceptance by receiving countries. On both counts, the desire to buy and sell labor in this case would seem to be irrelevant, and indeed some receiving countries prohibit people in this category from working. Nonetheless, when refugees and asylum seekers *do* work, it seems reasonable to consider them foreign workers. They come with many of the same characteristics that distinguish other types of foreign workers from "native" workers: they are typically from poor countries, their presence is considered undesirable by much of the receiving country population, their labor and political rights are restricted, etc. Most importantly, they typically add to the supply of low-wage labor and are often seen as different and problematic by the receiving society.

The point is reinforced by the widely held perception – which is distasteful to some but which cannot be dismissed simply on that basis – that many asylum seekers are not actually fleeing persecution but instead are economic migrants much like other types of foreign workers. Such persons try to enter under asylum provisions, it is claimed, simply because opportunities for other types of migration have diminished in recent decades; asylum is their only chance. To the extent that this is true, there is certainly no difficulty including them in the category of foreign workers.

To summarize, we can begin with the laypersons' notions that foreign workers are either employed persons who are non-citizens and/or foreign-born. But the discussion above makes clear that not all non-citizens are really foreign workers, and some people are foreign workers despite not being foreign-born. The former point requires us to exclude professionals/managers, workers who migrate under common labor market arrangements, and other workers from wealthy countries. The latter point means that we will include the second generation in *jus sanguinis* countries.

The conceptual definition developed above is summarized in Figure 2.1. (An x in a cell indicates that the combination is incoherent or does not exist in the real world; for example, the notion of free labor market mobility is irrelevant to native-born citizens, i.e., those working in their "own" countries.) The text in each cell denotes prominent instances of people having that particular combination of characteristics. Foreign

			Foreign born			Native born	
			Free labor market mobility			Free labor market mobility	
			yes	no		yes	no
Foreign citizen	Low level employment	yes	x	guestworkers, refugees, other immigrants e.g. Hispanics in the US		x	children of guest workers, e.g. in ius sanguinis countries
		no	EU, Nordic Common Labor Market	American, Japanese professionals, managers, in US, Japan & vice versa		children of EU workers in ius sanguinis countries	children of other immigrant professionals, e.g. in Japan
Native citizen	Low level employment	yes	x	unsuccessful colonial immigrants, e.g. in UK, France		x	native born citizens
		no	x	successful colonial immigrants, e.g. in UK, France		x	native born citizens

Figure 2.1   Attributes of foreign workers.

workers are those who fit into the highlighted cells. Thus foreign worker status depends in the first instance on foreign birth or foreign citizenship (i.e., no one in the lower right quadrant fits the description). As discussed above, however, these markers are necessary but not sufficient to denote foreign worker status; an additional requirement is low-level employment. In this regard, the category relating to free labor market mobility is not strictly necessary in the table: I am assuming that those with free labor market mobility will not be employed at a low level the way workers from poor countries typically are. I include this category here simply because it is such a prominent feature of the labor migration phenomenon (especially in relation to the EU).

This conceptual definition fits with intuitive understandings of what a foreign worker is; in that regard there is nothing terribly surprising about the approach I am presenting. The value of the table is that it clarifies how particular instances should be treated; specifically, it highlights the need to exclude certain types that are often counted as foreign workers by default (not to say unthinkingly).

Empirical applications: implications and difficulties

Ignoring the entire preceding discussion, we could turn to a source such as SOPEMI or EUROSTAT and quickly form a straightforward impression of how many foreign workers are present in various receiving countries; the tables regarding "stocks of employed workers" would be quite helpful. If we follow the approach elaborated above, however, things become more difficult. The analysis that follows is by no means a comprehensive application of this approach to the entire universe of relevant cases. Instead, I merely illustrate the impact that adopting this approach has on our sense of how many foreign workers are present in various countries (including the difficulties we will have in coming to that determination). In general, the effect is to reduce the numbers of workers counted, considerably in some cases, because of the exclusions discussed above.

Belgium.   The case of Belgium illustrates the significant effect of applying the approach described above on our understanding of how many foreign workers a country has. The total number of foreigners employed legally in Belgium is 1989 was 194,600; estimates of the illegal immigrant population were ranged from 50,000 to 100,000, and we will assume that the true figure was 75,000 and guess that two-thirds of those were employed. The total figure then would be 244,600. In a labor force of 4.1 million, foreigners thus accounted for 6 percent of the labor force. But 82,000 of those foreigners came from elsewhere in the EU. Removing them from the category of foreign workers reduced the percentage to 4 percent. This is a decrease of almost one-third – a significant change in our understanding of foreign workers in Belgium. This change does not include any adjustment for foreigners employed as managers and professionals; this additional adjustment would decrease the percentage still further.

The Smaller Nordic Countries. Much of the labor migration to Finland, Denmark, and Norway (as well as Sweden) has taken place under the auspices of the Nordic Common Labor Market, operating since 1954. The agreement goes beyond simple freedom of labor mobility to include equalization and transferability of welfare state benefits, health services, and pensions. The extent of movement has been relatively limited, perhaps surprisingly so, given the favorable conditions. While there was a large net movement of Finns to Sweden, net migration among Finland, Denmark, and Norway has not been significant (Fischer and Straubhaar 1996). This statement holds even for earlier time periods, when there was a more substantial difference between the level of development in Finland and that of Denmark and Norway. In more recent years, the majority of intra-Nordic migration has involved white-collar workers; Finnish emigrants, for example, have above-average levels of education relative to their compatriots. This experience reinforces the idea that migration within common labor markets is distinct in important ways from labor migration under other circumstances.

Migration flows from poorer countries have been relatively minor in size as well. Finland has always maintained tight controls, and Norway began restricting immigration in 1972, before inflows had become significant. Restrictions on immigration have come in large part as a response to trade union demands (Fischer and Straubhaar 1996).

In 1992 there were 74,000 foreign workers in Denmark, but 17,700 were from elsewhere in the EU and 13,000 were from other Nordic countries. Thus at most there were about 43,000 low-wage foreign workers in Denmark, or 1.5 percent of the labor force; in fact the percentage is probably lower because an unknown number of those 43,000 are North Americans. In addition, there were 21,000 unemployed among the total figure (74,000), and unemployment among foreign workers is concentrated among immigrants from poorer countries (e.g., 49 percent among the 13,700 Turks) (all figures from SOPEMI 1995); the demand for such workers is rather lower than the supply.

Finnish estimates concerning foreign workers place the 1993 stock at 25,000 (SOPEMI 1995). Subtracting an approximate 3500 Nordic nationals and 1000 North Americans, we find an estimated maximum of 20,500 low-wage foreign workers in Finland, or 0.8 percent of the labor force. One-fourth of these are ethnic Finns or "Ingrians" from the former Soviet Union (Fischer and Straubhaar 1996). As in Denmark, unemployment among foreign workers is very high, more than 40 percent, and is concentrated among the unskilled workers, mainly from Eastern Europe, Africa, and Latin America.

Norway had a total of 47,900 employed foreigners in 1993. Of these, 16,400 were Nordic citizens and 11,200 were from Western Europe or North America, leaving a maximum of 22,700 low-wage legal foreigners, or one percent of the labor force (not including the unemployed – foreigners have an unemployment rate of almost 20 percent) (SOPEMI 1995). There were an estimated 5000 illegal immigrants in Norway; if all of these people were in the labor force, the percentage of low-wage foreigners would rise to 1.2 percent. This figure has remained relatively constant throughout the postwar period.

This analysis reinforces the point that there are some countries where the presence of foreign workers is quite limited. This presence would be adjudged quite low even without the modifications just applied to the rough figures, but the effect of those modifications is to reduce their numbers significantly. As I have argued at length elsewhere (Bartram 2000), these countries constitute significant anomalies with respect to extant theories of labor migration and thus ought to be of significant interest to migration scholars.

The conceptual definition elaborated above leads to some interesting outcomes that might be considered problematic. One such case is treated here – Switzerland, which raises the question of what happens to our sense of foreign workers' presence over time.

Switzerland. The percentage of foreigners in the labor force has been higher by far than in any other OECD country (discounting the city-states): between 20 percent and 32 percent throughout much of the last three decades. The absurdly low unemployment rate among Swiss citizens (for many years below 1 percent) has helped justify the extensive use of foreign labor.

But the majority of foreign workers in Switzerland have come from wealthy neighboring countries in Western Europe, including France and Germany. In other words, these workers came from countries that not only imported labor themselves but provided extensive welfare-state protections (including unemployment benefits) to their citizens. Many foreign workers, then, did not seek out employment in Switzerland because of hardship in their home countries. The employment offered to them therefore had to be at least as attractive as what they could have found at home. "Professionally, foreign workers in Switzerland are closer to their Swiss peers than guestworkers in the Federal Republic are to the Germans: foreign workers in Switzerland have higher qualifications and the proportion of unskilled workers is smaller. ..." (Hoffman-Nowotny 1985: 226). It thus makes little sense to think about French or German foreign workers in Switzerland as foreign workers, even though there is no official common labor market arrangement among these countries. I therefore exclude these workers from the category.

The question of how to treat workers from Italy is more interesting. I argued above that workers from wealthy countries should not be classified as foreign workers. But what exactly do we mean by a "wealthy" country? Italy is certainly wealthy by a global standard, but many Italians who went to work elsewhere in Europe came from the very poor southern part of the country.

In this particular case, I suggest that we pay attention to Italy's entry into the EU (or, more precisely, its precursor, the European Economic Community), by which Italians were granted labor mobility within the EEC beginning in 1968. This event gives us a way of coping with the fact that Italians working elsewhere in Europe in the first few postwar decades fit our intuitive sense of what a foreign worker is, while Italians working outside Italy in more recent years do not fit into the category nearly as well. According to the rules outlined above, Italians working in France, Germany, etc. before 1968 are counted as foreign workers; those who worked in such countries after 1968 are not counted as such, and the point is that they should not be counted as foreign workers in Switzerland either. After all, entry into a common labor market arrangement is understood to signify that the country in question has essentially developed to a level comparable with the other members of that arrangement (see Tables 2.1 and 2.2).

In practical terms, the implication is that the number of "foreign workers" declines once Italy enters the EEC's labor mobility provisions (and not just for Switzerland, of course). The decline is perhaps artificial in the short term but reflects an important reality over a longer term: Italians working in Switzerland in recent decades are different from those working there in the 1950s and early 1960s, and it no longer makes sense to group them together with, say, Romanian guestworkers in Israel. A precise "turning point" concerning Italian workers is both

Table 2.1   Foreign workers, 1964 (thousands)

	Labor force	Total foreign	Percent foreign
Austria	3,331	40	1.2
Belgium	3,566	350	9.8
Denmark	2,253	12	0.5
France	19,251	1,200	6.2
Germany	26,523	1,058	4.0
Japan	47,100	140	0.3
Luxemburg	138	25	18.1
Netherlands	4,557	61	1.3
Norway	1,467	15	1.0
Sweden	3,814	162	4.2
Switzerland	2,508	782	31.2

Sources: Descloitres 1967, p. 26; Immigration Bureau, Japan 1990.

Table 2.2   Foreign workers, 1974 (thousands)

	Labor force	Total foreign	Percent foreign	Common market	Maximum low-end foreign	Maximum % low-end foreign
Austria	3,252	218.0	6.3	2.0	216.0	6.2
Belgium	3,844	278.0	6.7	85.0	193.0	4.7
France	22,147	1,900.0	7.9	210.0	1,690.0	7.0
Germany	27,320	2,360.0	8.0	446.0	1,914.0	6.4
Israel	1,088	59.3[a]	5.2		59.3	5.2
Japan	53,098	149.2[b]	0.3		149.2	0.3
Netherlands	5,145	193.4	3.6	70.8	122.6	2.3
Sweden	4,043	190.0	4.5	105.0	85.0	2.0
Switzerland	3,264	887.3	21.4	335.0	552.3	13.3
UK	27,533	775.0	2.7	56.5	718.5	2.5

Notes: "Low-end" foreign workers here refers to employed non-citizens who do not enjoy freedom of labor mobility under a common labor market arrangement (specifically, the European Union or the Nordic Common Labor Market).
[a] Israel Central Bureau of Statistics.
[b] Immigration Bureau, Japan 1990.
Sources: Labor force: Datastream; other figures from SOPEMI except where noted.

awkward and necessary; on the one hand, there was no great transformation of Italy from 1967 to 1968; moreover, for the most part the Italians who worked in Switzerland in 1968 were probably the same individuals who worked in Switzerland in 1967. But discerning a more gradual transition would make for an unworkable method of operationalizing "foreign workers" as regards Italians.

A more general survey

The primary difficulty with the conceptual definition I have developed here relates to the problem of getting appropriate data. Migration researchers routinely complain about the quality of data, especially regarding its comparability. In my case, I am truly asking for the moon. Since I will not get it, I need to explain the strategy that informs the empirical presentation below.

To operationalize the concept of low-wage foreign labor in other countries, I draw mainly on data from SOPEMI. In the first instance, the difficulty is that many countries are covered by SOPEMI only for quite recent years. The last column of Tables 2.2 through 2.5[5] (relating to more recent years) excludes foreign workers in the labor force who are (1) from countries with which the host country has a common labor market arrangement such as the Nordic Labor Market; (2) clearly identifiable in SOPEMI data as teachers, professionals, or managers; or (3) from wealthy countries (Japan, Canada, Australia, the US, and Western Europe – though not Spain and Portugal before 1993), even if there is no common labor market arrangement between the sending and receiving countries. (The latter two categories are collapsed into "elite workers" in Tables 2.3, 2.4, and 2.5.) For example, many of the approximately 94,000 foreign workers with professionals' work permits in Japan are from countries like the US and Britain (SOPEMI 1995); it violates common sense to put these individuals in the same category as unskilled workers from China and Iran. Likewise, Finnish workers in Sweden and the other Nordic countries are not included in the last column; the same applies to all workers from EU countries working in other EU countries.[6]

This latter adjustment has not been possible in all cases: SOPEMI provides information on country of origin in many but not all instances, so that it is not possible from available data to know how many North Americans are included in the figures for Germany, for example. This raises the possibility that for some countries the number of low-wage foreign workers is overstated by the last two columns of Tables 2.2 through 2.5. If this were true, then these tables would overstate the extent of the variation I intend to capture. I cannot entirely dismiss this possibility. However, there are good reasons to conclude that the problem is not serious. Consider Germany, for example, where the percentage of low-wage

Table 2.3   Foreign workers, 1983 (thousands)

	Labor force	Total foreign	Percent foreign	Common market	Other elite	Maximum low-end foreign	Max. % low-end foreign
Austria	3,294	145.3	4.2			145.3	4.2
Belgium	3,634	190.6	5.0	63.8		126.8	3.3
Canada[a]	11,978	468.5[a]	3.8			468.5	3.8
Denmark	2,389	51.9	2.1	12.2	9.9	29.8	1.2
France	21,154	1,578.4	6.9	138.5		1,439.3	6.3
Germany	24,690	1,983.5	7.4	273.4		1,710.1	6.4
Israel	1,238	87.8[b]	6.6			87.8	6.6
Italy	22,564	766.5[c]	3.3			766.5	3.3
Japan	57,330	170.6[d]	0.3			170.6	0.3
Luxemburg	158	53.8	25.4	51.0		2.8	1.3
Netherlands	4,932	174.0	3.4	78.0		96.0	1.9
Norway[e]	2,183	49.5	2.2	17.2	11.3	21.0	0.9
Spain[e]	14,889	58.2	0.4		19.2	39.0	0.3
Sweden	4,224	222.0	5.0	121.0		101.0	2.3
Switzerland	2,994	629.9[f]	17.4		339.5	295.8	8.0
UK[g]	27,415	744.0	2.6	361.0	53.0	330.0	1.2

Notes: "Low-level foreign workers" refers here (and in Table 2.4) to employed non-citizens who do not enjoy freedom of mobility under common labor market arrangements; the term also excludes workers from wealthy countries – Western Europe (but not Spain or Portugal), the US, Canada, Australia, Japan – and workers identified in SOPEMI as professionals, managers, and teachers.

Figures from SOPEMI generally exclude foreign workers who are unemployed (the exception is Finland); but whether the unemployed are excluded is unclear for Denmark, France, Germany, Ireland, Japan, Spain, and Sweden.

[a] 1980; from Beaujot *et al.* 1981. Calculated as follows: Beaujot *et al.* identified 179,000 immigrant-headed families and 200,000 single immigrants who fell into the Canadian low-income status category. On the assumption that half of the families had two members in the labor force (and the rest had one), then $200 + 179 \times 1.5 = 468.5$. This figure includes an unknown number of workers who had already become naturalized citizens.

[b] Israel Central Bureau of Statistics.

[c] 1984; from Calavita 1994, p. 307; includes an estimate of 464,900 illegal workers.

[d] Immigration Bureau, Japan 1990.

[e] 1988.

[f] Includes seasonal workers.

[g] 1984.

Sources: Labor force: Datastream; other figures from SOPEMI except where noted.

foreign labor registered in the last column is relatively high. Here it is well known that very large numbers of foreigners with work permits are from Turkey and the former Yugoslavia, and that most of these workers are employed in sectors such as manufacturing, construction, and low-wage services.[7] It is very unlikely that I have failed to account for so many elite workers that the relevant (percentage) figures would change very

Table 2.4 Foreign Workers, 1993 (thousands)

	Labor force	Total foreign	Percent foreign	Common market	Other elite[a]	Maximum low-end foreign	Max. % low-end foreign
Austria	3,679	277.5	7.0	19.1		258.4	6.5
Belgium[b]	4,095	194.6	4.5	82.0		112.6	2.6
Denmark[c]	2,886	74.0	3.3	30.7		43.3	1.5
Finland	2,508	25.0	1.0	4.5		20.5	0.8
France	25,155	1,541.5	5.8	658.7		1,346.5	5.0
Germany	30,949	2,575.9	7.7	493.4		2,082.5	6.2
Greece	4,034	500.0[d]	11.0			500.0	11.0
Ireland[e]	1,354	40.0	2.9	30.0	4.0	6.0	0.4
Israel[f]	2,110	159.5[g]	7.0			159.5	7.0
Italy	21,609	994.7	4.4	80.0		914.7	4.0
Japan	66,150	771.7[h]	1.2		95.4[h]	676.3	1.0
Luxemburg[c]	167	92.6	35.7	82.7		9.9	3.8
Netherlands	6,406	219.0	3.3	91.0		128.0	1.9
Norway	2,131	47.9	2.2	14.9	11.2	21.8	1.0
Spain	15,319	365.4[i]	2.3		4.8	360.6	2.3
Sweden	4,320	221.0	4.9	95.0		126.0	2.8
Switzerland	3,389	980.3	22.4		697.8	282.5	6.5
UK	28,271	862.0	3.0	359.0	99.0	404.0	1.4
USA	129,525	7,801.0[j]	5.7		2623.0[j]	5,178.0	3.8

Notes: See Table 2.3.

[a] "Other elite" workers includes those employed as professionals, managers, and teachers as well as workers from wealthy countries (Western Europe, the US, Japan, Canada, Australia, New Zealand) even when there is no common labor market arrangement.

[b] 1989.

[c] 1992.

[d] See Glytsos 1995.

[e] 1991.

[f] 1995.

[g] Includes 40,600 Palestinian workers, 68,900 other workers with permits, and an estimated 50,000 illegal workers. See Bartram 1998 for further details.

[h] SOPEMI, citing Japan Labor Ministry estimate of 297,000 overstayers, 303,000 workers with permits (including students and Nikkei workers); and 171,000 permanent residents in the labor force, data from Immigration Bureau, Japan 1990. "Other elite workers" refers to foreigners whose permits allow them to engage in "specific professional activities."

[i] From SOPEMI, 115.4 workers with permits, and from Cornelius 1994 (p. 335), an estimate of between 200,000 and 300,000 illegal workers (entered here as 250,000). The SOPEMI figures already exclude workers from elsewhere in the European Union.

[j] US Current Population Survey, "The Foreign-Born Population," P20-486. "Other elite" workers in the US refers to employed non-citizens earning more than $20,000.

Sources: See Table 2.3.

Table 2.5 Foreign workers, 2000 (thousands)

	Labor force	Total foreign	Percent foreign	Common market	Other elite[a]	Maximum low-end foreign	Max. % low-end foreign
Austria	3,882	242.2	6.2			242.2	6.2
Belgium[b]	4,330	386.2	8.9	261.3		124.9	2.9
Denmark	2,824	96.8	3.4	30.5		66.3	2.3
Finland[b]	2,548	37.2	1.5	6.5		30.7	1.2
France[c]	26,624	1,617.6	6.1	608.4		1,009.2	3.8
Germany	39,303	3,546.0	9.0	1,027.0		2,519.0	6.4
Greece[d]	4,482	585.0	13.1		5.3	597.7	12.9
Ireland	1,739	59.9	3.4	47.5	2.8	9.6	0.6
Israel[e]	2,655	220.0	8.3			220.0	8.3
Italy	23,369	759.7	3.3			759.7	3.3
Japan	67,660	710.0	1.0		50.2	659.8	1.0
Luxemburg	267	152.7	57.3	141.7		11.0	4.1
Netherlands[d]	7,761	235.0	3.0	116.0		119.0	1.5
Norway	2,327	111.2	4.8	40.4		70.8	3.0
Spain[b]	17,220	310.2	1.8	110.4		119.8	1.2
Sweden	4,418	222.0	5.0	90.0		132.0	3.0
Switzerland	4,196	873.3	20.8		625.8	247.5	5.9
UK[c]	29,372	1,229.0	4.2	483.0	145.0	601.0	2.0

Notes: [a] "Other elite" workers includes those employed as professionals, managers, and teachers as well as workers from wealthy countries (Western Europe, the US, Japan, Canada, Australia, New Zealand) even when there is no common labor market arrangement.
[b] 1999.
[c] 2001.
[d] 1998.
[e] Israel Central Bureau of Statistics.

much if I had more detailed information. The same point should hold for Austria, Belgium, France, Israel, and Switzerland, other countries where the indicated percentage of low-wage foreigners is relatively high. Nonetheless, there is no question that the quality of these data is not excellent: it has been necessary to use different methods and types of data to arrive at figures concerning use of low-wage foreign labor. Even when data concerning many countries are collected in one place (e.g., SOPEMI, Descloitres 1967), the fact that different countries use different definitions and methods of collecting data means that strict comparability is far from ensured (Coleman 1997).

It does appear, however, that the data are good enough to allow us to see a different picture than the one often presented in discussions of international labor migration. In some countries, the percentage of low-wage foreign workers in the receiving country labor force at some point between 1964 and 1993 exceeded six percent (Israel, Greece, Austria, Belgium, France, Switzerland, Germany). In others, the percentage remained below two percent throughout the entire period (Ireland, Finland, Norway, Japan, Denmark). When the data are viewed this way, claims about foreign labor as a "structural" part of advanced capitalist economies become a bit suspect.[8]

The point is reinforced by further consideration of some of the low-percentage countries. For Denmark and Finland, for example, the figure in the "Maximum Low-wage Foreign" column includes foreigners with work permits who are unemployed. In Denmark, almost half of low-wage foreigners are unemployed, and in Finland the rate is 40 percent. Substantial numbers of foreigners in some other receiving countries are unemployed, but they are already excluded from the relevant figures in each row. Unemployment among foreigners residing in wealthy countries erodes the labor market position of employed foreigners by threatening the latter with displacement and moderating wage demands. In this respect, the employment of foreigners indicates a demand for very cheap and vulnerable labor. But the substantial unemployment rates also indicate that that demand for cheap labor is quite limited: even when foreigners are already present and have the willingness (presumably) and the legal right to work, employers in some countries have no use for them.

Foreign workers in wealthy countries

The variation in use of foreign labor emerges quite clearly in Tables 2.1 through 2.5, which reveal (in the last column) the percentage of each country's labor force that is composed of low-wage foreign labor. Table 2.6 merely summarizes and synthesizes the data from the previous tables.

Conclusion

The unmistakable conclusion emerging from this survey is that low-wage foreign workers have had a varied, uneven presence in advanced capitalist countries. Contrary to some theoretical perspectives, there is no imperative of capitalist development that demands large amounts of cheap imported labor as citizen populations become wealthier and/or choosier about the kinds of work they will accept. In fact, some of the world's wealthiest countries are among the ones with the smallest

Table 2.6 Low-level foreign labor as percentage of labor force

	1964	1974	1983	1993	2000
Austria	1.2	6.2	4.2	6.5	6.2
Belgium	9.8	4.7	3.3	2.6	2.9
Denmark	0.5		1.2	1.5	2.3
Finland				0.8	1.2
France	6.2	7.0	6.3	5.0	3.8
Germany	4.0	6.4	6.4	6.2	6.4
Greece				11.0	12.9
Ireland				0.4	0.6
Israel		5.2	6.6	7.0	8.3
Italy			3.3	4.0	3.3
Japan	0.7	0.7	0.7	1.0	1.0
Luxemburg			1.3	3.8	4.1
Netherlands	1.3	2.3	1.9	1.9	1.5
Norway	1.0		0.9	1.0	3.0
Spain			0.3	2.3	1.2
Sweden	4.2	2.0	2.3	2.8	3.0
Switzerland	31.2	13.3	8.0	6.5	5.9
UK		2.5	1.2	1.4	2.0

Notes: Use of or citation from this table without detailed reference to the contextual material and methodological discussion in this chapter is strongly discouraged. For example, the apparent decline in foreign workers as a percentage of the Swiss labor force is entirely a product of changing definitions and data quality and is not a real decline. For 1964, there is no indication of how many workers in Switzerland came from neighboring countries, and in 1974 only workers from Italy have been deducted (and not the many workers from France and Germany).

Sources: Compiled from previous tables.

percentage of low-wage foreigners in the labor force (Japan, Norway, Finland). At all levels of development among advanced capitalist countries, there are many countries that do receive large numbers of foreign workers, but there are also a few countries that do not. The range of variation is significant enough in absolute terms – more than 11 percent in Israel, versus less than one percent in Ireland and Finland – but in relative terms the variation is even more impressive: the high and the low values differ by more than a factor of ten. Even discounting the upper outliers, the extent of variation is substantial: four of the main guest-worker countries in the postwar period (Germany, France, Austria, and Switzerland) have used at least three times as much low-wage foreign labor, in relative terms, as five other countries (Japan, Finland, Ireland, Norway, and Denmark).

The question then becomes: why do some countries end up importing large amounts of foreign labor while others rely almost exclusively on labor provided by natives/citizens? How do we explain the variation? The rest of the book takes up this question through an examination of contrasting cases.

3
Foreign Workers Policy in Israel

The discussion in the previous chapters allows us to approach the study of positive cases of labor migration with a fresh perspective. The question we will ask concerning labor migration to Israel is no longer simply: why did Israel import foreign labor? The question also becomes: why did Israel fail to follow another strategy for solving its labor supply problems? The relevance of this question is reinforced by the fact that many Israeli policymakers did not want foreign labor and held a clear preference for an alternative solution. The heart of the matter is that such a solution was not achievable, given certain features of the Israeli state.

I will argue here that the importation of foreign labor in Israel is directly connected to the structure of the Israeli state, a structure which frustrated efforts to implement the kind of policy measures that would likely have significantly reduced the demand for cheap foreign labor. The policy process for at least some economic issues in Israel exhibits a number of characteristics that sharply distinguish it from economic policymaking in a developmentalist state such as Japan. In particular, this process is highly politicized, fragmented, and marked by short-term thinking. These characteristics mean that in many cases private interests have the ability to block changes that threaten their interests, and in particular their profits. This statement is especially true concerning the difficult changes that would have been required for restructuring the construction industry in Israel, a precondition for limiting the number of foreign workers while also achieving other goals important to the government.

Because the government was unable to bring about changes that would have reduced labor requirements, and because increasing the housing stock was an important national priority, policymakers perceived that they had no choice but to accede to contractors' demands for imported labor when Palestinian workers became unavailable. Some policymakers believed that, in making this decision, they were simply acting like policymakers in any other advanced capitalist country, where foreign labor was taken to be an inevitable outgrowth of economic development. We have already established grounds for rejecting this view. The Israeli decision to import labor was inevitable only in a certain institutional context that put alternative solutions to labor shortages out of reach. As we will see, Israeli policymakers did not *want* to open its labor force to non-citizens any more than Japan did. In addition to the economic costs of foreign labor, we can consider that Israel is an ethno-nationalist society to the extent that the presence of foreigners is considered highly undesirable, except as tourists.[1] Nor was the structure of the two economies different in a way that predisposed Israel to "need" foreign workers in the mid-1990s more than Japan had experienced such a need 25 years earlier.[2] The factor that effectively distinguishes the two countries on this question is the institutional structure of the state as it affects the capacity for economic policymaking. If the Israeli government had been able to implement a different policy, it almost certainly would have done so, and the presence of foreigners in the labor force would have remained quite small.

I begin with a brief discussion of perspectives on policymaking in Israel, to provide a context for understanding the policymaking process concerning foreign workers and to clarify some misconceptions in the literature. I then summarize the history of Palestinian workers in Israel, an important precursor to the more recent experience with other foreign workers. The analysis of foreign workers themselves, focusing on construction workers, then has three sections: a descriptive summary of basic parameters, an examination of why efforts to pursue alternative solutions failed, and a discussion of the policy process that led to the decisions to allow imported labor. I also include a brief treatment of foreign workers in agriculture.

Policymaking in Israel

To interpret the policy process concerning foreign labor, we must understand to what extent that process shares characteristics with other policy areas that have been central to Israeli governance, especially concerning the economy. As a first step in this discussion, I will attempt to sort out some of the claims made by a variety of observers concerning economic policymaking in Israel. I argue here that a common perception concerning the strength of the Israeli state is misguided: while Israel has strong political parties, the institutions of the state (especially in more recent years) are relatively weak, in particular because they are dominated by the parties and their constituencies (Grinberg 1993b). This position is elaborated in general terms here and will be a central theme in the discussion of foreign workers policy below.

The dominant position would seem to be that Israel is characterized by a strong state whose government plays a central role in the management of the economy. Government officials have (or have had) a variety of tools to guide economic activity (Pack 1971). In particular, the government was long the overwhelmingly dominant factor in the capital market, especially by virtue of its control over inflows of foreign capital (e.g., Plessner 1994). In the early years of the state, policymakers did not trust private capital to invest in ways that would achieve national goals and used their power to direct investment to particular types of industries and regions (Ben-Porath 1982; Kleiman 1997). The government's ability to direct economic activity in this way has led one observer to conclude that Israel has a developmentalist state similar in many ways to those of Taiwan and South Korea (Levi-Faur 1998). In another discussion, the Israeli state is held to be similar to the strong states of Germany and the Netherlands – as against the weak American state – because of the high density of its policy networks (Maman 1997).

Many observers assert that the power of the government in directing economic activity was especially great in the first two decades of statehood. Shimshoni (1982) has referred to governments of that period as having a "dual-presidential" structure, where the prime minister dealt with foreign policy and some domestic issues while the finance minister had absolute authority/autonomy over matters of economic policy (see also Aharoni 1998). More recently the government's power has declined: finance ministers have less autonomy from other political actors (Shimshoni 1982), and a wider variety of actors participates in economic policymaking, resulting in a multiplication of veto points (Zalmanovitch 1998). But on balance there is a widespread perception that the economy is still highly politicized and that the Israeli state continues to be strong in this respect, relative to many other capitalist countries (e.g., Aharoni 1998).

This view is challenged by Grinberg (1993b), who argues that Israel has strong political institutions, but not a strong state. In this approach, political institutions are usefully conceived as separate from state institutions, in particular because the relationship between them can assume a variety of forms. This argument has significant implications for our understanding of foreign worker policy: as we will see, one of the key determinants of this policy has been the fact that political leaders, as distinct from officials in the bureaucracy, are the real power holders in such decisions.

Even in the early decades of statehood, Grinberg argues, the state was dominated by (Mapai) party-affiliated organizations, especially the Histadrut trade union federation. Mapai depended on the Histadrut for maintenance of its political power in a way that often limited state policymakers' ability to pursue the economic policies they preferred – even though those policymakers were central Mapai figures. The state may have had powerful tools for directing private (as well as public) economic activity, but the state's relationship with dominant party institutions reduced state officials' ability to use those tools as they saw fit. In particular, professional finance ministry staff were often unable to pursue macroeconomic policies which they believed would strengthen the economy in the long term. Political factors, such as Mapai's need to woo Histadrut members, determined that state budgets would contain large subsidies for both labor and capital (see also Shalev 1992). State support for labor – or, more exactly, elite labor[3] – was especially generous before 1967.

After the Six-Day War, and with the economic boom spurred by massively increased defense spending[4] (e.g., Bichler 1986), subsidies for capital increased substantially. Concentration of the economy accelerated, mainly as a result of state-sponsored investments in research and development as well as production for the emerging local defense industry. The five "core conglomerates," which had come to prominence already in the 1960s, saw their profits increase dramatically during the 1970s (Nitzan and Bichler 1996). There is no question that the state was responsible for the increasing fortunes of these organizations, but the end result was perhaps different from what policymakers originally had in mind:

> Having built up an industrial sector characterized by an extremely concentrated core, acute dependency on patronage and subsidy, and intimate formal and informal links with the political elite, the state had unwittingly created a centre of power capable of making compelling claims on its resources. (Shalev 1989: 131)

The accession of the Likud (with its liberal Herut partner) in 1977 was expected to lead to a decline in the extent to which both producers and consumers were subsidized, in particular via exchange rate manipulation, but initial moves in this direction were quickly abandoned (see also Ben-Porath 1982).

The state did achieve some additional degree of autonomy from capital with its anti-hyper-inflation Stabilization Plan of 1985 (Bruno 1993), but the liberalization program widely perceived to have been taking place since then has had uneven results at best (Shalev 1998): the state has ended many subsidies for many producers, but these losses have been offset by business tax cuts of a similar size. Moreover, certain incentives targeted at specific firms have remained very significant. The meaning of some of these changes is ambiguous: they are certainly intended (i.e., by the government officials responsible for their design) to enhance the autonomy of the state from private actors, but the continuing subsidies testify to the limits of that effort.

The Israeli state in the 1950s and 1960s resembled the basic image of a developmentalist state in some important respects. This was a period of very fast economic growth in Israel, and the government played a major role in organizing and catalyzing that growth. On the other hand, political leaders and not the professional bureaucratic staff were the real policymakers, indicating a significant deviation from the ideal type.

What really matters here, however, is that the capacity of the Israeli state for coherent economic governance has declined significantly since the 1960s. The earlier capacity of the government derived in large part from the weakness of (un)organized capital and Mapai's position as a dominant party (Shapiro 1996). Neither of those conditions has held now for some time (on the rise of organized capital, see Shirom 1984). Whatever one makes of arguments concerning state autonomy in the earlier period (and there are reasons at least to make such arguments more subtle), more recently the increasing power of capital has helped define a new period in Israeli political economy. The state's economic policy capacity has also suffered from the increasing fragmentation of Israeli politics and the demise of Mapai/Labor as the dominant party (Shalev 1990). As Shimshoni writes, "In a quasi-feudal coalition government structure, professional analytical or planning effort, which is not closely coupled with those who have the power for ongoing action, can have very limited effectiveness" (1982: 254; see also Roniger 1994). "Those who have the power" refers primarily to political leaders, and the fragmentation of the bureaucracy described in Shimshoni's work points to the difficulty that the professional staff usually have in asserting their preferences against those of the political elite.

Grinberg's and Shalev's arguments lead to the conclusion that analyses of economic governance, especially with respect to more recent periods, cannot be satisfied with statements about state "strength." There is no question that Israel has had a strong state in many respects: the positions summarized earlier in this section are correct on their own terms. But if we are concerned with *how* economies are actually governed, or with the *content* of the policies that strong (or weak) states adopt and implement, then we must refocus the question. Instead of asking whether or to what extent the government intervenes in the economy, we can ask *how* the state shapes economic activity. Instead of asking only whether the state is weak or strong, we can ask, why has the state implemented certain types of policies and not others? And, just as important, why has the state failed to implement certain kinds of policies in spite of good intentions and official adoption?

Answers to those questions must come from an investigation of the internal structure of the Israeli state and its relations with other central institutions in Israeli society.[5] Relevant items include shaky coalition governments (especially after the decline of Mapai/Labor – see Shalev 1990) and the fragmentation and weakness of professional bureaucrats (Schecter 1972). These characteristics emerge, for example, in a study of an urban renewal project in the late 1970s (Lazin 1994). "Project Renewal" was supposed to relieve slum conditions among Eastern (Mizrachi) Jews, following up on a campaign promise Menachem Begin made in 1977. The program had some beneficial effects, but in general it did not achieve most of the goals its creators intended. Implementation was hampered by the fact that different parties in the governing coalition controlled the various ministries and other government bodies responsible for the project. The Housing Ministry, for example, was controlled by a smaller party, and the Housing Minister refused to cede his authority to the inter-ministerial committee that was supposed to coordinate the whole effort – because that committee was controlled by a Likud-nominated figure.[6] Moreover, in the absence of a political culture and legal system demanding strict adherence to rules, project funds – some of which had been raised from foreign donors – were diverted from their intended use and used to supplement or replace ministry operating budgets. We will encounter similar themes in our analysis of foreign worker policy as well. (For additional examples see contributions to Nachmias and Menahem 2002).

In addition, and in direct contrast to the Japanese case, the bureaucracy as a whole carries relatively little prestige in Israeli society. Preference for civil service employment is strongest among those with the least education (Nachmias and Rosenbloom 1978). "Clerks" are often despised, by the public and senior politicians alike. "Despite considerable effort at its establishment, a high degree of administrative professionalism remains elusive" (Nachmias and Rosenbloom 1978: 47).[7] There are formal hiring procedures and a Civil Service Commission, but there is a substantial gap between theory (i.e., law) and reality here: political parties generally have the ability to make the civil service appointments that suit their needs.

The Israeli state is a strong state in some respects. The government plays a central role in determining what kind of economic activity takes place (e.g., for export vs. for domestic consumption), under what conditions, to what degree of profitability, etc. But the content of this economic policy regime is quite different from the developmentalism of states like Japan and South Korea. The logic behind many of the policies actually implemented is often not a logic of economic growth but instead a logic of political survival and advancement of party and personal private interests (for a direct discussion of rent-seeking in Israel, see Kleiman 1997). While such a logic characterizes all regimes to a certain extent, the particular institutional context in which Israeli policymakers operate determines that some types of goals are often frustrated. This chapter on foreign workers in Israel will illustrate and defend this contention; this general description of the Israeli state is entirely consistent with the recent experience of policymaking concerning foreign workers.

Palestinians from the occupied territories

The primary focus of this study is the entry of foreign workers to the Israeli labor market in the early 1990s. The essential background to this more recent episode is Israel's long-standing reliance on Palestinian workers from the occupied West Bank and Gaza in some key economic sectors. In many respects, non-citizen Palestinians represent a paradigm of cheap foreign labor: their lack of citizenship in the host society as well as the underdeveloped economy in the sending region determined that their entry to the Israeli labor market would take place at the bottom, expanding the supply of cheap unskilled labor. On the other hand, Israel's occupation of the "sending country" distinguishes this particular labor flow from more familiar labor migrations to other advanced industrial countries: the occupied territories are part of the "Israeli control system" (Kimmerling 1989; see also Lustick 1980) in a way that most sending countries are not (relative to the respective receiving countries).[8] In some other ways as well, Palestinian participation in the Israeli economy is distinct from other instances of labor migration, as we will see. The similarities arguably outweigh the differences, but there are differences.

Israel already had a highly stratified labor market by 1967, when its army occupied large amounts of Arab territory in the Six-Day War. Palestinian citizens of Israel, constituting 14 percent of the population, were at the bottom of the job market; internal military restrictions hampered their freedom of movement until 1966, and a host of social, economic, political, and cultural factors determined that they would hold the least attractive jobs.[9] Jews from Middle Eastern and North African countries were also disadvantaged relative to Ashkenazi (European) Jews, who held most of the elite government, professional, and business positions. Palestinians thus entered the labor market at the bottom, while other groups advanced in the queue (Semyonov and Lewin-Epstein 1987; see also Neuman 1994 and Makhoul 1982).

The decision after the 1967 war to allow residents of the occupied territories to work in Israel did not come automatically but was the product of a prolonged discussion among the government, the army, employers' associations, and the trade union federation (the Histadrut). The specific policy adopted reflected the prevailing balance of interests and power (Grinberg 1993a). Economic and political factors converged to "overdetermine" this choice (Rosenhek 2003). The army and the security establishment favored allowing workers to enter Israel, as they wanted to ensure that Palestinians in the territories would be able to make a living now that connections with Egypt and Jordan were inhibited; economic prosperity was required, so the thinking went, to prevent civil unrest. The Finance Ministry and employers were interested in cheap labor at a time of rapid economic expansion. Some employers also wanted to invest in the territories themselves, taking capital to the workers instead of vice-versa. But some ministers rejected this idea, arguing that Israel needed to maintain the option of withdrawing from the territories without worrying about employers' interests there. The Histadrut also favored allowing workers to enter, at first glance perhaps a strange position for a labor movement to take. But the federation had its own interest as an employer controlling about 20 percent of the economy. Federation officials also saw that they could restrain business sector wages and maintain control over Israeli workers by introducing cheap competition from Palestinians, while protecting the position of the public sector workers who had real power in the unions (Grinberg 1991, 1993a).[10]

Some writers (e.g., Aronson 1987) have argued that the Israeli government opened its labor market to Palestinians as part of a design to make the territories dependent on Israel and thus to preclude the eventual establishment of a Palestinian state. Dependency of Palestinians on Israeli jobs was clearly one result of Palestinians' entry into that labor market. But Grinberg (1993a) has shown effectively that Israeli policy-makers at that time were more concerned with solving immediate problems such as maintaining public order and paid less attention to long-term consequences. Only later did they appreciate that labor market dependency would hinder Palestinian national aspirations.[11] On the other hand, the opening of the labor market was accompanied by other Israeli policy responses to its acquisition of territory in the war. The Allon Plan called for settling strategic areas of the territories, separating Palestinian population centers and inhibiting future territorial concessions. And Moshe Dayan's policy of "open bridges" allowed Palestinians to export their produce to Jordan, so that Israeli producers (especially farmers) would not have to face competition from a less-developed economy (Aronson 1987). The link between "security" concerns and economic policy is further illustrated by survey results demonstrating that a majority of commuting workers from the West Bank began working in Israel only after their family's land had been confiscated (Kadri 1998).

Palestinians began crossing the border illegally in small numbers, and only in 1969 did the government begin issuing permits. A Cabinet memo of 1970 governed the conditions of Palestinian employment (Angrist 1994). Permits were issued on conditions similar to those required of foreign workers in other countries; in particular, the state's Employment Service was supposed to ensure that no Israelis could be found before offering a job to a Palestinian, though in practice the two labor forces quickly became largely complementary and not competitive. Eventually, permits were granted only to Palestinians with no record of "security offenses," a term subject to wide interpretation by the authorities and generally connoting any active form of resistance to the Israeli occupation. In practice, though, not having a permit was no real barrier to finding work: border control and permit enforcement were haphazard at best, as the Israeli government tolerated illegal border crossings much in the same way the US government has long tolerated such crossings by Mexican workers in the American Southwest.

Palestinians found jobs mainly in construction, agriculture, and services. By the mid-1980s, around 110,000 were employed in Israel, though less than half of these had permits (Table 3.1). They constituted 6 to 7 percent of the Israeli labor force, though one-third of the West Bank labor force and about half that of Gaza. In sectoral terms the percentages

Table 3.1   Non-citizen Palestinian workers in Israel (thousands)

	N	% of employed persons	Construction N	Construction %	Industry N	Industry %	Agriculture N	Agriculture %	Other N
1970	19.8	2.0	10.8	11.9	2.3	1.0	5.0	5.6	1.7
1975	63.9	5.4	35.2	28.1	11.9	4.2	9.2	12.7	7.6
1980	70.4	5.3	33.8	29.9	15.0	4.8	9.6	12.1	12.0
1985	89.2	6.1	42.5	37.0	15.9	4.8	14.1	18.0	16.8
1990	107.7	6.7	64.1	45.7	11.2	3.4	12.6	20.3	19.8
1991	97.8	5.8	67.0	41.1	7.5	2.2	11.7	21.1	11.5
1992	115.6	6.5	85.9	44.4	6.9	1.9	10.4	18.0	12.4
1993	83.8	4.5	60.8	33.3	4.8	1.3	8.6	11.9	9.6
1994	46.7	2.4	29.8	17.8	3.5	0.9	5.0	6.9	8.4
1995	40.6	2.0	26.8	12.4	3.3	8.0	3.7	5.0	6.8

Note: Data are from labor force surveys and thus include at least some workers without permits.
Source: Central Bureau of Statistics.

were more impressive: at the peak, Palestinians held 25 percent of Israeli agricultural jobs and 45 percent of construction jobs (Central Bureau of Statistics 1994). This was a highly mobile work force: almost 50 percent changed jobs at least once a year (Portugali 1989).

The employment of Palestinians as cheap labor had strong effects on the development of the two main sectors where their presence was significant (construction and agriculture). In particular, relative wages fell substantially. Using an index of 100 to describe average wages in manufacturing, construction wages fell from 104 in 1967 to 77 in 1991, and wages in agriculture fell from 62 to 50 (Condor 1997).

These figures are probably related to weak labor productivity growth as well (Bar-Natan 1984). Official figures paint an exaggerated picture of increases in construction labor productivity from the 1970s onward. Using official figures, it is possible to arrive at the conclusion that construction labor productivity increased at an average annual rate of 1.3 percent from 1970 through 1995. But we arrive at this result by dividing output by employment, and official statistics on employment do not record the substantial presence of illegal or undocumented workers (both Palestinian and foreign), particularly in construction. An increase in the base would decrease the value of the result. Using relatively conservative estimates,[12] let us assume that the number of illegal workers in construction grew from 20,000 in 1985 to 50,000 in 1990. Average yearly increases in construction labor productivity would then drop to 0.5 percent. A similar point holds for figures on wage increases: official figures on increase in construction wages are also likely overstated by the fact that the data refer to official, recorded wage payments. If we included the wages received unofficially by many Palestinian and other foreigner workers, the average would most likely drop significantly. Moreover, foreign workers tend to work very long hours (an average of 280 hours a month): average wages calculated on an hourly basis would be even less impressive than those calculated on a monthly basis.

Palestinian workers in Israel are subject to a host of administrative requirements and legal constraints. Work permits are granted for limited durations and for specific jobs. Changing jobs means getting a new permit, which is often an intrusive and time-consuming process (International Labour Office 1989). Workers must return to the territories at the end of each day; they are forbidden from spending the night in Israel, though some workers, with the help of their employers, sleep at their work sites during the week to save time and transportation costs (Gharaybah 1985). As non-residents, Palestinian workers are prohibited from forming their own unions in Israel, nor may they join the main Israeli trade union federation (the Histadrut). Their non-resident status also bars them from receiving unemployment and certain other benefits, though they are subject to the same paycheck deductions as Israeli workers. The state defends these deductions as a way of "equalizing" the cost of Palestinian and Israeli workers so that employers do not have even greater incentives to prefer Palestinians over Israelis, though this policy certainly carries fiscal benefits to the state as well.

Israel's experience with Palestinians from the occupied territories is of course an essential precursor to the later entry of foreign workers from outside the region. In many respects, however, this experience is not an exemplary case of labor migration: a number of unusual circumstances contributed to the government's decision to allow Palestinians' entry into the labor market. Most importantly, it is very unlikely that Palestinians would have gained access to the Israeli labor market if the army had not conquered the territory and assumed responsibility for its inhabitants. Even the resumption of economic growth that characterized the postwar period was in many respects a result of the war and its subsequent effects on the Israeli political economy (Kanovsky 1970; Mintz 1983; Shalev 1992). This growth contributed to the strong demand for labor that Palestinian workers met, particularly in the construction industry. The government's choice to address unmet labor demand in this manner was by no means inevitable. This was perhaps the first real opportunity for effecting some sort of structural transformation in labor-hungry sectors such as construction and agriculture.

But the army's interest in maintaining order and stability among the residents of the territories meshed in an irresistible way with the interests of employers in this period.

The fact that this cross-border migration resulted from a confluence of these two interests makes it very difficult to speculate as to what might have happened in the Israeli labor market had the war not occurred. It seems extremely unlikely, however, that Israeli governments would have opened the country's borders to (Arab) workers from the region, given the latent and sometimes open hostilities of the time.

A more conceivable option, assuming the emergence of labor short-ages, would have been to import labor from countries that were not involved in the regional geo-politics. This idea was raised among employers during the boom years before the war, but it was not the sub-ject of serious discussion in policy circles (YA 13.4.64; INT-Sanbar; for source codes on newspapers and interviews, see Appendix). At the time Israel was facing not only a labor shortage but also a serious balance of payments crisis and a widespread perception that labor was becoming too undisciplined (Ginzberg 1964; Grinberg 1993b; Weinshall 1976). Labor's share of national income was rising (Halevi and Klinov-Malul 1968); a policy of importing labor could have helped employers reverse this trend.[13] The government's response instead was to engineer a reces-sion (Aharoni 1998; Beham and Kleiman 1968; Greenwald 1973; Shalev 1984; 1992). This policy did in fact solve the balance of payments difficulties, but more to the point is that the main mechanism for doing so – the intentional exacerbation of unemployment – also directly resolved the problem of labor shortages, at least for the moment.

The foreign labor option was not viable as an alternative policy in part because allowing non-Jewish immigration of any kind was incompatible with the Zionist ideology of the time. Israeli leaders were very serious about the notion that Jews/Israel should be self-sufficient, an idea that was supposed to mean even refraining from employing Arab citizens (INT-Smit). (While some Arabs did work in the Jewish sector during this period, there was clearly room, from an economic point of view, for increasing employment of this relatively inexpensive labor – see Makhoul 1982.) There is no reason to think that this posture would have changed by the late 1960s, which suggests that the resumption of growth (i.e., in the absence of the war) would not necessarily have led to guest-worker programs even involving workers from non-Arab countries.

In addition, the weakness of capital – or, to put it differently, the relative strength of the state – during this period probably worked against the foreign worker option as well. The fact that the idea went nowhere when it was raised in 1964 is probably related to this weakness: employers pushed the idea no doubt because they perceived it was in their interest, but they were unable to realize that interest. Especially in light of the fact that the government did not respond to labor shortages in the mid-1960s by facilitating structural reform (e.g., in the construction sector), it would not be fully plausible to discern "developmentalism" in the Israeli state at this juncture. Still, the balance of power between capital and the government was clearly in the latter's favor, as discussed above.

While Palestinian workers are clearly relevant for understanding the later experience with foreign workers, then, this particular episode of imported labor is in some ways very different from the sort of labor migration that occurred in Western Europe during this time. Most importantly, not all European countries used their military forces to occupy the areas that sent them labor. France is the major exception, of course, but Algerian workers were at least formal citizens of France. The decision to import Palestinians was "overdetermined" by the unusual circumstances that characterized the policymaking process of the time (Grinberg 1993a).

More importantly, however, it would be a mistake to conclude that Israel's more recent experience with foreign labor is nothing but the replacement of one set of foreign workers by another. Many foreigners have recently taken jobs formerly held by Palestinians. But the new foreigners also work in sectors that never employed Palestinians (e.g., domestic help, care of elderly persons – see e.g., Raijman *et al.* 2003). In addition, the scale of foreign labor in Israel has reached a new order of magnitude in recent years: Palestinians constituted just over seven percent of the labor force in 1987, but Palestinians and other foreigners together have more recently almost doubled the foreign share of the labor force in a rather short time (depending on the reliability of various estimates concerning illegal workers). The labor force itself – the denominator of the percentage – has been significantly enlarged by the immigration of Russian Jews since 1989, and so the increase in foreign labor in the last decade is a very significant phenomenon that is by no means entirely attributable to the previous employment of Palestinians.

Moreover, the difficulties that arose concerning Palestinian workers (discussed in more detail below) did not *have* to mean that finding a substitute cheap foreign labor supply was imperative. Some Israeli policymakers saw these difficulties precisely as an opportunity for escaping the country's dependence on cheap foreign labor. Much of this chapter will focus on the reasons this opportunity was not exploited.

Israel's new foreign labor force

In this section I present a descriptive history of the country's recent experience with foreign labor. This description lays out many of the basic parameters of that experience, without yet exploring the structural factors that are relevant to explaining it. Those structural factors are the subject of the subsequent section.

Legal (Contract) workers – prehistory

The history of foreign labor in Israel and Palestine extends back to the pre-state, *Yishuv*, period, when workers from Egypt and the Sudan were employed in agriculture and some service jobs, especially in upscale hotels (Kleiman 1996). During the first two decades of Israeli statehood, however, the foreign component of the labor force was limited to a very small group of foreign professionals and technical advisors.

In 1979 an American company hired an almost all-foreign (mainly Portuguese and Thai) labor force to build a new army airbase in Israel's southern desert (HA 16.12.79; D 30.5.80). The airport was financed by the American government as a replacement for the Sinai base the Israelis gave up when they returned the Sinai to Egypt under the Camp David agreement. The agreement itself specified that an American company would build the base with foreign labor. Moreover, the numbers involved were rather small (about 1400) and all but five left the country when the project was finished (M 15.1.88). All told, it is best to view this instance as a product of unusual circumstances, substantially unrelated to Israel's other experiences with foreign labor: the conditions were not yet ripe for large-scale importation of non-Palestinian labor.

Foreign workers with permits in the 1980s were also few in number (1400 permits in 1984, or less than 0.2 percent of the labor force) and were mainly limited to specific sectors such as tourism, nursing, and geriatric care (YA 4.9.84; D 29.3.85). By 1987 the number had risen to 3000, many of whom were metal and textile workers from Portugal (M 1.1.88).

It might have been expected that the number of foreign workers would rise substantially with the beginning of the Palestinian uprising (*intifada*) in late 1987. But the increase was quite moderate, despite pressure from employers (HA 14.1.88). One month after the uprising began there were still only 3000 permits, including those granted previously (HA 22.1.88), even though the absentee rate among Palestinians was close to 50 percent in some sectors and the citrus harvest was threatened (HA 18.1.88). The Labor Minister, Moshe Katsav, alternately informed employers that they would not get foreign workers and threatened to flood the labor market with foreign workers so that the Palestinians would know they were replaceable (HA 22–26.1.88), but by mid-March the government had added a mere 50 permits for agricultural workers and 300 permits for construction workers.

Press assessments of the uprising's economic effects revealed little worry from a macroeconomic point of view: the uprising was not creating an economic crisis in Israel, though the effects were more severe in the territories themselves. By May 1988 an average of 82 percent of Palestinians employed in Israel were showing up for work, though the figure was only 65 percent in the construction sector. But individual firms were suffering, and the number of requests for foreign workers tripled by July, relative to the end of 1987 (HA 22.7.88). And even if a high percentage of workers continued showing up, they often did so irregularly, so that over the long term the issue for employers and employer associations became worker reliability rather than absolute numbers available. In one of the more interesting episodes in this effort, agricultural employers began importing Thai workers in larger numbers (HA 25.11.90), calling them "volunteers." These "volunteers" did not need work permits (until the government put a stop to the charade) but nonetheless received regular wages. (See also Cohen 1999 for more details on Thai agricultural workers in Israel.)

In 1989, after the disintegration of the Soviet Union had begun, Russian Jews began moving to Israel in large numbers (as citizens, not as foreign workers). Almost 200,000 arrived in 1990 alone, adding more than four percent to the population in a single year. This immigration had myriad effects on the Israeli economy and on the labor market in particular. First, the government had to worry about creating employment for the new immigrants; without work, the Russians were more likely to leave Israel for the US, a failure of Zionism the government was extremely keen to prevent.[14] Replacing Palestinians with Russian Jews thus became something of a national mission; as one Member of Parliament (Knesset) put it, "Soon anyone who employs Arabs will be forced to explain to neighbors, friends and business connections why they still prefer to employ Arabs instead of giving livelihood to Jews" (HA 25.11.90). And where the government saw a mission, employers saw an opportunity to escape from dependence on what they regarded as unreliable, dangerous workers. Thus in November 1990 the Citrus Forum of the Farmers' Association announced its intent to replace the bulk of its Palestinian labor force with new immigrants and other unemployed Israelis (HA 25.11.90). The government encouraged the construction sector as well to hire immigrants, with the Construction Ministry adopting a plan to pay a wage supplement equal to unemployment benefits to Israeli workers who accepted construction jobs. These efforts were not very successful among new immigrants. By the beginning of 1991 only 5000 new immigrants had taken jobs in construction (HA 21.1.91). Russian Jews had no more reason than other Jews to want "Arab jobs." Forty percent of them had been highly educated professionals in the Soviet Union (compared to nine percent of the Israeli labor force), not construction workers or grapefruit pickers (Ofer *et al.* 1991). Those who accepted the latter jobs did so temporarily, until they could find work suiting their qualifications and experience. Other Israelis (including Arab citizens) did join the construction sector in large numbers, but there was still a shortfall because of substantially increased demand.

In another respect the immigrants exacerbated the demand for cheap labor, by greatly increasing the demand for housing. The lack of adequate housing was another main factor in the decision of many Russians to re-migrate to the US and elsewhere. To prevent this, the government and private contractors thus embarked on a massive building project. Demand for inexpensive construction workers increased accordingly. Already in 1990 the Bank of Israel (1990) advocated, on essentially neoliberal grounds, a substantial increase in the permits allocated to foreign construction workers.

The government decided as early as 1991 to import foreign labor to solve bottlenecks in construction. Shortly before the Gulf War in January, Housing Minister Ariel Sharon convinced the government to grant 3000 permits for foreign construction workers, a number that probably would have been much larger but for the strenuous opposition of the Ministry of Labor, members of Parliament, and the Histadrut labor federation (D 8.1.91). Opposition was partly ideological and partly practical.[15] Government officials and MPs argued that foreign labor would exacerbate unemployment. Some MPs also held that Israel would not succeed where western European countries had failed: they knew that "temporary" workers in the latter had settled permanently, and they argued that Israel would not benefit from the presence of another large non-Jewish population, in addition to the country's Arab citizens.

But problems in the construction industry were becoming acute. Builders were accustomed to a ready supply of cheap labor (Palestinians) and were either unable or unwilling to invest in modernizing their building processes. Without cheap labor, contractors were finding themselves unable to meet contract deadlines. The penalties they had to pay to their customers were then passed on to future buyers, fueling inflation in the sector and in the economy as a whole (INT-Porshner). Inflation was being driven by housing cost increases that arose simply because the supply was insufficient.

During the 1991 Gulf War the government imposed a near-total closure on the territories, and building sites came to a standstill. After the war ended Palestinians were again allowed to enter, but the days of tolerating massive illegal border crossings and employment were supposed to be over, though in practice the percentage of illegal crossings simply dropped from around 65 percent to slightly less than 40 percent (HA 17.5.91, 31.10.91). Another closure (of Gaza) in May 1992 fueled employer demands for more foreign workers, but the real push was still to come as the extent of Palestinian terrorist activity within Israel increased.

Until this point, access to Palestinian labor was hindered but not severely disrupted. Border closures were relatively brief, and it was still possible in many cases to enter the country illegally, circumventing the closures.

The recent mass immigration

After a series of murders on Israeli territory by Palestinians in March 1993, the government announced a general closure of the territories. For the first time since 1967, Palestinians were unavailable to employers for an extended period. The construction boom was still on, and employers began to clamor, arguing that the government, having deprived them of their labor force, was responsible for finding an alternative. Agricultural employers made similar demands. The government again resisted their demands, instead trying again to make construction and agriculture jobs more attractive to unemployed Israelis by subsidizing their wages and offering free training courses.

The situation of the government was very difficult. Unemployment was at unprecedented levels (210,000, or more than 11 percent) and was especially high among the Russian immigrants. One hundred thousand people were receiving unemployment benefits, and another 30,000 were receiving income guarantees after exhausting their unemployment benefits (HA 15.3.93). The perception was that many people on unemployment were young, healthy, and otherwise capable of heavy physical work. Ministers thus began announcing that under the circumstances the government would start withholding benefits from those refusing to accept any job offered; they argued the money would be better used to subsidize wages in the needy sectors (HA 17.3.93). Meanwhile Labor Minister Ora Namir was presenting a tough stance against employers, declaring that she would not approve even a single additional permit for foreign workers (e.g., D 31.3.93).

Again, however, few Israeli workers responded to the government's pressures, and those who did accept work in construction and agriculture did not last very long. The government's initial resistance to employers' demands for foreign workers at this stage lasted only a month, until Prime Minister Yitzhak Rabin accepted the housing ministry's proposals and put an end to vacillation in the cabinet (INT-Ben-Eliezer; INT-Mizrahi; INT-Arbel). All the same, the number of permits grew slowly at first, reaching only 6000 in construction two months after the extended closure of the territories began (YA 16.5.93). Contractors complained that the building industry was operating at 40 percent of capacity. Farmers were getting no satisfaction and finally sued the government in the High Court of Justice, arguing that the government had a responsibility to ensure them a labor supply after interrupting their access to their traditional labor supply by closing the borders to the territories (HA 13.5.93). The government finally relented and granted permits, and the suit was dropped.[16]

But even if the numbers grew slowly, they grew steadily, so that in mid-1996 the government had granted 103,000 permits to employ foreign workers in Israel, not counting Palestinians. This figure may overstate the number of legal workers actually present: it is not clear that employers always use all the permits they receive, as there are discrepancies between the number of permits allocated and the number of workers for whom wage deductions are reported to the National Insurance Institute. The latter approach indicates a figure of approximately 80,000 legal foreign workers between 1996 and 2002 (see Table 3.2).

Foreign workers with permits have come primarily from three sources: Romania (primarily working in construction), Thailand (agriculture), and the Philippines (domestic services), though in 2001 permits were given to workers from 103 countries (HA 5.3.02). Illegal workers, discussed below, also come from a very large number of countries, including Poland, Bulgaria, Ghana, Bolivia, Chile, China, Sri Lanka, and Turkey, to name just a few.

The process of increasing numbers displayed a very clear pattern (INT Fefferman; INT-Zohar; INT-Porshner). After each bombing or series of individual attacks, the government would close the borders completely to Palestinian workers. Employers would then present demands for more foreign workers, and the government would comply, typically

Table 3.2 Estimates of foreign workers (non-Palestinian) (thousands)

	Legal workers	Illegal workers	Total	% of civilian labor force	% of employed persons
1987	2		2	0.1	0.1
1988	3		3	0.2	0.2
1989	3		3	0.2	0.2
1990	4		4	0.2	0.3
1991	8		8	0.4	0.5
1992	8		8	0.4	0.5
1993	10		10	0.5	0.6
1994	41	11	52	2.5	2.7
1995	70	22	92	4.2	4.5
1996	80	43	123	5.4	5.8
1997	83	67	150	6.4	6.8
1998	79	84	163	6.7	7.3
1999	77	110	187	7.4	8.0
2000	78	142	220	8.3	9.0
2001	89	149	238	8.7	9.5
2002	93				
2003	71				

Notes: For 1996–2002, "legal workers" refers to workers for whom employers reported wages to the National Insurance Institute. Housekeepers and home-care workers are excluded. Prior to 1996, "legal workers" refers to the number of employment permits issued by the Ministry of Labor.

Source: Israel Central Bureau of Statistics (web site: 147.237.248.51/reader/shnatonhnew.htm).

granting about 20,000 new permits at a time. The government would also gradually increase the number of Palestinians allowed to enter and work in Israel in spite of the general closure. But with another terrorist incident, these workers would be barred anew, prompting more employer cries for more foreign workers, as employers capitalized on the government's weakness and preoccupation with other aspects of the fallout from the attacks. Employers' desire for foreign workers was consistently high and was satisfied incrementally according to the vagaries of Palestinian terrorist activity;[17] the number of permits, then, did not necessarily accord with a demand that could be conceived objectively.

The slow but steady increase in foreign workers during this time also derived from the Israeli government's geopolitical aims. Government ministers, particularly Prime Minister Yitzhak Rabin, became more and more convinced that the success of the peace agreement with the

Palestinians required "separating" the two nations, reversing the process by which the pre-1967 boundaries had become very blurred. One aspect of this separation involved eliminating Israel's dependence on Palestinian labor. This dependence could not be eliminated overnight, however, and the government thus began to view imported foreign labor as a temporary transitional measure that would give the country time to restructure its economy so that cheap labor would no longer be needed to the same extent. Over the long run, however, this restructuring did not occur. Geopolitical pressures were immediate and alternative solutions to labor shortages such as restructuring required a slow process: the turn to foreign labor in the first instance makes sense in these terms. But the fact that foreign labor rather than restructuring has become the long-term *de facto* policy vitiates the argument concerning geopolitics, as I will argue in greater detail below.

Various governments have proclaimed initiatives to reduce the presence of foreign workers. The Netenyahu government announced in 1996 that it would try to reduce drastically the numbers of foreign workers; the goal was no more than 20,000 workers by 2001. Pressure from employers, however, has continued to be intense and the government is not even close to meeting this goal in mid-2004. The structural argument advanced below would suggest that significant and sustained reductions would be difficult to achieve.

Illegal workers

Illegal workers other than Palestinians were present in small numbers as early as the late 1970s (D 28.7.80). In 1980 the Interior Ministry threatened to expel about 1500 workers, including family members, from Yugoslavia, Turkey, Vietnam, and the Philippines, all of whom had overstayed their visas and in any case were working without permits in construction and industry. If the Interior Ministry found 1500 persons, the number actually present was of course probably rather higher. There were also Thais working in agriculture in the Jordan Valley, though their numbers were minuscule relative to more recent years. African and Filipina domestic workers also became increasingly visible in the 1980s (YA 18.6.87).

In the first half of the 1990s, as the Israeli government allowed increasing numbers of legal foreign workers, there was an explosion in the number of illegal workers as well. Some observers have offered estimates as high as 250,000 illegal workers, but these numbers appear to have no factual basis. Reasonably responsible estimates (e.g., from the Central Bureau of Statistics) for 2001 are in the region of 150,000, bringing the total to 238,000 (see Table 3.2 above). Foreign workers (not including Palestinians) thus constituted almost 9 percent of the labor force, a figure higher than those for all western European countries except Switzerland and the city-states.

Illegal workers entered the country and the labor force in familiar ways. Many posed as tourists but then found jobs and overstayed their visas. Others entered as legal workers and overstayed their permits, left the employer authorized to hire them, or both. Probably very few crossed the borders at other than official checkpoints, a risky endeavor. Some entered on forged passports.

Manpower companies in Israel have devised ingenious means for circumventing the Interior Ministry's attempts to limit the entry of "tourists" likely to become workers. Knowing that individuals from certain countries will encounter meticulous scrutiny at border checks, manpower companies sometimes arrange to have an entire planeload of "tourists" arrive at once. When the Border Police try to turn them back, the "tourists'" embassy often protests, accusing Israel of racism, and the Foreign Ministry pressures the Interior Ministry to back down to avoid a messy diplomatic controversy. In one incident, 600 Indians arrived, ostensibly to attend an international agricultural exposition; the Interior Ministry discovered that the Indians were all young men and nearly illiterate and tried to deport them, convinced that they were destined for the illegal labor force. The Foreign Ministry protested and the Agricultural Minister personally went to the airport to usher them through the border control (YA 13.5.96), prompting a major newspaper to write that the "incident proves, with great irony, that the ones who are really showing contempt for the law are government offices themselves" (HA 15.5.96).

Much of the demand for illegal workers, especially in the construction sector, comes from small employers, many of whom had previously employed Palestinians without permits: the government has allocated legal foreign workers according to previous legal employment of Palestinians, thus ignoring the needs of those employers who had previously ignored the law by hiring Palestinians illegally (INT-Fefferman). A survey commissioned by the Labor Ministry (Bar-Tsuri 1998) indicated that about half of the illegal labor force is employed in construction, perhaps one-fourth are employed in domestic services, and the balance are in industry and business services. Forty-four percent of the sample received less than the minimum wage.

Fines assessed on employers of illegal workers are generally low and easily absorbed by employers as a business expense (Asiskovitch 2004;

Condor 1997). Employers forced to pay fines can sometimes recoup their losses (or even emerge with a net gain) simply by failing to pay the final wages of the worker whose employment led to the fine. The government is not known for being energetic in enforcing the wage claims of illegal workers; after all, the government's main interest is to deport such people.

A sustained deportation effort was underway in 2003 and 2004; in the 18 months of the campaign, approximately 32,000 people were deported (HA 21.4.04). Many others left of their own accord, perhaps because of the climate of fear surrounding the deportation efforts (eloquently described in regular contributions to *HaAretz* by reporter Ruth Sinai, among others). Even at this pace, however, it would take at least six years to deport all existing workers – a rate that might perhaps seem reasonable but for the fact that it does not address the sizable continuing inflow. Israeli law partly constrains the government against illiberal arrest and deportation policies, though the Israeli government is less inhibited by these constraints than other western states (cf. Hollifield 1992).

Even the recent success of deportation efforts is not necessarily sustainable. These efforts have taken place in a context of severe economic crisis, including economic contraction. The construction sector in particular has seen significant declines in levels of activity. Under these conditions, employers are more prepared to tolerate government efforts to reduce permit numbers and deport illegal workers (Asiskovitch 2004; Rosenhek 2003), even if employers' public stance would suggest otherwise. It is not clear that these reductions will lead to the sort of structural change in the sector that would prevent increased pressure from employers in the event of renewed economic vigor.

The failure to attract Israelis to construction

The received wisdom concerning foreign labor in Israel is that it is necessary to import labor because Israelis are unwilling to supply labor for certain types of jobs. Nearly everyone connected with the issue, however, believes (or at least professes to believe, as in the case of employers of foreigners) that it would be preferable to hire Israelis, if only they were available. This is certainly the view of government officials, to the extent that it forms the basis for official policy, which specifies that employers may receive a permit to import and hire a foreign worker only if no Israeli can be found for the job (Amir 1999). Already before the large influx of foreigners had begun in 1993, Israeli governments had created committees to address the problem of foreign workers; the committees recommended reducing the (very small) number of permits that had previously been issued, and these recommendations were briefly carried out (Condor 1997). In practice, however, this view has amounted to very little, as we have already seen above.[18] Nevertheless, the government has made several efforts to facilitate the entry of Israelis into jobs now held largely by foreigners. The reasons for the failure of these efforts are an important piece of the story concerning why imported labor has come to be the predominant solution for solving labor supply problems in certain segments of the Israeli labor market. In this section we focus on failed efforts in the construction sector.

The occupational training approach

Israeli building methods, particularly for residential construction, are relatively primitive and have not advanced in many years (Amir 2002; Bar-Natan 1984; Amir draws on the opinions of construction project managers, some of whom are reported to say that the extent of labor intensive construction has even increased in recent years). In some cases, particularly in residential construction, it is considered techno-logically advanced to have a motorized winch for hauling buckets of wet concrete to an upper floor, where it is then laid by hand, a bucket at a time. Drywall is almost non-existent in residential construction; concrete blocks and wet plaster is the rule. The work is not necessarily unskilled, but the skill involved is perhaps akin to the skill of sewing shirts by hand. For housing starts initiated by the government, the amount of construction done with industrialized methods actually declined during the height of the building boom, when the labor market was widely believed to be marked by shortages (Table 3.3).

The relevant variables were quantified in a study commissioned by the Ministry of Housing and Construction (1998). Capital investment in Israeli construction occurred at the rate of $8000 per worker, compared with an average of $30,000 per worker in 14 other advanced industrial countries. Moreover, the sector is relatively undercapitalized to a greater extent than other Israeli economic sectors: in construction the ratio is 27 percent (8000 ÷ 30,000), whereas the ratio for other economic sectors is closer to 35 percent. Unsurprisingly, worker productivity is therefore relatively low as well: yearly output per worker is about $50,000, compared to an average of $80,000 to $100,000 in the other 14 countries, and is higher only than that of Italy. The study concludes that wages are so low that contractors simply have no incentive to substitute capital for labor; indeed, wages in shekels were stagnant (and thus declined in

Table 3.3 Construction methods – percent of building starts initiated by the public sector

	Conventional	Industrialized	Other
1987	63.5	36.5	
1988	80.5	19.5	
1989	81.9	18.1	
1990	77.0	20.2	2.8
1991	60.7	28.1	10.9
1992	51.1	34.2	6.8
1993	92.6	6.8	0.6
1994	91.0	8.4	0.6
1995	87.4	7.6	5.0
1996	94.8	3.6	1.6

Note: These data relate only to publicly initiated housing starts; data are not available for private starts.

Source: Ministry of Construction 1996.

Table 3.4 Construction labor force data

	Workers (1,000s)	% Day workers	Daily wages (shekels)	Monthly wages (shekels)
1992	134.1	56.6	123.5	5,332
1993	130.8	46.8	129.5	5,018
1994	137.4	38.9	121.1	4,999
1995	137.5	37.9	139.2	5,063
1996	181.1	42.0	133.2	4,990

Note: "Day Workers" refers to workers hired for a day's work only at street-corner "slave markets."

Source: Ministry of Construction 1996.

dollar terms) from 1992 to 1996, a period characterized by increased construction activity and labor demand (Table 3.4).

Given in addition the low pay and the unpleasantness of the work, certain construction jobs are very unattractive to Israelis. Israelis are almost completely absent from jobs involving work in concrete, plaster, ironwork, and flooring. It is not the case that there are no Israelis employed in the construction industry; in fact the majority of jobs in the industry are held by Israeli citizens (many of them Arabs). But Israelis are generally not employed for what is known in Hebrew as "wet" work.[19] Regarding the construction industry, this is the heart of the labor supply problem and the main reason given for importing foreign labor.

Some Israeli policymakers have long recognized the disadvantages of being unable to attract citizens to this type of work. One policy response in the recent period, when Palestinians became "unavailable" as workers precisely at a time of increased labor demand in the industry, was to try to encourage Israelis to accept work in construction. There has been a substantial offering of training courses to make Israelis attractive to construction employers. There was indeed a substantial increase in the number of Israelis employed in construction during the early 1990s, but it is far from clear that this increase resulted primarily from the training initiative or the wage supplements. What *is* clear, however, is that these efforts failed to solve the problem of labor supply for the low-end jobs discussed above.

A closer look at some of the parameters of this policy helps explain why the problem persisted. This analysis will also help us begin to understand the particular characteristics of government policymaking in this type of policy sphere. The Israeli government spent what many policymakers considered a large amount of money – something like $25 million over a five-year period ending in 1997 – attempting to train Israelis for work in the construction industry (INT-Artum; INT-Geffen; INT-Michaelov). About 26,000 people participated in the program, which had two separate streams. One stream involved soldiers who were released from the last three months of their mandatory three years of service to participate in training courses. The other stream involved unemployed civilians who opted to participate in the training as a way of extending or restoring their unemployment benefits. In both cases, the Labor Ministry and the National Insurance Institute paid a subsistence allowance to the trainee, an amount approximately equal to the minimum wage. The Labor Ministry also paid for the operation of the courses. After three months of classroom instruction, the trainees were placed for an additional three months of on-site training with a contractor. The government continued to pay the subsistence allowance, and the Contractors' Association paid the released soldiers a wage supplement equal to about $350 a month. If the released soldier then found a job and remained in the sector for six months, the Contractors' Association paid a bonus of 5000 shekels, or about $1700 (INT-Artum).

The relevant indicator of the program's success is the tendency of trained Israelis to continue working in the sector. The results were disappointing to many of those involved. One Labor Ministry official (INT-Artum) determined that only 20 percent of those trained were still working in construction jobs two years after the training period ended. A representative of the Contractors' Association disputed that claim but allowed that the figure was less than 40 percent (INT-Shtern). The modal path, particularly for released soldiers, was to work in construction only long enough to get the contractors' bonus and then to use the money for an extended period of foreign travel – a common experience for Israelis after their military service. Few returned to construction work upon arrival home. Those who did return to the sector, as well as those who never left, were very unlikely to continue working in the "wet" trades that were experiencing labor supply problems. Instead, many found work in other types of construction jobs or even became small contractors themselves – and then looked to hire others to do the wet jobs (INT-Shabbat; INT-Hecht; INT-Artum).

Some of those interviewed therefore reached the conclusion that the main function of the government's training effort was to provide a source of cheap labor for the contractors (INT-Hecht; INT-Michaelov). The three months of on-site training were deemed an apprenticeship, where the worker was not paid by the contractor but instead received a subsistence allowance from the government. There were some who seriously questioned whether the contractors were at all interested in hiring the trainees once the latter began to require actual wages; one official claimed that the contractors simply did not want to employ Israelis because they were too expensive and not as malleable as Palestinians or other foreigners (INT-Hecht). This assertion received support from an episode in 2001, when a jobs fair to attract unemployed Israelis to the construction sector was cancelled when the Employment Service received an uncooperative response from the Contractors' Association when the former asked the latter for information on wages and benefits to be offered (HA 23.11.01).

The Labor Ministry official who supervised the training program for a time asserted that training for the relevant methods of building really only required one month of on-site work (INT-Hecht). The adoption of the more extensive program was the result of political pressures from the Minister of Labor herself, who was essentially interested in making the contractors happy and in creating good public relations for the ministry (INT-Artum; INT-Hecht). Perhaps most tellingly, the government employees with whom I discussed this program who were involved in design or implementation said that they had either actively opposed its creation or predicted that it would fail (INT-Geffen; INT-Hecht; INT-Artum). They claimed further that the decision to proceed was made by the political leadership and on political grounds; in particular, the politicians needed (so the argument went) to create the *appearance* of "doing something" about the twin problems of high unemployment among Israelis and the shortage of labor in the construction sector. The professional people involved in its implementation uniformly referred to this effort as a waste of money and time.

The justification informants gave for this prediction or opposition was that there was no way to convince Israelis to make a serious commitment to working in the construction sector without first changing its basic parameters (INT-Geffen; INT-Pialkov). Israeli workers shun the sector because of low wages and unpleasant, low-status work. The training program was not designed to address these structural problems; it proposed, instead, simply to provide some small cash incentives for undergoing training and remaining in the sector for a short time. Bureaucrats in the Labor and Finance Ministries continue to hold that training was and is largely irrelevant to the question of employing Israelis in construction. What these officials say *would* make the sector more attractive to Israelis is to increase the wages available and to change the nature of the work involved – changes that depend on restructuring the sector. The fact that the program emerged at all is perhaps testimony to the rewards of rent-seeking in the Israeli state: whatever the contractors' individual intentions were, what the program provided in fact was not a steady, long-term labor supply but a short-term fix of cheap labor that resulted from the political interests and power of certain actors.

The failure of structural transformation

We arrive, then, almost at the heart of the matter: the failure of various efforts to bring about precisely the type of restructuring in the construction sector that many policy people believe would in fact make it possible to attract an Israeli labor force. The foreign labor question is directly related to this topic: many Israeli bureaucrats and other analysts believe that the single most effective step towards this sort of structural transformation in the construction sector would be to cut off the supply of foreign labor (INT-Pialkov; a senior Finance Ministry official who requested anonymity also made this point). In other words, if construction employers had no alternative but to employ Israelis, the economics of the sector would likely quickly evolve to the point where investing in building methods with a higher labor productivity would make economic sense to the employers. Furthermore, the higher wages and less unpleasant work would (again, at least in theory) make the jobs more attractive to Israeli citizens. So we are almost in a position to discuss the development of foreign worker policy itself. But the government did take other steps to encourage restructuring, both in spite of and because of the foreign worker problem, and we will discuss those efforts first.[20]

One main point of restructuring – either using industrialized methods on site or relying on more prefabrication – is of course to save labor, which in this context would in all likelihood mean a reduction in employers' perceived needs for foreign workers. Warsawszki *et al.* (1999) estimate that it may be possible to save half of the labor involved in residential construction (which accounts for 70 percent of construction in Israel) by moving to prefabrication or on-site industrialized methods: conventional building requires approximately 20 hours per square meter, while the more advanced methods require approximately 10 hours per square meter. In the prefabrication scenario, the reduction in total labor demand would be smaller than that: there would also be an increase in the need for workers in factories producing the prefabricated components. But this work is not generally counted as construction labor; in this case it certainly should not be counted as such, because there is no reason to suppose it would be difficult to find Israelis willing to do this kind of manufacturing work. A transition to greater prefabrication, then, could be expected to result in a transfer of labor demand from construction – work Israelis disdain – to manufacturing – work Israelis accept; the notion, commonly found in the migration literature, that foreign workers and citizens are complements and not substitutes needs rethinking.

Was restructuring a feasible option? The claim that the government "failed" in its efforts to restructure the construction industry and to attract citizens to construction jobs would be rendered meaningless if it could be shown that such efforts were obviously too expensive – to buyers, contractors, the government, etc. In particular, it might be imagined that the wage increases that would have been required (both to attract citizens and to convince contractors that using labor intensive methods was no longer a sound business decision) were simply too large. While I cannot definitively demonstrate how restructuring would have affected all the relevant variables concerning costs, I can address the central issue of wages and business decisions.

The Ministry of Construction commissioned a study in 1998 to determine the level of wages at which contractors would begin to find it profitable to invest in more technologically advanced and productive methods of building (Ministry of Construction 1998). The average monthly wage in the sector in 1998 was 4500 shekels (about US$1200). According to this study, once wages began to exceed 6000 shekels, contractors would begin to make capital investments to begin substituting for labor. Because selling prices are determined more by housing demand than by building costs, it is not clear that this increase in the cost of labor would be passed on *in toto* to buyers (thereby fueling inflation in general, something the government greatly wished to avoid). Nor would such an increase in labor costs (i.e., of 33 percent) represent a 33 percent increase in building costs: labor costs account for about 45 percent of the cost of all inputs, and the cost of inputs of all kinds represents something like 50 percent of the final cost to the buyer (depending on definitions). In other words, labor costs on average account for less than 25 percent of the price buyers pay for new housing. For an average house or apartment costing US$150,000, then, a 33 percent increase in labor costs amounts to a lost profit and/or increased purchase price of approximately $12,000 per apartment – hardly the catastrophe the contractors predicted would ensue had the government failed to allow imported labor. It is not clear from this study whether 6000 shekels was above the reservation wage in construction for Israeli citizens. However, given a transformation in contractors' investment decisions, the work itself would likely become less objectionable as well (Warsawszki *et al.* 1999), perhaps lowering that reservation wage.

Informants claimed that relevant sections of the government have believed for many years that it is not in the country's best interest for construction employers to rely on a cheap foreign labor force, e.g., the Palestinians. In 1987, soon after the outbreak of the *intifada*, the Construction Ministry offered a program to encourage builders to use more productive methods. The ministry granted bonuses to contractors who used prefabricated curtain walls on building exteriors and drywall for interiors. But ministry officials were unable to assert that the program had made any measurable difference in the building methods used in the sector. Even figures on bonuses actually awarded would not indicate whether bonuses went to contractors who formerly used conventional methods and then switched or to (the few) contractors who had already been using more advanced methods (INT-Pialkov). This failure to measure the impact of an intended transformative program itself indicates a serious weakness in the capacity for state economic policy.

While there have continued to be proclamations to the effect that the Israeli government is encouraging "industrialized" building, more recent efforts actually to induce change have had even less practical import. In the words of one Construction Ministry advisor, a "program" instituted in 1993 was primarily "declarative," involving exhortations (INT-Pialkov). There is a certain amount of confusion among officials in different ministries concerning exactly what industrialized building means and what it would take to bring about this sort of structural transformation. One Finance Ministry official, a Budget Department liaison to the Construction Ministry, went as far as to say, "We don't really know how to do it" (INT-Eiges). Chamish (1992) goes even further and charges that Construction Ministry officials, lobbied by local contractors and banks, frustrated the efforts of an American contractor to offer (relatively) inexpensive prefabricated houses in 1990.

The confusion perhaps became most apparent in a renewed effort in 1995 to foster industrialization, repeating an idea that had been tried in 1990 (INT-Pialkov). The government again offered monetary incentives, but the mechanism was perverse: bonuses were given to contractors who completed buildings within a specified reduced time period, a goal that was presumed to be facilitated by increased use of technologically advanced methods. What emerged instead was that employers simply increased their demand for labor and used the labor they had more intensively, i.e., extended workdays (INT-Eiges). Moreover, the program was terminated after irresolvable disputes arose between the Finance Ministry and the Construction Ministry concerning how to measure the period between initiation and completion of building (INT-Eiges). The Finance Ministry took the position that completion meant the house was inhabitable. But inhabitability depended not only on the condition of the house or apartment but of the infrastructure (e.g., electricity, water and sewer hook-ups, roads), which was ultimately the responsibility of the Construction Ministry itself. The latter, not wanting to draw attention to its own lapses in this matter, strenuously objected to the Finance Ministry's interpretation (INT-Pialkov). It does not matter which interpretation was more reasonable – what is relevant here is that there was no mechanism for resolving this kind of inter-ministerial dispute in a way that would have facilitated the orderly implementation of a proactive policy.

The contractors themselves expressed various contradictory positions concerning a government policy on the "industrialization" of the building sector. The director of a subdivision of the Contractors' Association earnestly stated that the contractors "really wanted" to adopt more productive methods of building and employ more Israeli workers (INT-Himmelfarb). But when asked about an actual proposal of the Construction Ministry to alter the incentives in this direction, this same person said the Association opposed the policy: "We would be profitable, but *less* profitable." The Vice Director-General of the Association referred to the entire effort as a "legend," saying the government hasn't even really tried to implement such a policy (INT-Arbel).

It might be suggested that part of the difficulty with the notion of restructuring the construction sector through greater investment has to do with a general shortage of capital, especially in a context where massive defense spending drains resources from other activities. While it is true, however, that more capital would be available for investment in construction (and other sectors) if defense spending were lower, a shortage of capital is one of the main problems that all developing economies face – there is never "enough." This is precisely the problem that a developmentalist state typically sets out to address, by mobilizing resources that are not directly available to private actors acting alone. The Israeli government has not made this a priority with regard to construction – nor would it make sense to do so, given the availability of labor and the resistance of the contractors to the notion of structural change.

The contractors' opposition to the industrialization proposal is anything but surprising. Housing prices have only a weak relationship to the contractors' costs (INT-Dar; INT-Mizrahi), so any change that increased costs would represent a significant deduction from profits. If selling prices represented the cost of production plus a standard markup, then an increase in production costs for all contractors would not represent much in the way of lost profit opportunities for any particular contractor; such increases would be paid by consumers. But this is not the case in the housing market: prices are determined much more strongly by relative demand (typically in Israel, a strong demand relative to a weak supply) as well as the high cost of land.[21] In this situation there is no reason to expect that the contractors would support any proposal that increased their costs.

The question then becomes whether the contractors have the power to prevent adoption of such a proposal. The widespread perception among the professional bureaucrats and others is that they do have power of this sort. A former Director-General of the Labor Ministry (INT-Ben-Shalom) asserted that the Construction and Finance ministers in the 1992–96 Labor government were very dependent on support from the contractors, a position echoed by numerous other informants. The president of the Contractors' Association in the early 1990s was also a senior Labor Party figure (Mordechai Yona – INT-Hecht). Representatives of the contractors themselves admitted as much, though in more subtle terms. The Vice Director-General of the Contractors' Association put it the following way: "Labor, Likud: we can talk to them, to the secular parties" (INT-Arbel). And, in the more cryptic words (whose meaning was nonetheless clear in context) of a former Labor Ministry official: "There are many ways to get to heaven" (INT-Ben-Shalom). The practical import of such statements is of course extremely difficult to verify, but their suggestiveness, combined with a clear record of no significant action, seems compelling, especially given the lack of evidence to the contrary (e.g., rising bankruptcies). All democracies involve opportunities for private actors' influence on policy outcomes. What matter in this case, however, are the structural characteristics of the state that determine that such influence is decisive for policymaking, particularly when that influence runs against stated, official policy. The lack of clear jurisdiction as well as the relatively large decision making role of the political leadership is especially relevant here, as we will see again in the next section.

The Israeli government, then, lacked the institutional capacity for crafting and implementing a program that would have significantly changed the incentives for construction firms to invest in a different type of production (and employ fewer but more productive workers). This conclusion relies on the assumption that some critical mass of policymakers in fact wanted to bring about such a change. The *desire* for such a policy was readily apparent in the numerous interviews I conducted. Moreover, a number of informants expressed their views in a way that made it clear such an approach was the "official" policy of the government. It is precisely this gap – between policy as officially stated and policy as a coherent set of actions having an impact in the world – that indicates a lack of state capacity, at least in this particular area.

In part, however, the government's failure to really pursue a policy of facilitating industrialized building reflects not only a structural incapacity but a philosophical ambivalence about this sort of "unwarranted intervention" in a market economy. The widespread influence of famous Chicago economists (Aharoni 1991) dictates against government initiatives towards structural transformation. This influence was readily apparent in numerous interviews, even when the informants themselves did not share a strict neoclassical view. Clearly, there are certain glaring contradictions apparent in this particular approach to governance of the construction sector. It is not clear whether restraining government in this context means (1) allowing the sector simply to adapt to prevailing conditions, including a labor shortage – i.e., refraining from solving employers' labor supply problems through a proactive foreign worker policy – or (2) refraining from regulating the labor market through immigration restrictions in the first place, so that cheap labor from wherever would be freely available. Still, the influence of the liberals mitigates against a developmentalist approach, no matter what the interpretation.

A developmentalist approach to structural transformation in the construction industry was a real, practical possibility, as we will see in the next chapter. The Japanese government helped alter the incentives and the market structure in a way that made non-traditional construction a realistic and even profitable endeavor for contractors. The circumstances under which these efforts were made were similar in important respects to the conditions prevailing in Israel: intense demand for housing, leading to rapidly increasing prices, and a shortage of construction labor acting as a bottleneck in production. The contention here is that Israel's different way of addressing the problem is best explained by its different state structure, and in particular its impaired ability to implement policies designed to restructure markets in a way that frustrate employers' immediate interests. This theme is continued in the next section.

The decision to import construction labor

The pressures on the Israeli government to ensure the production of new housing throughout the early and middle 1990s were very intense, as discussed above. The problem of housing for new immigrants was acute, with many families living doubled up in small apartments. The public consensus, at least among Jews, was that this was the government's problem to solve, and political leaders accepted the responsibility in word and deed. This was the worst possible time for political troubles in the occupied territories to render contractors' traditional labor force unavailable. Under these circumstances it is perhaps not at all surprising that the government turned to a "quick and dirty" solution to problems of labor supply. It is common among Israeli citizens and some policymakers to believe that the combination of these two factors – a serious housing shortage and a shortage of construction workers – accounts perfectly well for the government's decision to begin importing labor. The question then becomes whether these contingent factors are sufficient as an explanation for that decision. I contend they are not and that we must look deeper into the structure of the Israeli state for a more satisfactory explanation.

Two factors support the contention that the contingent factors are not satisfying at the explanatory level. The rhetoric surrounding the policy debates on foreign labor was dominated by the notion that Israel had "no choice" but to import labor (see e.g., D 1.4.93; M 7.4.93). This notion was simply not coherent (which is not to say that its assertion did not have an impact). What policymakers really mean when they say there is no (alternative) choice is that the costs associated with the alternative choices are too high. More precisely, they are too high for some particular interests that have the ability to avoid being forced to bear those costs. Labor markets in capitalist societies are markets where commodities are traded. Social factors influence, to a greater degree than for other commodities, the determination of prices for the commodity called labor power – but that commodity nonetheless has a price at which it can be traded. Israeli construction employers were indeed unable to attract Israeli labor – but only because they were unwilling to pay the wages Israelis would have demanded to accept such work. Understood in this context, the problem of housing immigrants and the closure of Israel's borders with the territories did not *determine* that the country would "have to" import labor. These factors merely changed the market conditions affecting the (potential) price of labor, by increasing its demand (i.e., as production needs increased) and restricting its supply.

The second factor concerns the decision making process and thus brings us to a discussion of the state itself. In Israel, formal authority for issuing labor permits to non-citizens lies clearly and unequivocally with the Ministry of Labor (upon whose recommendation the Interior Ministry issues the corresponding entry visa). The Minister of Labor in the Rabin government, Ora Namir, first confronted the foreign labor question by refusing to grant such permits (as discussed above). *In a different type of state*, had she persisted in this refusal the (legal) foreign worker phenomenon in Israel would likely have significantly restrained. As it turned out, the Labor Ministry's authority in this matter was usurped.

In this context it matters deeply what type of state *did* exist; in particular, it matters that the decision making process in Israel was highly politicized. The series of decisions that constituted the Israeli policy of importing labor was made entirely at the highest political level of the government, by cabinet ministers. The bureaucracy was fragmented and the professional staff had no real influence on the outcome (cf. Schecter 1972, indicating continuity over time in this regard). As such, the policy process itself was marked by a very short-term time perspective. It was – most importantly – open to influence of private interests to a very significant degree. The rest of this section explores these contentions in greater detail.

Governments in Israel, particularly but not exclusively when led by the Labor Party, have a self-conscious "pioneer" quality. The lasting image of Zionist leaders from the pre-statehood and early post-statehood periods is that of the "doer", the decisive leader who solves problems with forceful decision making and with a pronounced disdain for official rules that interfere with one's purpose. British regulations during the period of the Mandate were widely perceived to thwart Zionist purposes, and disregarding them was tantamount to a national duty. Sprinzak (1993) relates a proverb invoked to justify the "illegalism" (e.g., state officials using public money for private purposes) that persisted in characterizing Israeli governance in the post-1948 period: "Don't muzzle the ox while it is threshing the corn." This attitude towards rules and bureaucracies has survived to a certain degree (Nachmias and Rosenbloom 1978; Roniger 1994), despite efforts to professionalize the government and rationalize procedures (e.g., Ben Gurion's *mamlachtiut* or "etatism" – see Cohen 1992). Government ministers sometimes even fail to obey explicit orders of the Supreme Court.[22] More generally, the clientelism of Israeli politics emerges in a system where "access to ... many public goods and publicly distributed private goods is mediated to a large degree by representatives of the major segments, be they religious groups, political parties, linguistic communities, local units or some other entity" (Roniger 1994: 171).

These features are evident in the decision making process concerning foreign labor. Again, the authority in this matter belonged to the Labor Ministry. Labor Minister Namir steadfastly refused to issue permits for foreign workers when the issue was first raised on a large scale in April 1993. The Minister of Construction (Ben Eliezer), under pressure from the contractors, therefore approached Prime Minister Rabin, in whom he found a sympathetic ear (INT-Mizrahi; INT-Arbel; INT-Ben-Eliezer). In negotiations among Rabin, Namir, and Ben-Eliezer, Namir "agreed" to cede her authority in this matter, and decisions were henceforth taken either by a committee of these three ministers or by the cabinet as a whole. The venue of the decisions did not follow any set logic from that point on: it simply happened on occasion that the Construction or Agriculture ministers would raise the issue at the weekly cabinet meeting, and the cabinet would proceed to take a vote, in spite of the fact that the issue had not been on the agenda (INT-Brodet).

The decision making process, then, became entirely divorced from the professional staff of the relevant ministries. One minister who might have been expected to vote against these proposals was Baiga Shochat, the Finance Minister. The top-level professional staff of the Finance Ministry opposed the idea from the outset (INT-Dar; INT-Brodet; INT-anonymous Finance Ministry official). In particular, David Brodet (Budget Director until the end of 1994 and then Director-General) asserted that he and his associates looked at the issue from a broad perspective and concluded that the cost to the society and the economy as a whole was higher than it appeared to advocates of the idea.[23] Brodet and the previous Director-General (Aharon Fogel – INT) claimed to have attempted reasoning with Minister Shochat, but Shochat voted in favor of granting permits until the middle of 1995. Fogel recalled arguing (perhaps with self-serving hindsight) that the government should at least tax the employment of foreign labor to eliminate incentives to prefer foreigners even when local labor was available (but more expensive), but to no avail.

Some officials argued that this experience was typical of economic policymaking in Israel. Brodet and Fogel (INT) affirmed that the Finance Minister frequently (though not always) disregards the opinions of his professional staff in favor of political considerations. This has been true most notably of decisions on wage policy, government pensions, and the budget process. In most cases, of course, the results are decisions that involve higher levels of spending, a phenomenon illustrated in very high budget deficits (in recent years those deficits have declined considerably, however). The staff were aware of the political pressures that could lead to such decisions and accepted such pressures as the "rules of the game" (INT-Brodet). The case of the Finance Ministry is important in this context because it is widely perceived as having the most professional staff – the fewest political appointments, the highest standards for recruitment, etc.

Aharon Fogel (INT) described a general policymaking dynamic that he claims, convincingly, operated in the case of foreign labor policy. Israeli politicians, he argued, take action only when there is a dramatic crisis. Even when professional bureaucrats can see that a catastrophe is imminent, it is difficult to convince politicians that advance efforts to avert the crisis are necessary. Such efforts could involve creating a small crisis to provoke action. If successful, however, Fogel argued that the politician could expect only to receive blame for creating the small crisis; no one would then give him or her credit for averting a catastrophic event, which no one would believe was imminent because in the end it didn't happen. Fogel characterized the Israeli experience with hyperinflation in the 1980s in this way, saying that the economic bureaucrats knew a huge crisis was coming but were powerless to do anything about it until the situation became critical.[24] Likewise with foreign labor, many among the professional staff believed that the decision to import labor is harmful, but the alternatives appear to be more costly in the short run, and the disadvantages were not compelling because they will only become apparent in the long run. Israeli politicians/policymakers, then, are often described as "putting out fires" rather than engaging in long-term planning.

Other officials echoed this overall view. One department head in the Labor Ministry (INT-Fefferman) argued that the professional staff frequently conducts studies concluding that various reforms should be made to various operations of a particular ministry. But the recommendations are rarely carried out; even when real changes are made, they typically do not reflect the conclusions of the research. The state's Employment Service, for example, has been the subject of numerous proposals for reform within the Labor Ministry, but no reform has occurred. Likewise with the effort to train Israelis for construction work: Finance Ministry officials, on the basis of a National Insurance Institute study showing that the program was not working, argued for its cancellation (INT-Michaelov; INT-Geffen). But the recommendations were ignored because, some argued, politicians wanted to present the image of "doing something" about the problem. A Finance Ministry staffperson concluded: "More research is always needed, but the real issue is teaching government offices how to use it. The conclusions are not implemented" (INT-Geffen). Entrenched interests (both public and private) as well as politicians' lack of interest in such proactive matters have created insurmountable obstacles to real institutional changes.

In this context it is noteworthy that nothing that could be called serious research was conducted to inform the decision to import labor (INT-Dar; INT-Barkan; INT-anonymous Finance Ministry official). At the beginning (in 1993), this is perhaps due to the perception that decisions had to be reached very quickly. But this mode of policymaking persisted through subsequent periods that produced recurring decisions to increase the number of permits. The reluctance to draw on the various ministries' ability to conduct research on such a topic reflected two facets of the policymaking process, both of which are connected to the fact that the professional staff were unable to have much of an impact on the decisions. Some bureaucrats, especially in the Finance Ministry, claimed (perhaps with the benefit of hindsight) that research on the need for and impact of foreign labor was unnecessary, because they already "knew" that importing labor would be harmful for the Israeli economy and society.[25] Many people working for the government who have a professional interest in this issue (as well as some politicians, including former Labor Minister Namir – see HA 8.3.88) were quite familiar with the European guestworker experience and hold the view that importing labor results in costly additional demands on infrastructure, health and education systems, and social integration, and that these costs outweigh the short-term benefits apparent in a narrow economic perspective (INT-Dar; INT-anonymous Finance Ministry official).[26]

On the other hand, however, those elements of the government who favored imported labor (the contractors and the Ministry of Construction) did not need to support their demands with research because their position was so apparently compelling (even obvious) to the average observer that it simply appeared as common sense. In both cases, this episode of Israeli policymaking, where consequential decisions were made with no systematic consideration of long-term impacts on the economy or society, presents a considerable contrast with the Japanese mode of policymaking, as we will see in the next chapter.

Given the government's stated interest in lowering unemployment, as well as an imputed public interest in minimizing the extent of foreign labor, it is perhaps especially noteworthy that no serious consideration was given at the time to the question of how high wages would have had to rise in the construction sector to attract Israeli workers (INT-Pialkov). According to the received wisdom, Israelis were simply not interested in doing construction work at all, or at least not in the "wet" occupations. This idea amounts to an unwarranted or overstated rejection of market forces as shapers of individuals' motivations to accept various types of work. It is undoubtedly true that Israelis do not accept construction work at prevailing wages. But there is a value at which this particular market would clear. The possibility of determining that value was not explored, according to informants.

In other words, the government gave no real consideration to the alternative policy option of allowing labor shortages in the construction sector to lead to wage increases that would eventually attract Israelis. As discussed above, at a certain wage, construction work would have become attractive, and not only to unemployed Israelis: workers employed in other low-wage occupations might also have begun to reevaluate their career options. The status considerations discussed above no doubt would have continued to operate; but it is more reasonable to think of such factors as determinants of a market-clearing wage than it is to think of them as preventing the operation of this particular labor market altogether. Some figures in the labor movement and the press clearly saw the construction labor shortage as a problem of wages and called for a rejection of the foreign worker option in favor of allowing the market to produce wage increases for construction workers (e.g., D 1.4.93; YA 14.4.93). But even the professional staff of the various ministries failed to consider this as a realistic possibility when the foreign worker question first emerged.

But given the political and structural factors described above, there was no reason the contractors *had* to accept lost opportunities for profit that may have resulted. That point also then leads to the conclusion that there is no reason to expect success from the Construction Ministry's more recent interest in using the results of its 1998 study to push a policy of industrialized building. The government remains deeply ambivalent about using "intrusive" steps to change the incentives for what it sees as private economic activity (INT-Pialkov; INT-Geffen; INT-Porshner; concerning Israeli politicians' anti-planning mindset, see also Bilski *et al.* 1980). Under these circumstances, some officials see their task as one of ensuring the short-term functioning of the sector, rather than trying to bring about long-term structural changes (which in the best of circumstances would involve transition costs).

Similarities with other policy areas

The policy process described above is one in which major decision makers are politicians (or political appointees) using political criteria to pursue policies that enhance the material welfare of selected private interests, without necessarily contributing to a public interest. The recommendations of bureaucracies' professional staff are routinely (though not uniformly) ignored. The focus is on resolving short-term crises rather than on long-term planning. Policy-making is fragmented among different sections of the government that find it difficult to cooperate and coordinate activities (recall Shimshoni's reference to a "quasi-feudal coalition government structure" 1982: 254); jurisdiction concerning policy areas is frequently unclear and contested, even if defined in law. The result, at least in the area of economic policymaking – and certainly concerning policy on foreign labor – is that structural reform is difficult and in some cases impossible to accomplish, even when there is an arguable consensus that such reform is desirable or even "necessary."

The point of this section is to show that in these respects policy on foreign labor is typical relative to policymaking in other areas, especially concerning the economy. If this were not the case, the arguments concerning foreign labor policy would have to be suspect. Instead, it will become clear that the characteristics described above are entirely in keeping with Israeli policymaking in general.

The State Comptroller's yearly report is without fail full of accusations that, contrary to clear regulations, government ministers routinely make political appointments to government bodies, and not only within the ministries themselves. Relevant examples include the charge that the Housing Minister in Rabin's government (Ben-Eliezer) appointed Labor Party figures and donors to the Israeli Building Center, a government corporation (State Comptroller 1996). Moreover, the tendency to make political appointments has not been declining: Kleiman asserts that perhaps 800 Likud activists held executive civil service jobs under the Netenyahu government, and "fully two-thirds of the directors in state-owned firms nominated by the government were known to be members of the centers of one or the other of the country's main political blocs" (1997: 160). The level of personnel turnover following elections is also significant: the Comptroller's 1997 report asserts that, after the Housing Ministry was given to an ultra-orthodox party leader, 17 of the ministry's 22 new hires were ultra-orthodox women. Moreover, the workers were supplied by a recruitment agency that failed to win the contract in a tender; the minister simply ignored the results of the tender and ordered the women hired. Considerations of coalition politics often prevent the government from taking action against illegal decisions such as this.

Examples of other types abound. Again in the Housing Ministry: when a contractor builds houses in an undeveloped area, the Housing Ministry provides infrastructure to that area such as roads, power lines, and water/sewer hookups. The ministry is supposed to bill the contractor for this work, and the contractor passes these costs on to the buyer of the house or apartment. The State Comptroller (1997) charged that the ministry in fact usually undercharges the contractors or fails to bill them at all – or fails to collect on bills actually sent. In 1990–94, the ministry failed to collect 3.8 billion shekels (about US$1.3 billion) of the 4.6 billion shekels it was owed. The Comptroller notes that the professional staff of the Finance and Housing Ministries prepared a plan to reform the problem, but it was never implemented. The amounts involved represent direct subsidies to the profits of the contractors.

A final example involves the Ministry of Industry and Commerce. A Law for the Encouragement of Capital Investment provides for grants to entrepreneurs involved in projects that advance specified government goals, such as providing employment in certain geographic regions or helping to reduce the balance of payments deficit. In 1985–94, such grants totaled 2 billion shekels (roughly US$1 billion). The Comptroller (1996) charged, however, that the ministry had no mechanism for determining whether projects for which companies received the grants met the goals specified in the law and in the grant conditions. In fact, the report noted, the majority of such projects did not meet the specified goals. Only one-fifth of new factories established with grant money succeeded in exporting even half of the target amount as promised in exchange for the grant. The fact that the policy failed to meet its objectives is itself significant. But even more so for our purposes is the fact that the ministry in question did not have the *means* to determine whether or not objectives were being met. This point speaks directly to the issue of state capacity for implementing developmentalist economic policies (recall Amsden's argument (1989) about the need for enforcing the conditions and terms under which government subsidies are given).

Outcomes: Enhanced profits for contractors and others

Foreign workers constitute almost 40% of the construction labor force in Israel, according to a recent estimate (Zussman and Romanov 2003). The contribution of foreign workers to labor inputs is larger than the per capita percentage, because foreigners work longer hours than Israelis. The entry of large numbers of foreign workers into the construction sector labor force has led to a pronounced stagnation of wages – and probably even to a significant decline in real terms. It has also enhanced the profits of contractors. There is of course a direct link between these two phenomena, a link which is illuminated by the concept of a *quota profit* (Amir 1999; the following discussion is based on Amir's piece). Quota profits emerge from the legal status of foreign workers in Israel, a status that is common in other foreign worker programs around the world. The worker receives a visa which allows him or her to work only for a specified employer; violation of this condition makes the worker's very presence in Israel unlawful. This relationship of indenture allows the employer to pay the worker less than the latter would receive in the free labor market: the worker accepts the lower wages as the cost for avoiding the risk of arrest and deportation associated with working for another employer (see also Drori and Kunda 1999). Here we see the rents discussed in more abstract terms in the first chapter.

The lower wages that workers with permits receive would have been passed on to consumers as lower costs if the housing market were very competitive and if all employers had access to workers with permits. Neither of these conditions holds in Israel. As discussed above, permits to employ foreigners have been distributed according to a contractor's previous *legal* employment of Palestinians: if a contractor previously held permits to employ Palestinians, then he was to receive permits to employ other foreigners. In practice, the permits are distributed by the Contractors' Association, which is controlled by the large firms and favors their interests (Amir 2002). So permits have been acquired mainly by the large contractors, while smaller firms have had to turn to illegal workers or unreliable and more expensive Palestinians. Thus the average cost of labor did not decline as much as it would have if all employers had access to legal foreign workers. The larger companies benefited from their lower labor costs relative to the average.

The larger companies have also been renting (the term is deliberately chosen) "their" foreign workers to other companies that have not managed to acquire permits of their own (Amir 2002). Firms with workers to spare sublet them to other companies for about $1 an hour (and then the latter pay the workers' "normal," permit-level wages). This fee is a good indicator of the size of the quota profit associated with employing a legal foreign worker: the firm that holds the permit can charge this much because the premium represents the marginal cost of an "illegal" worker over a worker with a permit.

This figure is supported also by surveys of workers, which showed that the average wage increase a foreign worker can get by abandoning his permit employer and finding "illegal" work is about $1 an hour (Amir 1999). With foreigners in construction working an average of 280 hours a month (see Drori and Kunda 1999), even a medium-sized contractor employing 100 foreign workers can "earn" something like an additional $28,000 a month by ensuring continued access to permits allowing him to employ foreigners. Small wonder, then, that many large firms have replaced most or all of their Palestinian workers engaged in "wet" work with foreigners in the last five years. Other employers have benefited too, given that the increased presence of foreign workers has depressed wages in the competitive labor market as well; wages for Palestinians in the relevant occupations have not changed in nominal terms since 1994, which means there has been a significant decline in real (dollar) terms (see Table 3.4 above; recall as well the discussion of Condor's 1997 analysis of long-term wage trends in construction). There are thus clear and compelling incentives to use whatever political pressure can be mustered to ensure that government policy decisions on foreign labor continue to favor the interests of the contractors.

The profits associated with use of foreign labor are enhanced additionally by the fact that the prices contractors receive for houses and apartments are only weakly related to the costs of construction. Instead, as noted earlier, prices are determined by demand for housing in a situation of chronic undersupply. Prices rose rapidly with the onset of the Russian immigration wave in 1989 (though they have declined since 2000 with the renewal of violent conflict and general recession). Under these conditions, most of the money a contractor can save on labor costs is probably additional profit. What matters here is the overall abundance of labor: a sufficient reserve of labor ensures that workers will be unable to bid up the average wage, even in a boom period. Importing workers contributes directly to this broad condition, and those with access to the quota profits associated with legal workers reap an even larger benefit.

Data from publicly traded construction companies,[27] obtained from financial reports filed with the Israel Securities Authority, show that gross profits almost trebled from 1993 to 1996 and remained above 1992 levels until the severe economic recession that began in late 1999 (Figure 3.1). The increase in the profit rate is even more important: gross profit rates rose from 12 percent in 1993 to almost 20 percent in 1997. The increase in gross amounts is of course in part a consequence of increased levels of construction activity (which were facilitated by the availability of extra labor at the "right" price). The increase in rates, however, also feeds the increased gross amounts. While profit rates are affected by a range of factors, the notion that the increase in foreign workers played no role is thoroughly implausible.

The points made above, however, are to a certain extent independent of trends in absolute profits. The clear implication of the argument made above is that, whatever the numbers concerning the profits contractors actually made, those numbers are higher than they would have been in the absence of foreign labor. Other factors certainly contributed to contractors' profitability in recent years: most importantly, the high level of demand, spurred in large part by the high levels of immigration, undoubtedly increased profits by driving up purchase prices faster than the cost of inputs. Ideally it would be possible to analyze profit data and attribute variation in trends to different factors such as level of demand and extent of use of foreign labor. Despite the fact that this is not possible,

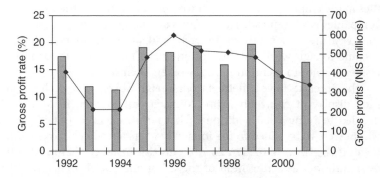

Figure 3.1 Profitability of Israeli construction companies.
Source: Computed from data from the Israeli Securities Authority; columns are profit rate, line is gross profits.

the force of the argument remains: access to cheap foreign labor lowered contractors' costs without similarly lowering their selling prices, resulting in enhanced profits directly attributable to government policy decisions. Foreign worker policy has resulted in enhanced profits not only for contractors but for the newly emergent "manpower" companies in Israel. Such companies act as employment agencies or intermediaries for employers seeking both legal and illegal foreign workers. There is a widespread perception that these companies are making enormous amounts of money, collecting fees both from the workers themselves and from employers. Here it is impossible to get precise numbers, though there are reports of Chinese workers paying up to US$10,000, and the head of the visa section of the Interior Ministry claims that "it's a business in the billions" (YA 7.12.01).

The manpower companies emerged into a regulatory vacuum when they first became significant. Several pieces of legislation have been passed to regulate their activities, but, predictably, efforts at enforcement have been timid, to the extent that this part of the labor market is sometimes referred to as the "wild west" of the economy. The use of manpower companies to allocate labor in the construction sector plays an important role in the creation of the rents and externalities that result from foreign worker employment. In particular, these companies create a certain ambiguity concerning who the actual "employer" of the foreign worker is (Pilovsky 1999). Contractors and the manpower companies each claim that the other is the real employer. This ambiguity matters when the Labor Ministry tries to enforce requirements that the "employer" provide decent living conditions for foreign workers: the government does not recognize any official role for manpower companies in the employment of foreign workers, even though the use of such companies is widespread. These efforts are hampered to such an extent that vast areas of southern Tel Aviv and other urban pockets have become foreign worker slums, lowering the quality of life for nearby residents – not to mention for the workers themselves.

Other interests have benefited from foreign workers as well. In a stunning display of chutzpah, Prime Minister Ariel Sharon in May 2002 decided to bring 6000 additional Thai farmworkers to Israel – 16 of whom were to be added to the foreign workers already employed at his own ranch (HA 27.5.02; HA 23.7.02). In this instance Sharon used his own authority as acting head of the Labor and Social Affairs Ministry and the Interior Ministry, during a coalition crisis in which the religious parties that had held those ministries were temporarily out of the government; the latter had been resisting the move for several months.

Various government institutions have reaped direct rewards as well. The National Insurance Institute (NII) collects premiums on workers regardless of their legal status but has refused, with uncertain legal authority, to pay benefits to workers without permits. According to one analysis, the NII collected 48 million shekels (about US$10 million) from foreign workers in 2001 and paid benefits of less than half that amount (HA 14.7.02). Much of the difference comes from a well-known logic regarding the employment of foreign workers: that sub-population tends to hold demographic characteristics associated with a low level of claims.

The lived experience of many foreign workers in Israel is similar in key respects to the experiences of low-level migrant workers everywhere. Foreign workers are excluded from most features of the Israeli welfare state, particularly at the national level, as the government is unwilling to take steps that would legitimate their membership in the society or polity. However, the municipalities (especially Tel Aviv) do offer some services relating to health and education (Rosenhek 2000). Foreign workers have already created organizations designed in part to advance claims in the political sphere (Kemp *et al.* 2000), although the leaders of these organizations have been targeted in recent state efforts to deport illegal workers.

Foreign workers in agriculture

The context of foreign agricultural workers differs in important respects from that of foreign construction workers. It would not be possible to claim that foreign worker policy has facilitated enhanced profits for the Israeli farmers who employ them, simply because Israeli farmers are not very profitable, period. Nevertheless, the same basic argument concerning the state, institutional structures, and rent-seeking applies to foreign worker policy in agriculture as well as in construction. In some ways, the connection among these elements is even more direct, as we will see shortly. First, however, a few words about the parameters of agriculture in Israel are in order.

As in many wealthy countries, most agricultural production in Israel survives only with substantial state subsidies and protections (INT-Kedmon). Water in particular is provided at a price to farmers far below the cost of supplying it. Until the early 1990s, the government routinely bailed out the large agricultural purchasing organizations: the latter sometimes made bad investments, and the lending banks had been nationalized by the government after a gigantic price-fixing scandal shook the foundations of the entire banking system. Renegotiated terms for the loans were generous to the borrowers (Schwartz 1995). There are also extensive protective tariffs and import restrictions. Some basic products are therefore much more expensive than they would be if imports were unrestricted; some imported dairy products, for example, would probably cost consumers about half the current price levels (INT-Barkan). There are various justifications offered for these measures. A "security" argument holds that allowing cheap imported food would destroy the local producers and make Israel too dependent on unreliable foreign sources. There is also the usual concern for "family farmers." But if we look for explanations rather than justifications, we must look to politics: the agricultural concerns in Israel are extremely well organized, and close to one-third of Knesset members identify officially with the agricultural lobby (INT-Barkan). Ties between producer organizations (such as the Moshav Movement[28] and the various kibbutz organizations) and political parties are tight, especially with the Labor Party, which historically played an important role in the development of Israeli agriculture (Schwartz 1995). Farm organization figures have held important positions in the planning bodies of the Ministry of Agriculture as well as the leadership of the Labor Party.

Foreign worker policy, whether for Palestinians or Thais, is best viewed as another type of subsidy, emerging from the same logic: if farmers had to pay higher wages to attract Israeli workers, exports would become less competitive, and tariffs on imported produce would have to be even higher than they already are for Israelis to continue buying domestic produce. Importing foreign workers facilitates not enhanced profits but survival – which requires a *minimum* level of profitability. Part of the central argument concerning foreign construction labor is that Israeli workers are denied the opportunity of earning higher wages in the building sector because employers are allowed to profit by maintaining the sector in a primitive condition that relies on cheap labor. If employers had no recourse other than Israeli workers, they would try to find ways to increase labor productivity to "justify" the wages they would be forced to pay. There appears to be little room for that sort of structural change in Israeli agriculture, which is very efficient but also potentially very fragile (INT-Bassi). Farmer advocates have long argued that employers are especially sensitive to labor supply problems: not having the necessary labor at harvest time can mean not simply a delay in production but the loss of an entire season's crops.

The conceptualization of foreign worker policy as an opportunity for rent-seeking on the part of farm employers is nonetheless appropriate in a very particular way. Israeli farmers survive (by making profits) only because Israelis pay much more for food than they would have to in a competitive foodstuffs market. In addition to expensive dairy products, the high (but subsidized) cost of water makes some produce expensive relative to potential imports as well. The cost of labor is of course also quite high relative to competing producers in nearby countries. These subsidies help guarantee the reproduction of farmers as farmers, in part by supporting their consumption. Consumption, however, of a very particular sort: access to cheap labor allows farmers to "consume" the farm lifestyle, which accords them a high status position as the classical Zionist pioneers, settlers of the land. In many cases, on the other hand, farm owners leave much of the work to their new employees in a way that departs from traditional practice: a former senior figure in the Ministry of Agriculture asserts that access to foreign labor has enabled many owners to increase their leisure time (INT-Bassi). So foreign labor does not so much substitute for capital as it ensures that certain individuals can continue (or enhance) their chosen way of life, which is made possible only by transferring resources from taxpayers and consumers to producers.

This argument concerning rent-seeking and policy is very different from that made regarding the construction sector. But an even more important element of the Israeli agricultural foreign worker story brings us to more familiar territory. Similarly to the construction sector, foreign agricultural workers are imported to Israel through one intermediary organization: the Moshav Movement. This monopoly has facilitated the accumulation of substantial profits for the organization; it has also led to the widespread impression that the Moshav Movement has transformed itself into little more than a manpower organization, though it subcontracts much of the actual work involved (HA 22.1.99). The profits come largely from fees paid by the Thai workers for the privilege of working in Israel as well as various deductions taken from their paychecks. The workers must pay in advance a fee of $250, which is used by subcontractors to ensure that conditions of the employment contract are satisfied over the two years the worker is supposed to remain in Israel. The average worker stays only 18 months, however, and the balance of the handling fee is not returned to the worker; the Movement then collects additional fees from replacement workers. This mechanism creates approximately $700,000 a year in profits for the Moshav Movement (HA 22.1.99). The Movement also charges the workers about $80 more for return airfare than the tickets actually cost, resulting in an additional $800,000 a year in profits. There are other mechanisms for reaping profits as well. One analysis concludes that by 1999 the Movement had made at least $8 million since the flow of agricultural workers began in earnest in 1994 (HA 22.1.99). The volume of these profits results from the Movement's government-sanctioned monopoly over importing farm workers. On the other hand, it is not clear that breaking the monopoly would lower these profits: it might simply spread them around. It seems unlikely that Thai workers are in a position to force different manpower companies (whose services are indispensable to any Thai wanting to work in Israel) to compete by lowering their fees and deductions. Still, it is clear that these profits are rents, even if they do not constitute "quota profits" in exactly the same way as the profits made by construction employers.

The decision to allow imported farm workers was taken with as little forethought, planning, or research as the decision to allow imported construction labor (INT-Bassi; INT-Barkan; cf. Borowski and Yanai 1997). And while Israeli agriculture is often heralded for its efficiency and pro-ductivity, there are indications that the availability of foreign labor has depressed the tendency to make capital investments (INT-Bassi). Still, on balance, the question of foreign labor policy can be framed in terms of alternative choices only to a limited degree. The principal alternative, as discussed earlier, is to rely more heavily on food imports, to allow fur-ther decline of the agricultural sector in Israel. There is perhaps some room for technological improvements to labor productivity in some branches: an Israeli research center, with funds from the Agriculture Ministry, has been developing a robot for harvesting tomatoes, for example (INT-Bassi). And perhaps a serious, prolonged labor shortage would catalyze an inventiveness for labor-saving solutions that are cur-rently not even imaginable. But it seems more likely that a prolonged labor shortage would lead to widespread bankruptcies or disinvestment: the nature of the sector seems to demand a certain amount of simple labor.

On the other hand, we should not be too quick to conclude that the price farm employers can pay for such labor is "naturally" or inevitably lower than the wages Israeli workers are willing to accept. Farmers could pay higher wages if they got higher prices for their commodities. And farmers could get higher prices at least for domestically consumed com-modities if import tariffs and restrictions were more burdensome and if all employers faced similar wage increases brought on by labor short-ages. Consumers would see higher food bills. But we should not make rash assumptions about the size of such increases: concerning the US, Martin (1994) estimates that doubling the wages of farm workers would result in an average 10 percent increase in retail prices. As with construction, the commodity called agricultural labor has a market-clearing wage. But in the Israeli political and institutional environment, private interests can frustrate efforts by policymakers to create the conditions under which the market is able to clear.

Conclusion

To understand the relevance of these ideas, we need to return to the discussion of the externalities associated with use of low-level foreign labor. We might think that economic policymakers would balk at the notion of policies designed to reorganize markets in ways that would result in price increases for consumers. In fact, however, policymakers adopt such decisions regularly: for instance, a public interest in workplace safety is invoked to justify regulations that result in increased product costs. In the case of foreign labor, the logic is arguably just as compelling. Consumers are already paying higher prices for food and housing, though not directly. The foreign labor that keeps food and housing prices (relatively) low carries social and financial costs that are borne by the public either through increased taxes (to the extent that the problems associated with foreign labor are in fact addressed by the government) or decreased welfare (to the extent that they are not). The government already spends uncounted millions of dollars a year in dealing with the issue: money goes for deportation efforts, expanded immigration control at airports and seaports, increased policing, etc. On the other hand, the government has mostly not responded to increased demands on (mostly urban) infrastructure; in this case the increased infrastructure burden is experienced as a welfare decline by all residents (though more by some than by others). In addition, worker remittances mean that foreign labor constitutes an import; to the extent that wages are sent abroad and not saved or consumed locally, *ceteris paribus* there is a lower level of local economic activity.[29]

   The magnitude of these costs is not known; measurement would be a formidable task, complicated in particular by matters of definition and questions about how to value non-economic "goods." It is not possible to say whether the social and financial costs associated with low-level foreign labor would be outweighed by the direct economic cost of doing without such labor. I therefore do not mean to argue that Israel *should* make alternative choices: such a decision would require assessing values and utilities in a culturally specific way. I will return to this question in the final chapter.

There is more that can be said here, however. Again, assessing the costs of using low-wage foreign labor depends heavily on defining the terms of the analysis, determining in particular what to count. The costs are not limited to the items considered so far (i.e., problems of social order, deportation, administration, infrastructure). A broader view would include a discussion of how importing labor affects the rest of the labor market itself. Here we return to the fact that Israel turned to foreign labor at a time when unemployment among Israeli citizens was very high, close to 10 percent. The contention that foreign and native workers are complementary and not competitive is far too static (cf. Gottlieb 2002; Zussman and Romanov 2003). In assessing the impact of foreign labor, we need to consider as well what the Israeli government did *not* do (and perhaps could not have done). In particular, the government did not succeed in upgrading the type of work performed in the particular sectors that came to be populated by foreigners. Had it been able to so, the jobs might have become desirable to the point that citizens, including unemployed citizens, would have been willing to accept them. There is thus a serious opportunity cost associated with importing workers, to the extent that there was a failure to enhance the economic welfare of citizens by way of increasing the number of desirable jobs and reducing unemployment. The fact that such an endeavor would not be as simple as that formulation sounds does not mean that it is *a priori* impossible.

What we may conclude from this chapter, however, is that these questions are moot as long as the institutional structure of the Israeli state rewards private rent-seekers and inhibits positive structural change. The analysis of this chapter confirms a central element of Freeman's institutionalist argument concerning clientelism and migration policies: in (some kinds of) liberal democracies, forces that favor immigration are better placed to realize their interests than forces that oppose it. Freeman, however, stops short of considering the possibility that non-immigration countries can teach us something about immigration and policymaking, or that there are other modes of policymaking (besides clientelism) in liberal democracies. To gain a better sense of those alternatives, we now turn to Japan and a discussion of how labor shortages do not lead inevitably to the use of foreign workers. We will thus begin to develop a comparative perspective on migration that offers a real possibility for explaining variation in labor migration outcomes.

4
Alternatives to Foreign Labor in Japan

The Japanese engagement with issues connected to labor migration and foreign workers presents a stark and compelling contrast with the Israeli experience. By itself, the discussion in the last chapter supports the argument that state structure and the mode of economic governance were important determining factors in the entry of foreign labor to the Israeli labor market. The purpose of this chapter is to strengthen the general argument by analyzing the contrast between Israel and Japan. More precisely, we will consider why foreign labor has played such a small role in the Japanese labor market, in particular by relating this phenomenon to the way Japan's economy is governed. In doing so, I also intend to present an explanation for the Japanese case itself that is more cogent than existing discussions.

The most important observations to make about foreign workers in Japan are that, as a percentage of the labor force, their numbers are small (relative to those in other countries) and that the current flows began relatively late. If we include the non-citizen Korean population, foreign labor in Japan constitutes approximately 1.2 percent of the Japanese labor force. When we compare Japan to Western European and other advanced countries, where the foreign share of the labor force sometimes exceed 10 percent, what emerges is that Japan still stands out as a minor user of foreign labor. Moreover, the current influx that has attracted so much attention began only in the mid-1980s – long after Japan became an economic powerhouse with very high growth rates and relatively high standards of living. On these grounds, I offer the following assertion (which I will defend further as the chapter progresses): Japan in the post-Second World War period has not been a significant host country for foreign labor, and it does not belong in the same category as other countries that have long used imported workers, such as Germany and France.[1]

Migration scholars are well aware that the number of foreign workers in Japan is small. But even those who begin by noting this fact usually go on to ask and answer the following question: why are there foreign workers in Japan? Given that the numbers in Japan have been growing, this approach is understandable: we want to address an emerging trend. It is, however, the wrong question, or at least not the most interesting one. The real question is, why are the numbers so small, and why have they remained small for so long?

I will argue here that some of the common answers to that question, drawing primarily on demography and culture, are at best incomplete, especially when we put Japan in comparative perspective. To understand what makes Japan different from other, labor-importing countries, we must also look to political economy, and in particular to the way the Japanese state interacts with the economy. The Japanese government has mostly resisted business demands for access to cheap labor from elsewhere in Asia, indicating a greater degree of state autonomy than we saw in the Israeli case. But just as important is the fact that the state has also helped create the conditions under which Japanese employers were able to continue employing Japanese workers, even at high and rising wages. The developmentalist character of the Japanese state has declined in the more recent period, but the particular mode of economic governance in Japan has continued to sustain those conditions, though in a way that is arguably less beneficial to the economy as a whole. The differences between Israel and Japan with regard to economic governance and state policies have been very significant. I intend to show that they are essential to a theoretically informed explanation of the fact that Israel has used large numbers of low-wage foreign workers while Japan has used relatively few.

In the rest of this chapter, I first lay out some of the existing discussions concerning the Japanese engagement with the issue of foreign labor. I then present comparative data, drawing on the experience of some western European countries as well as Israel, to defend the notion that Japan is a compelling anomaly among advanced capitalist countries in this matter. The chapter moves on to a sustained discussion of functional substitutes for foreign labor in Japan; in particular, I look at the conditions that made possible the high and rising wages that continued to keep Japanese workers willing to supply labor in sectors typically staffed by foreign workers in other countries. Finally, I draw out the relationship between these developments and the institutional structure of the Japanese state regarding economic governance.

Japan in the labor migration literature

Analysis of questions concerning labor migration to Japan during the late 1960s and early 1970s is relatively scarce (particularly in English).[2] Most scholars who have paid attention to this period tend to downplay its importance to the question of foreign labor in Japan. Usually, the analysis points out that surplus Japanese rural workers moved into the urban industrial sector, obviating any "need" to import labor (e.g., Cornelius 1994; Lie 1997; Sellek 1994; Sellek and Weiner 1992). Reubens (1981) also emphasizes this point, though he discusses as well other factors that allowed Japan to refrain from importing labor, such as the fact that low-level work is not stigmatized in Japan the way it is in most Western countries. It is thus said to be easier to attract native workers to what in many other societies would be considered undesirable work. The implication of this domestic labor reserve thesis is that there was no real need for foreign labor at this time, and therefore the question of foreign labor is not worth pursuing further. Alternatively, Japan's insular culture is said to have inhibited the government from acceding to employers' demands for imported labor (Martin 1991a; Zolberg 1981; see also below).

Mori's analysis (1997) is much more detailed: in addition to discussing the central role of domestic labor reserves, Mori presents data concerning wage differentials and labor shortages according to firm size. He also describes the increasing labor market mismatch caused by the persistence of unattractive jobs in the face of increasing educational attainment. On balance, however, this analysis perhaps raises more questions than it answers: "… the existing labor force was more fully employed in the 1960s and early 1970s. One should take note here that the use of foreign labor emerged in response to the comparatively less tight labor market of the recent [1980s] expansion" (1997: 40). Mori does not sufficiently explore the implications of this essential point, which is based on the fact that the job "openings to applicants" ratio was higher in the early 1970s than in the late 1980s (see below). The central thrust of the argument, however, is the one introduced above: employers in the earlier period were able to find other solutions to labor shortages (primarily drawing on rural Japanese workers), while more recently they have had no choice but to turn to foreign labor because those reserves have been drawn down.

Again, however, the question of labor migration (or its absence) to Japan during this period has received relatively little attention. Some of those who discuss the later entry of foreign workers into Japan do not treat the earlier period at all (see e.g., Foote 1993; Nagayama 1992, 1996;

Okunishi 1996; Sassen 1993; Shimada 1994). Certain kinds of research concerning labor migration to Japan may not require extensive historical background. But addressing the theoretical question of what *causes* labor migration to a country such as Japan would seem to necessitate serious engagement with the question of why Japan did *not* import workers in an earlier period of tight labor markets.

While Japan's experience with foreign labor was minimal prior to the 1973 recession, more recently stocks of foreign workers have increased. This increase has led some observers to conclude that Japan can and should be analyzed in much the same terms as other labor-importing countries (e.g., Yamanaka 1993, 1994). Others have addressed both the recent influx and the fact that the numbers remain small relative to many other countries (Mahmood 1996; Mori 1997; Oka 1994; Shimada 1994). What is relevant is the way the problem is conceptualized. Given that foreign workers constitute approximately one percent of the Japanese labor force, the tremendous attention this influx has received seems a bit exaggerated. Even sophisticated treatments of the topic sometimes use overblown language: Mori speaks of their numbers having "increased dramatically" (1997: xi); Iguchi refers to "an enormous influx of foreign labor" (1998: 300); and Komai describes the introduction of the trainee system as "epoch-making" insofar as it opened the door for the "large-scale employment" of foreign labor (1995: 47–48). This type of description is consistent with a more general assumption that what needs explaining is the presence and mode of insertion of foreign labor in Japan. Such analyses are valuable on their own terms. But understanding Japan's implications for theories of labor migration requires first asking: what is this phenomenon a case of? In other words, what do we "see" when we look at foreign labor in Japan? Even in the more recent period, it may be more useful to "see" only a rather insignificant influx of foreign workers, or what I am calling a negative case.

Before the oil-shock – Was Japan different?

The question of Japan's limited use of foreign labor becomes especially compelling when we focus on one of Japan's most extraordinary periods of high growth rates, i.e., the late 1960s and early 1970s (the so-called Izanagi boom). This was the period in which significant labor shortages first became apparent. It was also perhaps the first time in the postwar period in which the Japanese government considered, but mostly rejected, the idea of importing labor from abroad (Evans 1971; Sellek 1994; Utsumi 1988). This period seemed to combine the elements that had led other countries to turn to imported labor to resolve shortages. Japan in the pre-oil-shock years, then, might stand as a major anomaly relative to the tendency in many advanced industrial countries to import foreign labor. The proportion of foreign labor in the Japanese labor force remained in the range of 0.7 percent, while in other industrial countries the percentage rose to a much higher level (Table 4.1). Moreover, most foreign workers in Japan were long-term Korean residents who had entered the country prior to the Second World War. They have long held jobs with lower status and lower pay, and this fact is no doubt related to social discrimination as well as to their distinct legal status as non-citizens; they are not eligible to work as civil servants and were long barred from professions such as teaching, for example (Hicks 1997). On the other hand, they were never "temporary" guestworkers of the classical European type.

But was Japan in the 1960s and 1970s really in the same situation as other industrial countries? Again, many analysts of this period (e.g., Boltho 1975; Galenson and Odaka 1976; Nakamura 1992; Reubens 1981; Sellek and Weiner 1992) point out that one of the reasons Japan did not import workers was that it had another alternative: Japanese workers from rural areas. Perhaps a country that could draw on its own citizens for labor cannot really be said to have experienced a labor shortage. In addition, perhaps Japan was quite different from other countries in other respects as well, e.g., economic growth rates, unemployment rates, inflation rates, etc. – all of which could have helped determine whether

Table 4.1 Percentage of foreign workers in labor force

	Japan	West Germany	France	Sweden	Israel
1960	0.3[a]	1.5[b]	4.9[c]	3.3[c]	
1964	0.3[a]	4.4[b]	6.2[d]	4.2[d]	
1969	0.3[a]	7.3	6.1[c]	5.6[c]	
1974	0.3[a]	8.2	7.1[c]	4.9	5.7
1979	0.3[a]	7.6	6.2	5.2	5.6
1984	0.3[a]	6.5	6.9	5.0	6.2
1988	0.8[e]	6.6	6.3	5.0	7.0
1992	1.2[e]	6.1	6.0	5.3	6.5

Notes: [a] Immigration Bureau, Japan 1990; [b] Herbert 1990; [c] Böhning 1984; [d] Descloitres 1967; [e] Mori 1997 and Immigration Bureau, Japan. All data on Israel from the Statistical Abstract of Israel.

Sources: Computed from the following sources: The denominator (total labor force) is from *OECD Economic Outlook*; unless otherwise noted, the numerator (foreign workers) is from *OECD-SOPEMI*.

Japan "really needed" foreign labor. We need to consider these issues seriously before designating pre-oil-shock Japan as an anomaly concerning foreign labor. In this section I therefore present and analyze data to highlight the similarities and contrasts between Japan and some other advanced industrial countries, especially regarding the labor force.

Japan indeed had a substantially higher proportion of its labor force employed in agriculture in 1960, around the time when some European countries began importing labor. For any given year through 1970, Japan's proportion in agriculture was more than twice that of Germany, for instance (see OECD Labor Force Statistics).

However, we should not compare Japan to other countries in the same years: other countries experienced labor shortages in earlier years and thus had to confront problems of labor supply earlier. West Germany and France started importing workers in the 1950s. By 1961, West Germany had signed recruitment agreements with Italy, Spain, Greece and Turkey, and the inflow of labor had begun in earnest. France had signed recruitment agreements even earlier. Japanese employers began to complain of sustained labor shortages only in the late 1960s. The proper comparison, then, is between Japan in the late 1960s and France and Germany in the early 1960s.

The proportion of the Japanese labor force employed in agriculture in 1969 (18.6 percent) is indeed higher – though not outrageously – than the comparable figure for West Germany in 1961 (13 percent), but it is *lower* than the French figure for 1961 (21.4 percent; all figures from OECD sources). In other words, the "reserves" of French workers employed in agriculture were proportionately greater than those of Japan, at the time each country confronted the problem of insufficient labor supply – but this fact did not keep the French government from allowing the recruitment of foreign workers. The fact that Japan could draw on reserves from agriculture was undoubtedly one of the factors that enabled the country to avoid importing labor. But the mere availability of surplus agricultural workers does not itself explain why Japan actually adopted this particular solution for alleviating labor shortages.

It may be, however, that Japan had other reserves of labor as well, so that it was not as difficult to tap other domestic supplies of labor as in other countries; in this case the question of foreign labor would not have been as relevant to Japan at this time. Possible candidates might include women not in the labor force, men not in the labor force, and unemployed persons. The data (from OECD Labor Force Statistics) show, however, that Japan had *fewer* such persons to draw on than other countries. Overall labor force participation rates were higher in Japan in 1969

(65.6 percent) than in France (55.7 percent) or West Germany (60.1 percent) in 1961 – in the case of France, significantly higher. Female labor force participation rates as well were much higher in Japan than in other countries: 50.1 percent in Japan versus 41.5 percent in West Germany (again, 1969 versus 1961). (If data were available for France in the early 1960s, they would surely show an even greater difference.) Japanese female labor force participation rates were even higher than those for Sweden throughout the 1960s, though the Swedish rate surpassed the Japanese rate in 1971. Unemployment rates for all countries in the 1960s reveal that there were very few people looking for work who did not find it: Japan's rate was only marginally higher than West Germany's throughout this period. On these measures, then, France, West Germany, and Sweden had more candidates in the domestic population for activation into the labor force than Japan – yet the former countries turned to foreign labor while Japan did not.

There is of course a difference between transferring labor from one economic sector to another and pulling inactive people into the labor force. The former are already active, while many of the latter are probably inactive for a reason and might well resist efforts to mobilize them. One of the most common ways of explaining the labor migration "problem" is to point out that there are jobs citizens are simply unwilling to do: citizens and foreign workers are said to be complementary, not competitive. But while it may seem unlikely that non-participating citizen women are good potential substitutes for foreign workers, the Swedish government in the late 1960s deliberately tried to decrease the need for foreign labor by encouraging more women to enter the labor force. "Encouragement" meant not exhortation but policy changes, including expanded community provision of child care and tax policy changes that penalized single-earner households (Cook 1978). The West German government, on the other hand, chose a different path: supporting "traditional family" roles for women and refraining from policies that would have facilitated working on the part of women with children (Kamerman 1979). The share of foreigners in the West German labor force rose to a rather higher level than in the Swedish labor force (9.8 percent in 1973 for Germany, 5.7 percent in 1976 for Sweden – see Table 4.1). Female labor force participation was certainly not the only factor accounting for the difference, but it seems unlikely that raising participation rates (in West Germany, for example) would have had no effect whatsoever on the demand for foreign labor. Japan arguably had fewer possibilities for this option, given that its female (and overall) participation rates were already higher than those of the other countries described here. On the other hand, a relatively high percentage of employed Japanese women work part-time, indicating that there was a greater possibility of relying more heavily on citizens for labor by increasing the working hours of Japanese women.

Another potential way to intensify the use of Japanese labor was to draw on the very large self-employed population: Galenson and Odaka (1976) note that the proportion of waged and salaried workers was much lower in Japan than in many western European countries. This point leads to a further discussion of the fact that France imported labor despite the fact that there were very large numbers of agricultural workers that might have substituted for foreigners. The reason this potential was not exploited to any great extent was that the French government had a long-standing policy of supporting the agricultural sector, with an explicit view to keeping peasant agriculture viable in the face of strong competitive pressures from other countries. (Japan and France have been rather similar in this respect.) The same point holds with regard to small business in Japan (as well as to the low rate of female labor force participation in Germany): there are very large numbers of self-employed workers in Japan in large part because government policies create the conditions for them to survive as such, to a degree that does not characterize other advanced industrial countries. In other words, the Japanese government made it possible for many self-employed workers to *refrain* from engaging in wage labor, a point illustrated by the fact that the self-employed population is still quite large relative to other advanced capitalist countries. In both countries, there is a politics of labor supply that helps determine to what extent workers will move into urban wage labor when demand for such labor increases.

In many of the discussions concerning labor shortages in Japan, the basic argument is that there were sufficient labor reserves to meet the demand. I have not tried to argue here that there were not reserves. Rather, I have defended two points: First, the reserves were not obviously of a different order of magnitude from those of some other countries that did import labor. And second, and partly as a consequence, the availability of labor reserves among the domestic population does not suffice to explain why they were in fact used. When analysts of Japan claim that the reason Japan did not import labor is that the country had labor reserves, they are implicitly claiming that there is a "tipping point" of some sort: when labor reserves "run out," a country "needs" foreign labor, and Japan still had not reached that point in this period. I do not argue in this section that such an argument merely puts the "tipping point" in the wrong quantitative place; instead, I have tried to show that the concept itself is problematic as an explanation for the absence of labor migration (and, therefore, for the *presence* of foreign workers in other places as well). The real question, addressed later in this chapter, has to do with the *conditions* that determine whether citizen workers are willing to accept jobs that in many countries come to be staffed by foreigners.

Another potential objection to the argument that Japan was in a situation substantially similar to that of other countries experiencing labor shortages might be that the Japanese economy was less developed and therefore had less of a "structural" need for foreign labor. Again, however, the (admittedly crude) data do not support this objection. In constant terms (1990 prices, 1990 exchange rates), the Japanese per capita GDP in 1969 was higher than the French or German figures for 1961: US$11,135 versus US$9165 and US$9248. In addition, economic growth rates, expressed as increases in per capita GDP, show that the Japanese economy was expanding substantially faster than the other economies (more than 10 percent annually in the late 1960s, as against approximately 4 percent in Western European countries), perhaps indicating that the Japanese demand for labor was expanding faster as well.

In sum, then, if we compare Japan to other countries for the relevant years, we see that the Japanese economy was growing more rapidly and was at a level of development comparable to other, labor-importing countries; the proportion of Japanese workers employed in agriculture was well within the range of other countries; and labor force participation, both overall and female, was higher than that of other countries that had already imported significant numbers of foreign workers. Thus the argument that Japan refrained from bringing labor from abroad because it had domestic labor reserves is at best incomplete and at worst does not stand up at all to comparative investigation. Japan did resolve labor shortages in this period partly by drawing on reserves of labor; but given that other countries might have done the same but did not, the real issue then becomes explaining *why* and *how* Japan followed this path. On these grounds Japan stands as a significant anomaly, having avoided importing labor through the high growth years of the late 1960s and early 1970s despite labor shortages that were arguably at least as severe as those experienced earlier by labor-importing countries. Japan is thus usefully conceived as a negative case of labor migration.

The remaining outstanding issue is that of culture. To some observers, the question of why Japan has few foreign workers (and few immigrants in general) is easily answered: Japan is a xenophobic society that prizes its putative homogeneity (to understand the adjective, see Michael

Weiner's *Japan's Minorities*, 1997). There is no denying this argument makes sense when Japan is considered alone. But as a more general explanation for why some countries receive many foreign workers while others do not, culture encounters some significant problems. First, regarding the comparison between Japan and Israel: It might be imagined that Israel, a country that already has an ethnically diverse population, is not characterized by the same cultural closure to foreigners. While Israel is open to immigration, however, it is of course open to immigration only of a very specific kind, i.e., of Jews. There is no plausibility in the claim that the presence of foreign workers in Israel derives from a greater openness to the increased presence of non-Jews from around the world; in fact, that presence was explicitly not desired at a popular level and has become highly problematic. The two countries differ culturally in a variety of important ways, but those differences do not add up to a distinction that helps account for their different policies with respect to low-level foreign labor. Despite some cultural differences, Japan and Israel share a marked particularism with respect to foreigners.

In fact this particularism is also shared by other labor importers, most notably Germany: it would certainly not work to argue that West Germany in the 1960s imported Turks and Yugoslavs because it welcomed an increase in cultural or ethnic diversity. In fact it would seem that the issue of guestworkers is likely to become salient precisely in those countries (experiencing labor shortages) that wish to maintain a sense of homogeneity: guestworker programs start with the notion that the workers will meet a temporary need and then leave when that need ends, thus posing no real long-term threat to homogeneity. Classic immigration countries such as the US and Canada can satisfy their labor needs by accepting more immigrants, i.e., as candidates for permanent residence and thus full social membership. These immigration flows have drawn on a diverse set of origin countries and cultures. The empirical contrast is not complete: continued American use of Mexican guestworkers testifies to the fact that some types of potential immigrants are in fact not welcome as full social members in the US, at least not in greater quantities. But that fact simply confirms the more general point: guestworker programs become relevant when workers are required but the actual people involved are considered undesirable as, well, people. What is surprising, then, given that Israel, Japan and Germany (among others) embody an ethno-cultural sense of nationhood, is not that Israel and Germany have imported guestworkers but rather that Japan has not. The claim that a desire for homogeneity explains Japan's aversion to foreign workers fails to appreciate the more general problem and thus starts with the wrong premise.

More importantly, however, while aspects of Japanese culture might lay the foundation for a *desire* to exclude foreign workers, culture is insufficient as an explanation for the country's *ability* to maintain both an exclusionary immigration policy *and* a reasonably successful economy (at least in certain periods). The ability to satisfy both economic and cultural "imperatives" is rooted in a particular state structure that facilitates a particular mode of economic governance.

Official and private perceptions of the problem

Even though Japan did have a sizable surplus agricultural labor force that would eventually be transferred to other sectors, this transition took place too slowly to satisfy the needs of many employers, partly because many of those working in agriculture were rather older and not inclined to take urban jobs (Dore 1986). There was a prolonged period in which the available labor force was simply insufficient to meet demand. The active openings-to-applicants ratio was quite high for a number of years and in fact was higher during this period than in the late 1980s, when the number of foreign workers in Japan started to increase significantly. Analyses of Japan in the early 1970s (e.g., Mori 1997; Reubens 1981) usually read as if the labor shortage were a single event that was resolved with a single-stroke solution: Japan had a labor shortage during a boom period, but this shortage was solved through recourse to labor from agricultural reserves. In fact, however, this was a prolonged period of economic difficulty for many individual employers, regardless of the fact that the economy as a whole was growing quickly.

Official and private publications from the period abound with references to "severe" and "critical" labor shortages. In the latter half of 1967 wages began rising at a faster rate than productivity (Labor Ministry White Paper, 1970–71). According to a 1969 Labor Ministry report, ten percent of firms surveyed reported that they had had to idle part of their production facilities because they could not get enough workers (*Oriental Economist*, May 1969). Fifty percent of firms surveyed predicted they would not be able to get enough suitable labor in the future, and another 38 percent said they would get enough labor only if they were not choosy about whom they got. Another Ministry survey later that year revealed that 80 percent of manufacturing enterprises reported they were unable to proceed with planned expansions simply because they could not get enough labor (*Oriental Economist*, August 1969).

The problems became more severe in subsequent years: a Labor Ministry White Paper from 1971–72 reported that openings for skilled workers were being filled at a rate of 19.8 percent and that the absolute number of openings was close to two million. Forecasts for later years were pessimistic: the Labor Ministry projected that if economic growth were to continue at an annual rate of 10 percent from 1970–75, the shortfall of workers would reach 4.1 million (relative to a labor force of around 50 million (Labor White Paper, 1972–73). In other words, it was not possible for the economy to continue to grow at such a rate, given population and labor force constraints. The government explicitly recognized that labor shortages would become a serious constraint on future economic growth (MITI White Paper on International Trade, 1970).

There was, at least in some parts of the government, a remarkable willingness to adjust growth rate expectations downwards because of labor supply constraints:

> The [Economic and Social Development Plan, adopted March 1967, for fiscal years 1967–71] set the growth rate at about 8 percent per annum. ... The establishment of this comparatively low growth rate was due to the expectation that the labor market, particularly that for young labor, would become smaller. (Miyazaki 1970: 377)

As Miyazaki notes, Japanese economic plans have tended to underestimate real growth potential: actual growth consistently exceeded estimates in the plans. Still, the fact that the government was willing to allow perceived labor shortages to dictate reduced *prospects* for economic growth stands in marked contrast to the path followed by many European countries – where growth was maintained in part by importing large amounts of labor.

From one angle, perceptions of this sort mattered more than reality itself: following W.I. Thomas, we should consider that to the extent the labor shortage was *perceived* as real by important interest groups, then that perception was real in its consequences. The importance of Japan's labor reserves was diminished by the widely held notion that such workers were not in fact available or were unsuitable because of age, gender, training, or location. Japanese employers resisted the ideas of extending the retirement age, retraining older workers, and employing more middle-aged women. They expressed preferences for different solutions, based on the reality they saw.

What many employers in fact wanted was that the government would allow them to import workers from abroad. The phenomenon of bringing in workers under the guise of "trainees" began during this period (Ochiai 1974), and the Labor Ministry announced plans to create an official program along these lines (though involving a mere 5000 workers), with the explicit acknowledgment that doing so would also help alleviate labor shortages (*Far Eastern Economic Review*, 3 October 1970). The Japanese Chamber of Commerce and Industry (representing small- and medium-sized businesses) adopted a resolution in 1970 urging the government to explore the option of importing labor. Many businesses and business associations, concerned about the shortage of unskilled and semi-skilled labor, submitted reports to the government urging that the trainee program be expanded (Kuptsch and Oishi 1995). The Tokyo Chamber of Commerce and Industry called in July 1970 for an expansion of the trainee program in a document entitled "The Demand on Next Year's Labor Policy"; it also insisted that employers be able to import workers from other Asian countries independently of the trainee system (Ochiai 1974).

The government's response was not altogether negative: a section of the Economic Planning Agency announced in 1970 that it would study the option in relation to its impact on future economic growth (*Japan Economic Journal*, 8 December 1970). In addition, the Economic Council, an advisory group in the Prime Minister's office, discussed the foreign worker question as it formulated a "New Economic Social Development Plan for 1970–1975" (*Japan Economic Journal*, 14 September 1971).[3] And the government – in particular, the Ministries of Foreign Affairs, Labor, and International Trade & Industry (MITI) – sanctioned small training programs for foreigners. These programs were developed in an atmosphere in which Japan was attempting (or trying to *appear* to attempt) to contribute to the development of poorer countries in the region. Following the 6th Asian regional conference of the International Labor Office, the Labor Ministry adopted a "Technical Development Plan" in 1971 which provided for acceptance of "technical trainees" from Asian countries. Despite official conditions specifying that trainees must not have on-the-job training, it became clear that many companies were using their charges for cheap labor (Ochiai 1974). In the end, however, a significant foreign worker program did not emerge during this period; it is important not to overstate the significance of the early trainee programs.

In the late 1980s, with a renewed economic boom, labor shortages began to reappear, prompting business groups to renew their calls for an opening to foreign labor. The government's response was two-pronged. The 1990 Immigration Law increased the number of categories of foreigners who were eligible for work permits – but this change merely increased the diversification among categories of professionals and other high-level workers. The main intent of the law was to reinforce the country's closure to unskilled foreign workers, and to establish (for the first time) penalties on employers who employed foreigners illegally (Meissner *et al.* 1993).

Most government ministries have consistently adopted negative positions on the idea of importing unskilled foreign workers. This is especially true of the two ministries that have direct jurisdiction over the matter, Justice and Labor. Justice's involvement is tied to its jurisdiction over immigration matters, and it is arguably the ministry with the most influence over policy in this matter (Oka 1994). The Justice Ministry's main concern is the prevention of illegal immigration and illegal employment, but Justice has also mounted strong opposition to the idea of a guestworker system based on employment permits (Komai 1995). The Labor Ministry, on the other hand, is more directly concerned with the potential impact of foreign labor on the Japanese labor force and the economy in general. While Labor has agreed to the creation of very small trainee programs (Imano 1997; see also below), in general the ministry has consistently and strongly opposed proposals to import unskilled labor. The Labor Ministry has issued a number of reports concluding that the fiscal costs of foreign labor would far outweigh any fiscal benefits; the reports also contended that introducing unskilled foreign labor would inhibit productivity and wage increases for Japanese workers, increase the stratification in the labor market, and result in very high social costs for the economy as a whole. These conclusions were based on a clear understanding that a certain number of workers would remain in Japan permanently and create families (Ministry of Labour, Japan 1993; see also Koshiro 1998).

Several other ministries remained opposed to unskilled foreign workers as well. MITI's opposition rests on the idea that unskilled foreign labor would inhibit rationalization in labor intensive industries. The Ministry of Construction, in spite of a reputation for very cozy ties with large contractors, is firmly against foreign labor, arguing that the image of the industry would suffer and Japanese workers would be increasingly inclined to avoid employment in construction – partly because wages would likely stagnate or fall (Komai 1995). Japanese labor unions are, unsurprisingly, opposed to foreign labor as well, though they have little or no influence on policy (Nimura 1992).[4]

The ministries in favor of opening the gates to unskilled foreign labor include Foreign Affairs, Transportation, and Agriculture (Komai 1995).

The Foreign Ministry is concerned that Japan's continuing closure on this matter will harm its relations with other countries in Asia that are interested in increasing the remittances earned by workers abroad (Meissner *et al.* 1993). The ministry speaks in terms of Japan's "responsibilities" (as an economic superpower) to its neighbors. Transportation and Agriculture are generally perceived as the ministries of transporters and agriculturalists, respectively (Katz 1998), and their main goal is to gain access to cheap labor for employers.

Perhaps most interesting of all is the fact that the Liberal Democratic Party's (LDP) "Special Committee on the Problem of Foreign Workers" has adopted a favorable position to unskilled foreign labor (Komai 1995). "Influential" members of Parliament from the LDP have also pressed for openness to unskilled workers (Iguchi 1998). The fact that this position has not been converted into government policy perhaps indicates that the authority on this matter rests with the bureaucracy, where the key ministries have for the most part rejected the idea. In other words, we already see some support for the claim that Japan's closure to low-wage foreign labor is related to the notion that economic policymaking authority lies more with the bureaucracy than with politicians beholden to private interests.

It bears reiterating that the number of foreign workers entering in the more recent period (i.e., the late 1980s and early 1990s) has been quite moderate as well. Unskilled or semi-skilled workers have come in four modes: trainees, Nikkei (foreign-born ethnic Japanese), students working illegally, and other illegal workers. The numbers in some categories are surprisingly small, relative to the attention they have received from scholars. Trainees, for example, constituted a mere 0.003 percent of the Japanese labor force in 1992 (see Mori 1997 for data). The category of "work permit" holders refers to foreign professionals and business managers of foreign companies; these persons are not low-level foreign workers as that term is being used here. The most significant categories (apart from long-term Korean residents), then, are clandestine workers, the Nikkei, and students working illegally.

The largest absolute numbers of foreign workers have been employed in manufacturing, trade and restaurant, services, and construction; apart from the very low numbers in agriculture, foreign workers in Japan are distributed in a way similar to foreign workers in other countries. Published data do a poor job of counting certain types of foreign workers, clandestine workers (including students) in particular. Also missing are long-term non-citizen Korean workers who have taken Japanese names.[5] If the estimated half-million workers omitted in data indicating sectoral allocations (e.g., Mori 1997 – see in particular his Table 6.1) were allocated evenly among the top four sectors of employment (manufacturing, trade/restaurants, services, and construction), the percentage of foreign workers in construction would still be less than three percent and the percentage in the other three sectors would still be less than two percent. (Recall that in Israel foreigners constitute approximately 40% of the construction labor force.)

Substitutes for foreign labor

We have seen that the shortage was perceived as a real problem that had to be addressed in some manner. The pressures from employers to import labor became much more intense in the 1980s, and there were some openings. But it would be quite off base, even in the more recent period, to characterize Japan's dominant response to labor shortages as one of importing labor.

The Japanese government had the opportunity to know that there were real drawbacks associated with imported labor. European countries had begun to experience problems in the 1960s, as discussed in Chapter 1. It is likely that Japanese policymakers were familiar with the West German situation in particular, as Japan frequently looked to Germany for guidance: "Because of the many striking parallels between the two countries, and because Germany modernized at an earlier date, Japan has a long tradition of seeking to draw lessons from the German experience" (Berger 1998: 319). I cannot provide direct evidence that Japanese policymakers decided to exclude unskilled foreign workers in the early 1970s because of lessons they drew from West Germany or other countries in Europe. But it seems implausible that Japanese bureaucrats were not aware of the concerns being raised there. In the more recent period that awareness is beyond question (see e.g., Awanohara 1986).

The government has essentially forced Japanese employers to rely on Japanese workers in most cases and has effectively created the conditions that have made it possible for this to happen. This section presents data on alternative solutions backed by the government and adopted by employers: automation and other means of increasing worker productivity and output; hastening the mobilization of "reserves" labor into the urban labor force; and exporting some types of production to low-wage countries. These were active solutions, but we will discuss "passive" solutions as well. The government's refusal to allow employers to import labor was likely a contributing factor to a variety of economic developments: inflation caused in part by increasingly militant wage demands; the increasing prices of non-tradables such as housing and services relative to tradable goods; and the transfer of income shares from capital to labor. These changes derived not only from the labor shortage but from other problems and goals as well. But each of them also had the effect of alleviating the labor shortage and thus diminishing the pressure for importing labor.

The data in this section demonstrate some features of Japan's impressive economic performance across the two periods with labor shortages. But the point of presenting these data goes well beyond documenting favorable economic performance. The more important goal is to show that the economy developed in a particular way, one that created the conditions under which Japanese employers could continue to employ Japanese workers in sectors and jobs that are frequently staffed by foreigners in other countries. As in the previous chapter, we begin with the assumption that the fundamental requirement for attracting citizen workers to jobs that are considered undesirable is high and/or rising wages. Other considerations are important as well, such as status, job security, and whether the work is unpleasant. But these factors can be considered to influence the value at which the commodity of labor power will be traded; the low status of a job affects (raises) the market clearing wage for that job, rather than preventing the operation of the labor market altogether. Whether employers will be able to pay that wage depends on the type and not just the magnitude of economic growth. We will see a strong contrast between Japan and Israel on both counts, a contrast that had significant implications for their different approaches to the question of foreign labor.

As a prelude, however, labor shortages (or, more precisely, the inability of employers to attract workers at prevailing wages) have likely played an important role in the migration of Japanese capital to low-wage countries, at least in manufacturing. Japanese foreign direct investment abroad began to increase significantly in the early 1970s. The cumulative total of investment abroad was US$3.6 billion in 1970 and increased by 287 percent over the next three years, to US$ 10.3 billion (Sekiguchi *et al.* 1979). In 1982 and 1986 the figures were $53 billion and $84 billion, respectively (Ng *et al.* 1987). More than half of this investment was directed to low-wage developing countries (especially in Asia, but also Latin America) and consisted of labor-intensive production in consumer goods industries making standardized products. In addition, small- or medium-sized firms made almost half of the number of investments (though in terms of volume large firms accounted for a much larger proportion) (Kojima 1983). On both counts it is clear that many of the firms investing overseas were precisely the ones that were having difficulty finding workers in Japan. Migration of manufacturing capital is probably an inevitable response to the confluence of rising wages and increasing international trade, but it is not the only response, as we will see shortly.

Data on the export of capital do not by themselves establish that Japanese employers' actions here were qualitatively different from those of employers elsewhere. In fact, businesses in other countries such as Germany and the US *have* moved production to low-wage countries, in large part because of wage pressures. To determine whether Japan was different in this respect, one would need to present data on the rates of capital transfer in particular sub-sectors of manufacturing that were experiencing labor shortages and wage pressures. Even if these rates were higher in Japan than in other countries, one would need to consider other hypotheses that might explain the export of capital, apart from labor shortages. While it may be the case that other countries did export capital, however, Japan clearly is different from many other countries (especially in Europe) insofar as it did not respond to wage pressures in manufacturing by importing labor. The most that can be said concerning countries such as Germany is that they did both.

There is little need to rehearse in detail the notion that Japanese employers, particularly during the earlier (Izanagi) economic boom, responded to labor shortages also by turning to domestic labor "reserves" such as women and workers from rural areas. This point is discussed in virtually every analysis of foreign workers in Japan. There has also been much discussion in policymaking circles about the need to increase labor mobility among firms, in part by deemphasizing traditions of "lifetime employment" and seniority-based wage formulas (see various Labor Ministry White Papers from the period). Another popular topic was the need to facilitate the continued employment of older workers, i.e., those who had been forced to "retire" at age 55. Middle-aged women were also increasingly seen as potential workers, though many employers were slow to adjust to the idea that such persons were suitable in this respect.

But given the consensus around the notion that domestic labor reserves provided labor at times when employers experienced shortages, there is a remarkable near-silence (at least in English) concerning the *conditions that made possible* the mobilization of those reserves. In existing discussions of the reserves thesis, there seems to be an assumption that the transfer of labor to labor-hungry sectors is a phenomenon that requires no explanation itself. Here is where we will (eventually) pin down the real factors accounting for the difference between Israeli and Japanese responses to labor shortages. The point is simple at first and will rapidly become more complex and ramified. The simple point is wages: Japanese workers in the labor-hungry sectors – construction in particular – have enjoyed real wage increases mostly unmatched by their counterparts in other advanced capitalist countries (with the apparent exception of Finland) (Table 4.2). Greater complexity will come when we look at related factors such as labor productivity, capital intensity, and consumer prices.

Real increases in wages[6] in construction were substantially greater in Japan and Finland than in the US, Israel, and Germany, three countries where immigrants/foreigners and their descendants are a large part of the labor force (Table 4.2). The figures presented relate to wages in national currencies, which means that in one respect they understate the size of the increase in Japan: the increasing value of the Japanese yen (especially during the mid-1980s) meant increasing purchasing power for imported goods.

For manufacturing, there is less of a contrast: manufacturing wages actually rose slightly faster in Israel than in Japan, for example. While this piece of evidence may seem to run counter to the thesis being presented, in fact the reverse is true: remember that foreign workers have had only a minimal presence in Israeli manufacturing.

The important point here, however, is not limited to the pace of the increase but to the structure of sectoral wages relative to the overall wage. The varying patterns here are depicted in Figure 4.1. The starkest

Table 4.2 Average yearly percentage increase in employee compensation, 1970–94

	Manufacturing	Construction	Retail/ hotels	Social services	Total
USA	0.8	−0.6	−0.2	1.1	0.5
Germany	2.6	2.1	2.2	2.0	2.1
Israel[b]	2.9	1.6[a]	1.9[a]		2.3
Japan[c]	2.7	3.2	1.7	2.4	2.7
Denmark	1.5	0.6	1.7	1.6	1.0
Norway	2.2	1.2	2.1	1.7	1.5
Finland	2.9	2.7	3.5	3.4	2.9

Notes: [a] As noted in Chapter 3, official figures on wage increases in Israeli construction and retail/hotel workers are seriously exaggerated, because undocumented foreign workers (including Palestinians) are not covered.
[b] For Israel, construction includes utilities workers.
[c] For Japan, hotels and restaurants are included in social services, not retail.

Sources: Computed from the OECD International Sectoral Database; for Israel, Statistical Abstract of Israel.

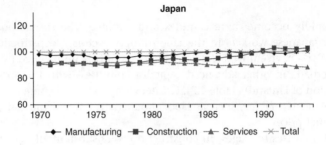

Japan

Source: OECD International Sectoral Database (for all but Israel).

Israel

Source: Israel Central Bureau of Statistics.

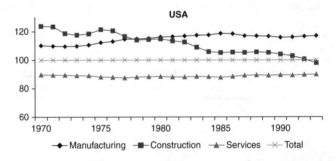

USA

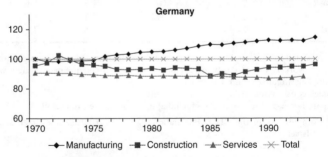

Germany

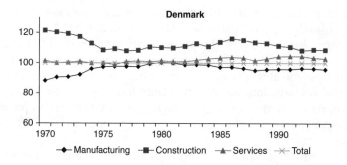

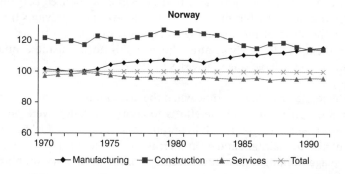

Figure 4.1 Sectoral wages as percent of average wage.

contrast is between Israel and Japan: construction wages as a percentage of the overall wage in Japan rose, while in Israel they fell (recall the discussion of Israeli wages in the previous chapter as well). In Denmark, Norway, and Finland construction wages were already quite high relative to the general wage level: the slower increases here are offset by the fact that construction was already a fairly lucrative occupation. Again, employers will find it easier to continue employing citizens in problem sectors when they can offer high and/or rising wages, relative to average wages.

The Japanese government's refusal to augment the labor force with foreign workers in the early 1970s contributed to a very significant development related to wage increases: the transfer of income shares from capital to labor, partly as a result of labor's enhanced bargaining position in a tight labor market. This was a reversal of previous trends, where the share of income going to Japanese capital had tripled since 1953 (Pempel 1978). Even after the first oil-shock, Japanese unions negotiated very large wage increases in 1974:

> The result – coming at a time when the disruption of the oil and commodity price rises and the efforts to control inflation were putting heavy brakes on the growth in output – was not only to fuel inflation but also to maintain and even increase real wages in spite of reduced average working hours, thus effecting a sizable shift in the proportion of national income going to wages at the expense of profits. (Dore 1986, 101–2)

As is evident from Table 4.3, the dramatic shift in 1974 was a continuation of trends of previous years. The shift was due in part to the recession (where profits fell faster than sticky-downwards wages), but labor's share never again dropped to the level of the 1960s. Moreover, labor's increasing share in the national income was *anticipated* (e.g., *Japan Labor Bulletin*, September 1973, citing a Labor Ministry White Paper). That is, not only did the transfer happen, but many observers believed it *would* happen. Capital's share rebounded in the late 1970s, though not to the level of the 1960s, and then a similar transfer of shares occurred again in the late 1980s and 1990s. It would be difficult to argue that these shifts were unrelated to the shortage of labor, though of course other factors were probably implicated as well, e.g., the 1971 "Nixon shocks" of currency exchange disruptions resulting from the end of Bretton Woods. Inflation, declining profitability, and restrictions on growth were precisely the kinds of problems other countries hoped to avoid by

Table 4.3   Distribution of national income

	% to labor	% to capital		% to labor	% to capital
1970	54.0	18.3	1983	69.3	11.0
1971	58.6	15.2	1984	68.9	12.1
1972	57.0	12.6	1985	67.8	12.8
1973	58.5	11.7	1986	67.9	12.7
1974	62.4	6.5	1987	68.1	12.9
1975	65.6	6.0	1988	66.7	14.1
1976	65.8	6.0	1989	67.1	13.1
1977	66.5	6.3	1990	67.9	11.3
1978	66.3	11.3	1991	68.6	10.7
1979	66.5	11.5	1992	69.7	9.5
1980	66.8	10.8	1993	70.9	9.2
1981	68.6	10.1	1994	72.4	8.3
1982	69.0	10.8	1995	73.4	5.6

Source: Computed from the Bank of Japan's *Economic Statistics Annual*. Capital's share refers to the category "entrepreneurial income of private incorporated enterprises, including dividends."

importing labor, and the fact that Japan refrained from following this path is quite striking.

The wage increases for Japanese construction workers merit more detailed attention, especially because construction is usually a key sector for employment of foreign workers, as the jobs are usually considered "dirty, dangerous, and demanding." There are foreigners employed in construction in Japan, many of them illegally, as the Construction Ministry opposes importing construction workers. But one of the really salient features of the Japanese labor force (i.e., citizens) is the very high percentage employed in construction. Construction employment as a share of total employment has remained steady at more than 10 percent, during a period (1970–94) when other advanced countries (with the notable exception of Norway) experienced significant declines. The Japanese construction industry is the world's largest, with an output of about $500 billion a year (Woodall 1996). Increases in construction wages have been very impressive, rising faster than average wages (uniquely among other advanced countries), to the point where construction wages are 103 percent of the average Japanese wage (i.e., in 1994; OECD International Sectoral Database). Big wage increases and high levels of employment in construction raise again the issue of what we "see" when we look at the foreign worker question in Japan. When many other countries experience declining native employment in construction, tepid wage increases (especially relative to other sectors), and a strong presence of foreigners, what stands out for Japan is the minimal role for foreigners and the strong tendency for Japanese workers to accept construction work in spite of the "dirty, dangerous, and demanding" work. The differences between Japan and the others seem more important than the similarities.

Wage increases in Japanese service sectors such as retail trade, hotels, and restaurants have been somewhat less impressive relative to overall increases. But again, closer analysis is called for. One of the important recent trends in economic restructuring among advanced countries is commonly held to be the emergence of a low-wage service sector, where increasing numbers of jobs are held by immigrants from poorer countries (e.g., Sassen 1991). Here, too, Japan seems noteworthy for the extent to which it has not followed this trend. The mix of employment and wage variables is somewhat different from that concerning construction. Wages have risen in an absolute sense, but they have shown indistinct trends relative to the average wage. But at least two other factors are also relevant here. First, growth in overall service employment has been relatively restrained: services in Japan account for about half of all employment, versus 58 percent in the US, and the increase in that proportion has been slower in Japan than in the US and Germany (1970–94).[7] It is clear from these figures – and from the relatively minor number of foreign workers employed in services in Japan – that the notion of an expanding service sector fed by low-wage immigrant labor does not characterize Japan's experience to the extent that it does in many other countries with more foreign workers.

That observation is also supported by data concerning consumer price increases at the sectoral level (Table 4.4). These figures show that consumer prices for services[8] – personal services in particular – have increased substantially faster in Japan than general prices. In other words, the fact that Japan has not witnessed the expansion of a low-wage service sector to the same extent as other countries has perhaps come at a price, at least to consumers. While the import of industrial products from low-wage countries has helped restrain prices for those goods (counteracting the wage increases for Japanese manufacturing workers), in this largely non-tradable sector labor supply constraints seem to be associated with price increases exceeding the general level of inflation. It then seems reasonable to conjecture that increasing relative prices for services have helped restrain demand for services as well, which would also be consistent with the relatively moderate gain in service sector employment.

Table 4.4 Consumer price indices, Japan, 1970 = 100

	Industrial products	Housing	Services	Personal services	General
1970	100.0	100.0	100.0	100.0	100.0
1975	170.6	167.8	169.8	200.0	171.6
1980	218.0	243.6	256.4	295.5	236.5
1985	242.6	285.3	305.2	355.6	271.0
1990	249.4	325.7	343.6	411.5	289.9
1995	257.9	370.7	383.2	481.1	310.1

Source: Nikkei Telecom.

The relationship between wages and prices is mediated to some degree by labor productivity, the next relevant factor in a discussion of how Japan has managed to rely on citizen labor to a greater extent than many other countries. There are certain difficulties associated with measuring labor productivity. Generally, productivity figures are affected by business cycles: layoffs during a recession can create a false impression of an increase in labor productivity. In addition, the figures (for all sectors) are derived by dividing value-added at market prices by employment (including self-employed and unpaid family workers). Using market prices as a measure of output creates problems in all sectors. Technological changes that increase the rate at which labor produces *physical* output may also increase the supply of a good such that its price declines significantly. It may then appear that labor productivity has actually fallen, depending on demand for the product; at the very least, the price decline will moderate the size of any productivity increase relative to the rate of increase of physical output. While it might be thought that this issue creates real problems for measuring labor productivity, the problem is mitigated somewhat by the fact that we are interested here in *relative* productivity performance: particularly for goods with a minimum level of tradability,[9] technological changes affecting the rate of physical output will show up in the relative rates of productivity growth for different countries.

Interpreting the figures for labor productivity in service sectors is more challenging. When the value of the service is measured in price terms, and when that price is determined almost entirely by labor costs – as in the case of personal services (which are included here under the category of social services) – then productivity will increase in large part as a function of wage increases. A typical example is the productivity of barbers. Haircuts are not performed more quickly than they were a generation ago, but the price has increased nonetheless: barbers insist on maintaining their income relative to the rest of the population, and consumers of haircuts are willing to pay the higher prices because their own rising incomes enable them to do so. But productivity in the sense of greater output per worker per unit of time has not increased. Wage increases for workers in sectors with these characteristics depend not so much on advances in production technology but on bargaining power in the labor market. Thus it matters greatly in countries like Japan and Finland that the various service sectors have not been flooded with foreign labor, as is true for some service sectors in Israel and elsewhere.

With these cautions in mind, we can assess the relative performance of the countries discussed here. The point of doing so relates to the fact that employers can afford to accede to demands for wage increases when workers are able to produce at an increasing rate (assuming markets do not collapse because of over-production). In this regard, increases in Japanese labor productivity have undoubtedly played a role in the extent to which Japanese employers have continued to employ Japanese workers, even when labor shortages have contributed to strong wage increases. Productivity increases have been the highest in manufacturing (Table 4.5) (though, again, some manufacturing employers have been able to get labor at a competitive wage only by relocating to low-wage countries). Construction labor productivity in Japan has increased more slowly than in other sectors and relative to Finland and Norway

Table 4.5 Average yearly percentage increase in labor productivity, 1970–94

	Manufacturing	Construction	Retail/ hotels	Social services	Total
USA[a]	2.7	−1.5	1.5	−0.4	0.9
Germany[a]	2.5	1.2	1.3	1.4	2.3
Israel	2.0	1.3[b]	−1.2		1.0
Japan[c]	3.7	1.1	4.6	0.9	3.2
Denmark	2.7	−0.2	2.9	0.9	2.0
Norway[a]	2.0	1.6	0.8	0.6	2.4
Finland	4.8	2.5	2.5	2.5	3.2

Notes: [a] Germany and the US: 1970–93; Norway: 1970–91.
[b] As noted in the previous chapter, official figures on labor productivity increases in Israeli construction are exaggerated. A more accurate estimate is in the range of 0.5 percent. See Chapter 3, page 84.
[c] For Japan, hotels and restaurants are included in social services, not retail.

Source: Computed from the OECD International Sectoral Database; for Israel, Statistical Abstract of Israel.

(and is on par with that of Germany). On the other hand, the increase contrasts with the poor performance of the Israeli construction industry (and even more so with the decline of construction labor productivity in the US).

Labor productivity is in turn to a certain extent a function of capital intensity (e.g., Dollar and Wolff 1993), and here the increase in capital stock per worker in Japan has been very strong in all sectors, relative to other countries (the US in particular – though of course the US started from a higher base in 1970; figures for Israel are not available) (Table 4.6). These figures attest to the *effort* by Japanese employers to invest in technologically sophisticated production processes, in part as a way to offset high labor costs. In manufacturing, in particular, this was a natural response to the competitive pressures Japan faced as the most advanced economy in East Asia and the one with the highest wages. To the extent that Japan failed to focus on more productive and higher value-added activities, its competitive position would have been undermined by low-wage countries that held advantages for labor-intensive activities. And while the threat of international competition in the non-tradable sectors is lower, employers in services and construction still had strong incentives to make capital investments and increase productivity in the face of essentially irresistible wage demands.[10]

The figures on capital intensity in the Japanese construction sector are impressive enough that the *attempt* to increase labor productivity merits further discussion. If increases in productivity have been modest, that has not been for lack of trying on the part of Japanese investors. Moreover, it is very likely that the overall average hides substantial

Table 4.6 Average yearly percentage increase in capital intensity, 1970–93

	Manufacturing	Construction	Retail/ hotels	Social services	Total
USA	3.6	−0.4	2.8	1.4	1.2
Germany	3.0	1.5	1.7	3.2	2.9
Japan	5.9	6.9	5.8	8.1	5.3
Denmark	3.4	4.2	3.2	2.8	2.5
Norway	5.3		3.4	6.2	2.1
Finland	4.6	4.9	3.7	3.2	4.3

Notes: Capital intensity is computed as capital stock per employee, where capital is measured in 1990 $US, adjusted for purchasing power parity.
Denmark: 1970–92; Norway: 1970–91.
For Japan, hotels and restaurants are included in social services, not retail.
Source: Computed from the OECD International Sectoral Database.

advances for the very large construction firms, while at the same time overstating the improvements that took place in the numerous (and not very productive) small firms.

The government's effort to industrialize the construction sector goes back at least to the early 1960s and received added impetus as a labor shortage intensified in the late 1960s, in a context where demand for housing has consistently been very strong. The Housing Bureau of the Ministry of Construction in 1969 adopted a long-term policy for the industrialization of the housing industry, continuing a policy of offering low-cost public financing for pre-cast concrete panel methods of construction (Minami 1973). A Government Housing Loan Corporation program offered low-interest long-term loans with significantly extended repayment periods (i.e., lower overall costs) for buyers choosing houses made with higher amounts of prefabrication processes, thus affecting the methods of contractors by manipulating the incentives of consumers (INT-Yashiro). The Ministry of International Trade and Industry was also involved and advocated in the 1960s that some of the sector be industrialized along the lines of the automobile and electronics industries. Some well-known manufacturers such as Toyota and Panasonic have diversified by developing subsidiaries that make houses with processes similar to those used for their core products (Gann 1996).

Incentives for research and development are built into tax and spending policies and government contracting procedures as well (Sidwell *et al.* 1988). As a very large client, the government manipulated public works spending to achieve certain goals, including the provision of sufficient resources for contractors' investments in technological progress: the Construction Ministry refrained from exerting significant downward pressure on procurement costs, so that contractors' profits would be sufficient to allow such investment (INT-Nomoto). In addition, construction companies wanting to bid on government-funded projects must enter the Ministry of Construction's classification system; if a contractor wants to bid on a Class A project, that company must hold a Class A rating. The rating system takes into account the capabilities of the contractor, and investment in technological development is an important component of capability (INT-Nomoto).

Construction research in the 1960s was focused on prefabrication and techniques for work mechanization. Here too contractors' activities were driven to a significant extent by government policy: government contracts for construction of public housing in the 1960s specified use of pre-cast concrete formations (INT-Yashiro). Prefabrication in general had a poor reputation in Japan (as it still does in Israel), a problem the government addressed through the creation of the Building Center of Japan: the Center developed an approval process concerning the quality and performance of prefabricated components, to increase the willingness of consumers to buy such houses (INT-Yashiro). Prefabricated housing construction grew to the point where it accounted for 25 percent of all new unit sales in 1995 (Gann 1996), and prefabrication processes are also used in a significant portion of traditional timber-framed houses (INT-Maruya). More recently factory processes have advanced to the point that even some construction firms – often considered one of the most inefficient sectors of the Japanese economy – use CAD and CAM systems (Hasegawa 1988).[11] We will discuss shortly the conditions that made these developments possible.

During the late 1980s and early 1990s as well, the economic press was full of reports on construction labor saving techniques and products as well as efforts to increase the manufactured component of buildings. To a certain extent, contractors have turned to robotics to "relieve workers from the execution of many dangerous and demanding tasks and to cut costs and improve productivity" (Sidwell *et al*. 1988: 34). New products included robots for painting walls, robots for hanging exterior walls on tall buildings, and robots for leveling cement floors (*Business Review Weekly*, 2 November 1990; *Comline Daily News*, 28 November 1988; *Japan Economic Journal*, 9 December 1989). The Ministry of Construction in 1990 began offering tax incentives to encourage contractors to expand their use of robots (*Comline Daily News*, 20 September 1991) and extended the program in 1992. "The Japanese have a strong central government policy to drive robotic research into construction, playing a positive role in coordinating the work" (Sidwell *et al*. 1988: 36). The research and development efforts of large construction contractors in Japan are probably unparalleled elsewhere (Bennett *et al*. 1987) – though company-provided information on the issue contains much public relations bluster as well (Bennett 1993), and some of the more ambitious components of the robotics agenda have been abandoned in more recent years (INT-Hikone).

Japanese contractors' adoption of industrialized techniques is far from total. Some contractors have limited their use of advanced methods because they are reluctant to upset long-term relationships with subcontractors (Bennett 1993). In addition, the impact of increased wages on productivity has been mixed: workers are said to be less willing to work long hours because they can meet their income objectives in a shorter time, such that per-day productivity has suffered. Construction costs have therefore been rising faster than inflation (Bennett 1993).

In addition, because public works spending in Japan is used in part as a substitute for welfare programs (for both workers and corporations), there is a tendency for construction employment to increase during recessions, a fact that contributed to a decline in labor productivity during the 1990s (INT-Suzuki, Maruya). Prior to 1973, however, labor productivity was rising rapidly (Hasegawa 1988). The recent exacerbation of the problem should only increase the pressure for contractors to adopt less labor-intensive methods.

Bankruptcies in the economy as a whole due to labor shortages quadrupled in 1989 (relative to 1988), and the construction sector accounted for a larger number of such bankruptcies than any other sector (*Japan Economic Journal*, 17.2.90). It is conceivable that the market share of those companies was picked up by larger firms that were more able to compete on the basis of higher labor productivity. There is still a very large number of small construction firms using low-productivity building methods in Japan (Woodall 1996), and so it would appear that there is room for a substantial amount of consolidation of this type as a macroeconomic labor saving strategy.

The preceding paragraphs support the claim that there is an association between the small presence of foreign workers in Japan and a number of trends in economic parameters related to the size and composition of the labor force. This association is reinforced by consideration of a number of other countries where the presence of foreign labor is small as well as two countries with a substantially higher proportion of foreign/immigrant workers. Not every piece of data is consistent with the overall argument. But the balance of the data support the existence of the association, and the strong contrast between Japan and Israel is of course central to the more detailed empirical argument of the book.[12] The contrast is especially relevant for construction (again, neither Japanese nor Israeli manufacturers have used foreign labor in any great quantity): wages for Japanese construction workers rose much faster than the average wage (which itself showed strong increases), while in Israel there was in relative terms a decline (and in all probability the decline was greater than that indicated by official figures). Construction contractors in Japan responded to labor shortages by investing at an impressive rate; in Israel, on the other hand, contractors responded by increasing their demand for cheap labor, while refraining from significant advances in production methods. Construction employers in Norway, Denmark, and Finland responded similarly to Japan; wage increases were not as strong in relative terms, but they were already at a relatively high level. Investment also proceeded at a higher level.

What seems clear, then, is that Japan (and, to a certain degree, the three smaller Nordic countries) followed a different path from the US, Germany (to a lesser extent), and most of all Israel – in terms of solutions to the problem of finding labor at a wage level acceptable to employers. Japan's refusal to open the doors to cheap foreign labor both reinforced the process of restructuring (indicated by the developments discussed above) and was made possible by it. The relationship between the two was entirely synergistic. If Japanese companies had been able to compete on the basis of lower labor costs, they would have had less of an incentive to make investments in higher value-added and technologically sophisticated processes.[13] Conversely, if they had not found it profitable to invest in higher value-added and technologically sophisticated processes, then cheap foreign labor would have appeared even more imperative as a means of competing on the basis of cost. Of course, some employers have long believed, and many continue to believe, that admitting foreign labor *is* imperative as a means of restraining production costs while securing the necessary labor. So the point here is relative: although there have been some bankruptcies as a result of labor supply pressures, on the whole Japanese employers have fared reasonably well by pursuing competitive solutions that do not rely heavily on production cost savings deriving from use of inexpensive foreign labor. What bears emphasizing is the distinctive relationship between these two elements in Japan: without tight restrictions on foreign labor, efforts to restructure towards more high-end production processes would have been undermined, and without such restructuring, employers would have had reason to try to subvert the government's efforts to restrict the inflow of foreign labor to a greater extent. In other words, the data presented above do not show simply that Japan performed well economically. They show that Japan performed well *without foreign labor*, demonstrating that Japanese economic growth was based not on low wages but on productivity-enhancing investment.

Economic policy and state governance

The changes described above helped alleviate the labor shortage and diminish the "need" for foreign labor, even if it would grant far too much coherence to government policymaking to argue that there was a grand design here, that the government developed a comprehensive approach to labor supply problems comprizing the above elements. In the context of an investigation of labor migration, what is significant about the data and arguments presented above is the fact that the economic developments described – increasing capital intensity and labor productivity, as a means for achieving a higher standard of living, i.e., higher real wages – were precisely the changes that the Japanese government was committed to achieving as part of its overall economic and industrial policy. Of course, these are precisely the changes *any* government would want to achieve as part of its economic policy – what government would oppose higher productivity and increasing investment in higher value-added activities? As we saw in the last chapter, the Israeli government was interested in bringing about similar changes, particularly for the construction industry, but the results stand in strong contrast to Japan's experience. So the conditions supporting Japan's success in this area are what really matter. Here we begin to explore the relevance of the "mode of economic governance" – relevance, that is, to the two Japanese experiences with labor shortages. I will argue that the structure and policies of the Japanese state have interacted with solutions to labor shortages in different ways in each period.

Early 1970s

It would be naïve to imagine that economic growth in capitalist societies could be determined entirely or even mostly by policies of the state. But it is also unwise to ignore the fact that there are distinct modes of economic policymaking and governance (e.g., Knoke *et al.* 1996) and that those modes have different implications for the rate and direction of economic development (Hollingsworth *et al.* 1994). Early arguments about the importance of the developmentalist state in Japan were clearly overly ambitious. But if the scholarly pendulum has swung back, it has also become clear that the fulcrum has shifted: a good deal of the earlier insights remain, even after the inevitable "complexifying" response.

The central insight of the developmentalist state argument is that economic growth and structural transformation can be – in the Japanese instance, were – enhanced by the existence of a relatively cohesive bureaucratic policymaking apparatus largely insulated from the pressures of politicians and private interest groups. Economic policymakers in Japan, particularly in MITI (supported in most instances by the Ministry of Finance) set goals that were in many cases beyond the reach of individual private investors trying to maximize their own interests. Any particular investor is concerned primarily with his or her own survival and profitability; to the extent that individual investors seek government assistance, they will try to maximize the extent to which such assistance benefits themselves, regardless of the impact on others. Lobbyists on behalf of individual firms can be expected to seek assistance that benefits that firm even at the expense of competitors within the relevant sector. Particular trade associations can be expected to seek assistance that benefits firms in that sector, at the expense of suppliers or purchasers. And advocates for capitalists as a class can be expected to push for policies that benefit capital, regardless of the effect on other groups.[14] When policy formation is driven by such interests, the possibilities for overall coordination geared to comprehensive national interests are diminished. A certain degree of bureaucratic autonomy from such interests increases the possibility for broader goals to prevail.

In Japan, this autonomy has been enhanced by virtue of the fact that the bureaucracy is staffed by highly competent individuals socialized to believe that they are an elite that is superior to, and therefore separate from, the world of private business people. As is well known, admission to the civil service is granted via performance on a highly competitive examination. Political appointments to the bureaucracies are limited both in number and in impact (Johnson 1982). Numerous observers have claimed that the policymaking elite in Japan (at least in MITI and the Finance Ministry, but to a certain extent in other ministries as well) therefore acts primarily according to a sense of national purpose; actions designed to benefit particular private interests at the expense of the general welfare are said to be less prevalent.

The third main condition assisting in the implementation of developmentalist policies in Japan was the long-term dominance of one ruling party, the LDP, which held power continuously from 1955 until 1993 (e.g., Pempel 1990). The LDP was dominant not only in the sense of holding almost continuous majorities in the Diet, but also in the sense that the other parties essentially failed to constitute an effective and viable opposition that could realistically form an alternative government. The hegemony of the LDP helped create a stable business environment where business leaders could expect basic continuity of policy direction – an important asset for policymakers pursuing goals that are necessarily long-term. The conditions for maintaining LDP hegemony have had a more equivocal effect on economic policies, as we will see below; but the continuity itself played an important role in the ability of the bureaucracies to pursue long-term goals and in the willingness of investors to accept "guidance" from the government. Moreover, while the LDP held majority power continuously for almost 40 years, it would be a mistake to conclude that the Japanese state as a whole is therefore monolithic: the LDP itself is factionalized, so that there is a great deal of competition and bargaining *within* the party. But Okimoto (1989) argues that such internal strife weakens the party enough so that it is less successful in dominating the bureaucracy than it would otherwise be;

bureaucratic autonomy is therefore enhanced rather than inhibited by intra-party competition.

The argument so far is that these institutional conditions enhanced the possibilities for certain types of economic and industrial policies, but so far we have said almost nothing concerning what those policies actually were. Here we need to understand what the government's conception of its role was, i.e., what the obstacles to development were that the state was uniquely able to address. There were at least two related main barriers to rapid industrialization and export competitiveness: insufficient capital/foreign exchange, and insufficient economies of scale. These were both problems that Japanese private investors probably would have overcome eventually without government assistance, but doing so arguably would have taken much longer (Yamamura 1982). The particular contribution of the government was to use specifically public resources – legal authority as well as budgets – to hasten the process.

One method of addressing economy of scale problems was to protect domestic producers against initially more efficient foreign competitors. Since established foreign producers could offer lower prices, one effective means of allowing domestic firms to grow was to make foreign goods either unavailable or more expensive. This has been standard practice in many late industrializing nations around the world (though of course protectionism is not limited to late industrializers), and there is nothing here that really makes Japan distinctive, even if it was a central part of the effort to build local industry. Moreover, there was no issue here concerning government initiatives that went against the preferences of Japanese investors, many of whom continue to press for import protection.

Another piece of Japanese developmentalism was MITI's various efforts to bring about mergers of firms within certain sectors – again, to achieve economies of scale, but also to pool resources for more effective investment, especially in research and development. The goal here was to prevent "excess competition" and to shore up revenues, in a competitive environment where firms' main goal was to maximize market share, even at the expense of short-term profits. The resulting "organized" competition was more conducive to continuous profitability, a requirement for continuous investment in increasing productivity through in-house research and development. The government's efforts to force mergers among smaller companies sometimes went against the wishes of private owners, though it was clear to bureaucrats that increasing concentration of capital was in the interests of the country as a whole.

The government's ability to make its demands prevail in this period was rooted in its control of scarce foreign exchange. Its influence over private decisions was both direct and indirect. Firms in need of capital for desired investments understood that their access to foreign exchange depended on the extent to which those investments were compatible with goals set by the bureaucracies. Moreover, foreign exchange was necessary not only for capital investments but for continuing operations, where such operations depended on imports of raw materials. The leverage of the government here thus extended not only to types of investment but more particular decisions concerning ongoing firm operations, via "administrative guidance." In the early 1970s, for example, there was

> a policy statement saying that housing contractors who built large projects had to cooperate in providing or helping to buy land on which to build elementary schools. When a contractor ignored these guidelines, the city capped the water and sewage lines he had built for the project with concrete. (Johnson 1982: 266)

Administrative guidance was also commonly used to coordinate production cutbacks (via "recession cartels"), when recessions or investors' efforts to increase market share led to overproduction that threatened to erode prices and end in bankruptcies. This is a clear indication of how the government used its power to impose a collective rationality that was not achievable through the uncoordinated pursuit of private interests.[15]

The paragraphs above briefly lay out some of the elements of the classic argument concerning Japan's developmentalist state. As noted earlier, this argument has been the subject of vigorous critique. One line of critique asserts that Japanese government policies were not essential to the undeniably impressive economic performance, that the economy flourished for other reasons and would have done so even in the absence of the government policies analyzed by the developmental state theorists. Friedman (1988) notes that government efforts have been focused mainly on the larger firms; he then argues that much of the dynamism in the Japanese economy has come from small- and medium-sized firms, which constitute about 60 percent of the Japanese economy in value-added terms (vs. 35 percent in the US) and 70 percent of the work force. In this regard, the actions of MITI – the foremost component of the developmentalist state – are asserted to be irrelevant to a large section of the economy. The difficulty with the developmentalist state argument, then, is that it sees economic success coincident with an activist bureaucracy and assumes that there is a causal association, without asking whether government actions really had an effect on the behavior of private investors.

Friedman's argument seems to overlook the particular relationship between small and large firms in Japan, however. Many of the small firms in Japan function as subcontractors for large firms, particularly in construction. While government policies may have been focused on large firms rather than small ones, the success of the small firms was to a significant extent predicated on the success of the large firms. While Friedman may be correct in his assertion that the dynamism of the small firm sector has been insufficiently appreciated, his argument that the actions of the state were essentially irrelevant to Japanese development is surely overstated.

Another line of critique looks at the failures of the government to achieve certain stated goals. MITI attempted to bring about mergers in the automotive industry, for example, but was compelled to back down in the face of opposition from firm owners. The auto industry, of course, is one of the great Japanese success stories. MITI also failed to achieve its main objectives in restructuring the banking and oil industries (Friedman 1988, Ramseyer and Rosenbluth 1993). Some analysts argue that, in a number of respects, the government did not really even attempt to implement policies that went against the preferences of private investors, but instead adjusted its own actions to those preferences. Samuels emphasizes the notion of "reciprocal consent" between business and government, and he writes: "we ask ... not why the Japanese state is so pervasive in the economy but why the pervasive state is so congenial to private firms" (1987: 260).

The argument that there were failed policies does not, however, dispel the notion that there were also successful policies (though it does add complexity to our understanding of Japanese economic history). Nor is it clear that the actions of the government were irrelevant simply because they were not objectionable to private interests. The core logic of the developmentalist state is that the government can use specifically public resources to create investment opportunities that would not otherwise be available (e.g., because they would be too risky) (Weiss 1998). Establishing the relevance of state policy, then, does not require showing that the government acted in ways that threatened private interests; indeed, such an argument would become self-defeating if carried too far. Rather, when the state helps create the conditions for accelerated investment, we should not be surprised if private firms find the state's presence "congenial." But the real point is that such a situation is clearly different from settings in which, for reasons of ideological preference or inability to act otherwise, the government merely allows firms to respond to unmediated market signals.

In challenging other pieces of the developmentalist state argument, other writers have raised questions about the structure and capacity of the state itself. Richardson, for example, argues (1997) that the government's control of the capital market has been overstated: government lending, even in the 1950s, is said to be relatively small compared to that of private sources, and so the government's attempts to send "indicative" signals to industry were less effective than is commonly believed. Moreover, questions have been raised concerning the overall cohesiveness of the Japanese state, which is necessarily a large and complex entity; we should not be surprised to find, then, that there have been internal struggles as well as uneven results (e.g., Moon and Prasad 1998; Okimoto 1989; Richardson 1997).

In offering what they believe are more sophisticated and empirically supported treatments of Japanese political economy, several writers have emphasized that the role of the Japanese state cannot be understood apart from the civil society context in which it operates. In other words, market and firm organizational characteristics were important as well as the state. Hart (1992) places great importance on the *keiretsu*, the Japanese version of the conglomerate, where each industrial group is closely associated with a major bank (see also Gerlach 1992). Each *keiretsu* has considered it very important to maintain a presence in major production sectors (e.g., automobiles, electronics). Hart asserts that this feature of firm organization has helped maintain a level of competitiveness that might have been lost if MITI had been able to reduce the number of major players in certain sectors through further mergers. More generally, Hart maintains that the *keiretsu* have played a key role in the government's effort to diffuse production technologies, which has been the fundamental condition of Japanese economic success as a late industrializer.

This point recalls Evans' (1995) argument that a state must be embedded in a society, not merely autonomous from it. Discussions of the organization and form of private actors are an important complement to the notion that states create varying modes of economic governance: *how* a state governs the economy depends in part on the organization of that economy and its social context. These discussions, then, are not damaging to arguments about the importance of the state and in fact form the basis for more recent theoretical writings on the state and development (Evans 1995; Weiss 1998).

If the responses to the earlier arguments about the developmentalist state have created a more nuanced and sophisticated understanding of Japanese economic development and the role of the state, it nonetheless remains true that the Japanese political economy is in some important ways distinctive from the dominant Anglo-American neoliberal model (e.g., Pempel 1998).[16] This point is especially relevant as a response to those who raise questions concerning the cohesion and capacity of the Japanese state. The arguments here are most compelling when made in a comparative way: the Japanese economy grew *faster* and *more dynamically* than some other late industrializers because its mode of economic governance was *different* from that of other countries. If the critical literature has succeeded in showing greater complexity as well as shortcomings in some aspects of the argument, then it should help sharpen our understanding of how Japan is different from other countries (as well as how it is not very different).

The crux of the argument in the current context, then, is that Japan's policy of not importing workers in large numbers was both (1) consistent with and (2) supported by the Japanese government's broader approach to economic policy. The initial assumption is that citizen workers will accept undesirable work if the price is right. That the price was right in Japan is demonstrated by the fact that Japanese and not foreigners continue to hold most of the jobs, even in sectors that are often staffed by foreigners in other countries. The wage increases discussed above are crucial. One of the main conditions for increasing wages is increasing labor productivity, which in turn is supported by productive investments in labor saving technologies. All three elements – wages, labor productivity, investment in advancing technologies – were precisely the goals of Japanese economic policy as embodied in the developmental state. Conversely, the government's strong preference for *not* importing labor from abroad prevented a "short circuit" solution to the problem of labor shortages and contributed to the strong increase in real wages, particularly in the early 1970s. A Ministry of Labor official made this logic explicit in a 1986 interview, contending that "it would be a mistake to maintain artificially, through the importation of labour, inferior working conditions in one part of the Japanese labour market, which may in turn work as a drag on the welfare of the whole" (Awanohara 1986, 25).[17] Rising wages provided another key incentive for employers to turn to advancing technology as a competition/survival strategy consistent with the government's overall emphasis on moving up the ladder of value-added production.

Most importantly, there is a strong contrast here between the Japanese and Israeli responses to labor shortages, a contrast driven in substantial measure by the different institutional structures of economic governance. In Israel, employers (particularly in the construction industry) were able to translate their natural desire for ever larger profits into a policy of importing labor. Their ability to do so was rooted in large part in the fact that politicians, not the professional staff of the bureaucracies, are the main decision makers for economic policy. Moreover, the fragmentation and weakness of the Israeli bureaucracy significantly reduced the possibilities for creating viable alternatives to the cheap labor upon which some parts of the economy had been built. In Japan, on the other hand, cheap labor was incompatible with a major premise of the government's intentions regarding economic growth. Employers might have found it easier and more profitable to employ cheap foreign labor, as opposed to paying the steadily increasing wages demanded by Japanese workers, and employers did make demands on the government to allow workers to enter. But these demands were not very effective in a context where employers' political power was not immediately convertible into influence over policy formation, given the relative insulation and cohesion of at least some parts of the Japanese bureaucracy during this period.

After 1985

The OPEC-induced oil crisis and the resulting serious recession in 1973 put an end to the problem of labor shortages in Japan for more than a decade. By the time labor shortages reappeared beginning in the mid-1980s (see Table 4.6), the functioning of the Japanese state with regard to economic governance had changed appreciably. In many respects it is appropriate to question the relevance of the term "developmentalist state" in Japan in more recent years. But if we look beneath the broad label and focus on concrete policies and institutions, we find a certain continuity in the government's approach to economic governance. However, because economic conditions in Japan had changed – and, in part, because policies had already worked in many instances – there was a major shift in the broad impact of the government's economic policies. Measures such as import restrictions, originally designed to increase productivity and efficiency, eventually came in some cases to have the opposite effect: protecting *inefficiency*, in particular (Katz 1998; Yamamura 1982). But there is a crucial paradox here relating to questions of labor supply: While the broad impact of economic policy after 1973 was different from the previous period, the specific impact of policy on labor supply was substantially the same. In a nutshell, government economic policies – ostensibly "developmentalist" but increasingly ineffective in achieving stated goals – continued to create the conditions under which employers were able to pay the increasing wages required to attract Japanese workers in key sectors.

The basic premise of the argument here is the same as in the previous section: when employers need workers under conditions of increasing scarcity, the most important factor determining whether (Japanese) workers will continue to supply labor is increasing wages. As I argued in the previous chapter, there is a market-clearing wage even for undesirable work. If employers can continue to pay that wage even as it rises, there will be less of a "need" to turn to foreign labor. When employers cannot continue to pay a market-clearing wage, some observers (and policymakers) conclude that there is a labor shortage and foreign labor is required. But another interpretation, just as plausible, is that employers cannot pay that wage because buyers no longer want their goods and services badly enough to pay the higher prices that would allow employers to pay that wage.

Employers in other countries have frequently turned to foreigners to supply labor in specific sectors: construction, agriculture, and some kinds of services. But Japanese employers in those sectors mostly employ Japanese citizens. Japanese workers, in strong contrast to Israelis, continue to work in the construction sector, for example, in huge numbers – more than 10 percent of the labor force, as discussed above. The market for Japanese construction workers, agricultural labor, and service sector employees is mostly clearing. The contention here is that the conditions enabling employers to pay sufficient wages were present in the more recent period, but these conditions were different from those prevailing in the previous period, at least for some sectors (construction in particular).

The main argument in the previous section was that substantial productivity increases allowed employers to pay increasing wages to workers, as they were essentially required to do, given that labor scarcities during the early 1970s put workers in a much better bargaining position than they had been in previously. That argument holds to a certain extent concerning the more recent period as well, but here we must pay closer attention to sectoral differences and dynamics. It is well known that some sectors of the Japanese economy, particularly those producing only for the domestic market, are inefficient relative to the export-oriented sectors. But if we look at Table 4.7, summarizing some of the developments in the Japanese economy, we see that the average yearly increase in real wages for construction workers was substantially higher than the average increase in labor productivity: 3.1 percent versus. 1.1 percent. We might then ask, what made it possible for wage increases to outstrip productivity growth to such an extent?

The answer lies in Japan's "dual economy" and the relations between the high-performance export-oriented sectors and the inefficient domestic-oriented producers. Since 1973, many of the export-oriented

Table 4.7 Japanese economy summary statistics
Average yearly percent increase, 1970–94

	Manufacturing	Construction/ housing	Retail/ hotels, etc.	Personal services	Total
Labor productivity	3.7	1.1	4.6		3.2
Capital intensity	5.9	6.9	5.8		5.3
Real wages	2.6	3.1	1.7		2.6
Consumer prices	4.2	5.7		6.9	4.9

Note: The figures presented here are by no means transparent in their meaning. The table is intended as a summary concerning Japan of data presented in earlier tables in this chapter, and the reader is referred to the text surrounding those earlier tables for discussion concerning interpretation.

Sources: Previous tables.

manufacturing sectors have continued to experience impressive gains in productivity, performing well under the pressure of international competition. The income generated in these sectors, however, has been used in part to subsidize and compensate for the poor performance of some domestic sectors, such as construction (Katz 1998). One possible interpretation of the fact that construction wages rose faster than productivity could be that construction firms have experienced a profit squeeze, and indeed there was a larger than usual number of bankruptcies in the late 1980s. But there is another plausible explanation. Productivity increases are not strictly required for wage increases: employers can pay higher wages without increased productivity if they get more income from selling their products, i.e., through higher prices. If this phenomenon were replicated throughout the economy, the result would of course be inflation, and so wage increases would be merely nominal and not real. But if wage and price increases were greater in some sectors of the economy than in others, inflation would be more restrained and we would see instead a transfer or subsidy from some sectors to others.

The notion of a subsidy is consistent with the fact that in recent years the outputs of the construction sector are very expensive, relative to previous periods (and to construction costs in other countries) (Woodall 1996). The difference is partly attributable to the fact that construction materials inputs are relatively expensive as well – the increased revenue for construction contractors does not all go for wages (or profits, for that matter). But we can then inquire concerning these inputs, and it turns out that basic materials industries such as cement and glass are also relatively inefficient and part of the same transfer/subsidy dynamic. The high prices paid to firms in these sectors indicate inefficiencies relative to production and prices in other countries, but the content of the inefficiencies has to do in part with higher relative labor costs.

The subsidization of domestic-oriented sectors by export-oriented sectors takes place through at least two mechanisms (Katz 1998 – see in particular Appendix J). First, the export sectors purchase some of their inputs (including physical plant) from the domestic sectors, at high cost. For example, a new factory requires cement and steel, which is very likely to be produced and purchased locally. Second, and probably more significantly, the high cost of some goods and services produced locally translates into a higher tax burden. The construction sector is especially relevant here, because of the high level and cost of public works con- struction. The export sectors bear this increased tax burden directly, through a business tax that is higher than it would otherwise be; employers in the export sector also bear it indirectly via the aggravated wage demands of their workers, who seek (though no doubt in some instances fail) to restore or maintain net relative income levels. "Bearing the burden" means that the prices exporters charge must be higher than otherwise (which implies that the success they have experienced in international markets is all the more impressive). But higher prices in a non-protected market mean lower sales and thus a lower volume of profit; they also mean diminished opportunities for wage increases. The resulting squeeze has forced many Japanese manufacturing plants to relocate to lower-wage countries elsewhere in Asia (Katz 1998).

The dynamic of subsidy from strong sectors to weak ones has played a significant role in the evolution of Japan's economy since 1973. It is driven primarily by effective protection against imports and foreign investment; although official barriers to trade have been dismantled, informal barriers and restrictions are rampant, to such an extent that imports as a percentage of GNP declined to a very low level by 1995. Low import penetration goes hand in hand with low levels of foreign direct investment in Japan (Kawai and Urata 1998); the absence of for- eign companies likely acts as an additional mechanism inhibiting price competition. In most cases the low level of imports derives from collu- sion among domestic manufacturers and distributors or suppliers.[18] Informal cartels – a key mechanism for preventing imports from under- cutting domestic prices – are widespread and have their origins in the policies of MITI (Katz 1998; Sheridan 1993; Tilton 1996).

The organization of Japanese firms into business groups (*keiretsu*) has also produced a tendency for firms to depend on Japanese suppliers rather than outsiders; preferential supplier–purchaser ties amount to "structural barriers to market entry" for foreign firms, both as investors and as sellers (Gerlach 1992).[19] Firms that attempt to cut costs by buying from outsiders can face severe retaliation from other Japanese firms with whom they have important relationships. Anti-trust and restraint-of-trade enforcement in Japan is relatively weak. In addition, MITI has continued to monitor imports and to provide up-to-date information concerning imports to relevant trade associations. Sekiguchi (1991) argues that the ministry helps provide an environment conducive to anti-import collusion among private firms.

The protection against imports has muted a key incentive for efforts to improve efficiency, e.g., through attempting to save on production costs such as labor. In other words, the high prices commanded by domestically produced goods and services[20] do not simply feed excess profits for construction contractors and other employers. Those prices also enable employers to employ more labor than would otherwise be necessary, and to pay their workers higher wages than would otherwise be possible. This is a key part of the substance behind the notion of inefficiencies in domestic production.

This system could not survive without the support of the Japanese government; in fact, the government arguably had basic responsibility for its emergence. In the early 1970s, as economic growth led large proportions of the labor force to move from the low-productivity farming sector to the higher-productivity (and urban) manufacturing sectors, the traditionally rural electoral base of the LDP experienced a process of erosion. There was a serious danger that left-wing parties would be able to break the LDP's majority in the Diet by capturing votes from the emergent urban working class. Under the leadership of Kakuei Tanaka, the LDP reversed this decline through a system of "money politics" – essentially buying votes through huge pork-barrel programs for voters, urban voters in particular (Schlesinger 1997). Politicians frequently made direct cash payments to individuals (e.g., as they attend funerals or weddings), but perhaps even more importantly they have implemented policies (such as large-scale public works and import protection) designed to maintain employment and profits in some declining and low-productivity sectors. In this way, the LDP has succeeded in "compensating" those sectors of the electorate who stood to suffer from the social upheavals following on rapid economic growth (Calder 1988). The government's failure to dismantle the informal (but highly effective) barriers to imports and foreign investment has therefore been a key part of its strategy for maintaining electoral dominance (Katz 1998).

There is thus a fundamental continuity between economic governance in more recent years and policy from the heyday of the developmentalist state, especially in the structural biases against imports and foreign capital. The difference, of course, is that in the previous period the protection was designed to give infant industries a chance to pass through initial stages of growth, to achieve the economies of scale that made large investments feasible (Yamamura 1982). More recently, the function of the rules is to spare domestic capital – and, by association, the labor it employs – from the pain of rationalization that would otherwise come from exposure to international competition. Protection against imports originated in the core policies of the developmental state, and the continuation of this policy mode is no doubt rooted in part in the fact that blocking imports and setting up cartels are what MITI knows how to do. There is also reportedly a feeling among MITI bureaucrats that the ministry's policies were partly responsible for getting some industries into a position where they were ill prepared to compete internationally, and that therefore the ministry has an obligation to continue to provide an environment where they can survive. Moreover, developmentalist thinking continues to inform policymaking to a substantial degree: "excess competition" is still considered a serious problem in the Japanese economy, and MITI officials still see it as their proper role to mitigate competition and provide a safe and supportive business environment (Tilton 1998). In other words, while the state's role in economic governance has evolved, it has not necessarily diminished: arguments about the "disincorporation" of Japan (Hollerman 1988) are overstated (Sheridan 1993).

The relevant implication of this complex of import protection and high costs/prices of domestically produced goods and services is that employers in these sectors can and do pay higher wages than they would otherwise. From the fact that they are mainly employing Japanese workers (and not foreigners), we may infer that these wages are sufficient to keep Japanese workers satisfied in, say, construction jobs in a way that Israeli workers are not. The mode of economic governance in Japan continues to create the conditions that allow employers to employ Japanese workers instead of turning to foreigners.

But the fact that the conditions allowing some employers to pay higher wages are arguably counterproductive for the rest of the economy raises the question: why has the Japanese state, formerly adept at economic governance, participated in the creation of such distortions? Katz (1998) argues that Japan has become an *anti*-developmentalist state. While such a formulation may be slightly exaggerated, others have argued that the role of politicians in economic policymaking has been increasing, at the expense of the professional bureaucrats (e.g., Johnson *et al.* 1989; Murumatsu and Krauss 1987). Such arguments indicate that the institutions underlying a developmentalist approach to economic policy may be breaking down. A developmentalist state is not merely a state that implements certain types of policies (e.g., protectionism) but one in which an institutional structure supports a coherent mode of policymaking appropriate to the relevant context. On the other hand, while there may be cracks in the walls (and perhaps even the foundation), this by no means implies that Japanese economic governance has become more like Anglo-American governance than it is like Japanese governance of the previous generation.

But the argument here is hardly that Japan in recent years has been free from clientelism. On the contrary, the relationship between the Japanese government and the construction industry for the last 20 years, for example, has essentially been *defined* by clientelism and blatant corruption (Krauss and Coles 1990; Woodall 1996). The Ministry of Construction is "among the most politicized bureaucracies in Japan" (Okimoto 1989: 99). Bidding for public works contracts is anything but competitive: participation is limited to members of officially recognized cartels, and the outcome is predetermined, in secret negotiations among the contractors themselves (*dango*). "Winning" contracts are padded with enough money to provide (LDP) politicians with the huge campaign contributions necessary to compete in Japanese elections.[21] Public works constitute about half of all construction activity in Japan, so the high costs are easily passed on to taxpayers. Bureaucrats and politicians associated with the system routinely "descend from heaven" into sinecures with the contractors and trade associations. The system itself contributes to bloated public works budgets and to the very high cost of construction projects; it has also helped the LDP maintain its hegemony since the mid-1970s when it was instituted. Public exposure of these practices in the early 1990s led to some very significant but token arrests (including the former Minister of Construction and the president of the Japan Federation of Construction Organizations), but McCormack (1996) asserts that the system itself was essentially left intact.

The point is also relevant to the agricultural sector. The argument presented here helps explain the almost total absence of foreign workers in the Japanese agricultural sector, a very significant anomaly relative to other advanced industrial countries. The relevant parameters of the sector are similar to those of the other inefficient domestic sectors: protection against imports, high costs of production, and incomes high enough to ensure that Japanese citizens are willing to continue supplying labor. Agricultural productivity has been stagnant, but protection against imports and continuing government subsidies have meant that there has not been a relative decline in farm incomes that would have led to a labor exodus making Japanese labor unavailable in sufficient quantities. Rural residents have been a key constituency of the LDP, which has pursued policies designed to boost farm incomes and reduce the gap between rural and urban incomes (Aoki 1988; Shimada 1991). These factors, combined with the prevalence of small-scale farming, help account for the minimal presence of foreigners in the agricultural labor force.

On the other hand, when clientelism as a form of political largesse is extended to very large segments of the population, then it is clear that we are dealing with a *type* of clientelism different from what we found in Israel. If clientelism between politicians and business leaders has brought political contributions to the former and enhanced profits to the latter, it has also brought substantial benefits to broad portions of the Japanese population. Japan's conservative political establishment has at times exhibited decidedly redistributive tendencies, implementing programs that benefited primarily farmers, labor-intensive manufacturing, small business, and other lower-income groups. At times, these programs have been adopted over vehement objections from big business (Calder 1988). Redistributive programs have emerged in particular when the dominance of the LDP has been threatened:

> Political crisis, because of the unusual threat it poses to fundamental goals of the big business and conservative political communities in a highly leveraged, high-growth political economy, opens a "policy window" which allows bureaucracy and conservative party politicians to entertain for stability reasons the prospect of major "new-large" policy innovations and significant shifts in budgetary shares that in normal times they would not countenance. (Calder 1988: 228)

When clientelism results in extensive public works programs and small business supports, what is actually being provided (i.e., what is relevant here) is resources that translate into employment opportunities for Japanese workers. This point is especially relevant for public works construction, given the tendency of construction employers in other countries to seek out foreign labor. What we find in Japan is that government budgets, subject to patronage dynamics, make available resources that enable construction employers to pay the wages that Japanese workers require (in addition to profits for contractors). Large-scale patronage thus functions in part as a substitute for welfare policies, which are small in Japan relative to those of other advanced industrial countries (Calder

1988). Insofar as clientelism leads to producer cartels, the impact on Japanese citizens is decidedly mixed: cartels bring higher prices, hurting consumers. But the point here is that there is a differential impact, with more benefits going to workers in sectors that might otherwise be more vulnerable to an influx of foreign labor.

Moreover, it is not clear that clientelism in the construction ministry/industry had any real implications for the development of foreign worker policy. A large portion of construction expenditures is simply not subject to competitive market pressures. Insulation from competition means that the larger contractors in particular do not have to trouble themselves with keeping labor costs down as a strategy for winning contracts. With respect to the economic and technological development of the sector, at least in some ways the Ministry of Construction has behaved exactly as we would expect from a developmentalist state bureaucracy: the ministry has justified its firm position against the introduction of foreign construction labor as part of a broader agenda of modernizing the sector and increasing productivity and technological sophistication. We encountered pieces of that agenda previously in this chapter; on the other hand, construction in Japan still ranks among the lower productivity sectors in the economy, and there is much room for labor saving productivity advancements that can function as an alternative to cheap imported labor.

How does Japanese construction sector clientelism fit into the general argument of the book, i.e., that a developmentalist state is less likely to allow the entry of low-wage foreign workers? First of all, it must be granted that Japan is not perfectly suited as a case that supports the argument – though the bulk of the evidence presented in this chapter does demonstrate that Japanese developmentalism helps explain why the numbers of foreign workers in Japan have been small. In an ideal scholarly world, Japanese developmentalism would have remained intact throughout the period discussed here, and the number of foreign workers would be zero rather than 1.2 percent.[22] The real world presents us with more ambiguities and gray areas. On the other hand, given that the Japanese state in the 1990s was less coherent (the fall of the LDP in 1993 is one indicator) and its economic policy manifestly less successful, we should perhaps not be surprised if the presence of foreign labor has begun to increase as well. In this respect, the Japanese case is arguably consistent with the general theoretical argument, though in a somewhat messy way.

But it would also be unwise to exaggerate the pervasiveness of clientelism and its effect on economic policy as a whole. Relations between the Construction Ministry and the contractors may be defined by clientelism, but that relationship does not imply the breakdown of rule-based, autonomous behavior on the part of the bureaucracy in general. This point is clearly true concerning immigration and foreign workers policy, which remains largely in the hands of the Justice Ministry and, to a lesser degree, of the Labor Ministry. Even in the more recent period, then, Japan presents a strong contrast with Israel, where the politicization of economic policymaking also meant that the Israeli Labor Ministry *de facto* lost its legal authority to limit the entry of foreign labor. Clientelism in Japanese construction is contained, while in Israel it became the dominant mode of policymaking concerning foreign labor.

The decision not to permit foreign labor on a large scale in the more recent period of labor shortages thus appears in a new light when we consider its relationship to the issues discussed above. Some of the issues highlighted by other writers are important pieces of the story. The Japanese cultural "closure" to outsiders was without question a key factor accounting for the fact that Japanese policymakers did not *want* to allow immigration. But, as we saw in the last chapter, Israeli policymakers did not exactly *want* to bring one hundred thousand foreigners as temporary residents and workers: this was perceived as a situation of "no alternative." In Japan, on the other hand, there were in fact alternatives to foreign labor, alternatives made possible by a mode of economic governance that contributed to increasing labor productivity (at least in the earlier period) and steadily rising wages. In the absence of a state structure that helped make this alternative path possible, cultural factors and the preference against foreign labor might not have produced the same result: the choice between cultural preferences and economic imperatives (as perceived by labor-hungry employers, in particular) might have been posed in rather starker terms.

Conclusion

The argument that a developmentalist state is associated with lower levels of labor immigration (particularly of low-wage workers) receives strong support from Japan's first postwar experience with labor shortages (i.e., in the early 1970s). Rather than allow employers simply to acquire more labor (i.e., from abroad), the government maintained a closed-door policy with respect to unskilled foreign workers (apart from a very minor opening to "trainees"). Cheap foreign labor, though potentially profitable for employers, was inconsistent with what economic policymakers had in mind for the Japanese economy. Policymakers preferred that employers continue to make investments that would increase labor productivity, supporting the wage advances that were in any case already being successfully demanded by Japanese workers. Even the construction sector, usually (and rightly) considered inefficient relative to the more advanced manufacturing sector, received government support for making productivity-enhancing investments. Wages rose faster than productivity beginning in 1967, and the increases were substantial enough to effect a sizable transfer of income from capital to labor until the recession in 1974 (and then again in the late 1980s). But advances in productivity in the early 1970s were also very significant and created the basic conditions for the wage increases that were key to retaining already employed workers as well as drawing in new workers.

Japan's more recent experience with labor shortages does not support the main argument to the same degree. Japan's developmentalist state is in some respects a thing of the past: government policies (such as the failure to dismantle the informal anti-import behavior of private firms and trade associations) are no longer unambiguously supportive of advances in productivity and economic growth. But, given the specific impact of economic governance on wages and employment patterns (as discussed above), this experience does reinforce the more general notion that labor immigration is in part a function of the (potential) receiving country's mode of economic governance. The import protection and producer collusion that make possible higher wage payments depend heavily on the Japanese government's acquiescence and even active support. The government's tendency to manage economic activity is still very strong, despite the lip service paid to western notions about liberalization and deregulation (Sheridan 1993).

It is frequently argued (e.g., Abella and Mori 1996) that further growth in the use of foreign labor in Japan is inevitable because labor reserves are exhausted and because the labor shortages experienced by small firms cannot be resolved through investment in automation or offshore relocation. Economies of scale in particular are said to dictate against automation as a labor saving solution for small firms. But this argument takes as given the survival of the small firm sector in its current form and dimensions. It may be, however, that some small firms cannot be profitable under conditions of restricted labor supply. If a certain number of such firms were to become unviable, we should not assume that the productive activity organized by those particular firms would cease to exist. Rather, demand for their goods and services would persist – perhaps at a reduced level, given increased production costs associated with more expensive labor – and surviving competitors would step in to fill the gap.

In this process of consolidation, there is a possibility that more firms would reach the size necessary to take advantage of economies of scale that justify increasing investments in automation and other labor saving solutions. Another related possibility is that market share for the larger firms would increase; in this case there would also be an increase in the amount of productive activity performed with more advanced methods. Some small business owners would suffer the hardship of bankruptcy, but the consolidation would be functional for the economy as a whole, at least in terms of increasing labor productivity.[23]

Finally, we may assess the arguments of this chapter further by considering some of their implications and whether those implications are consistent with the experience of other cases. For instance, the argument implies that if West Germany had faced the question of foreign labor at a later point and had had the opportunity to learn from the experience of other countries, German policymakers would have followed a different course and in particular would have refrained from importing guestworkers. This notion is perhaps troubling: after all, weren't guestworkers a key component of West German economic growth before 1973? There is no reason to doubt the consensus that, in fact, foreign labor played a central role: in quantitative terms, by providing additional labor, and in qualitative terms, by supplying a particular *type* of labor – unskilled and willing to accept low wages. In both respects, the presence of foreigners was useful not only to capital but also to German workers, who experienced substantial upward mobility during this period (e.g., Castles 1992). Moreover, Germany is commonly understood as a state with a high level of economic planning capacity, with elements that fit the basic definition of a developmentalist state, such as a strong and relatively independent bureaucracy.[24] Would such a state have jeopardized economic growth, even given more insight concerning the long term costs associated with foreign labor? The possibility of a positive answer to that question begins with the fact that foreign labor is not a *necessary* condition for economic growth, even if it was a factor in growth in many European economies during the postwar boom. This is after all one of the most important lessons of the Japanese case. It is a lesson also illustrated by some of the Nordic countries, Finland in particular, which have achieved impressive economic performance with minimal foreign labor.[25] There is no reason to rush to the conclusion that a West Germany without foreign labor would have been a dismal economic performer.

The possibility of good economic performance without foreign labor supports the notion that West German policymakers could have considered foregoing the guestworker option. To understand why they might have wanted to do so, we may briefly recall the central place that the "foreigner problem" (Castles 1992) has played in German politics for the last two decades. On one hand, the presence of foreigners has perhaps been functional for German politics: Huyssen (1995) argues that Germany has a long history of buying national unity by demonizing an "other." On the other hand, there is no question that this strategy, if it can be considered as such, has carried high costs for Germans as well as for the foreigners who have been its most recent objects. And in fact it no longer buys national unity, as the Social Democrats' recent proposal to ease naturalization restrictions for guestworkers demonstrates. In a country like the US, immigration is usually seen as having a net economic benefit (e.g., Simon 1989), though the benefits are enjoyed disproportionately by the wealthy and the disadvantages are suffered disproportionately by minorities and the poor (Beck 1996; Briggs 1996). In a country with an "ethnocultural" construction of citizenship and nationality (Brubaker 1992), however, reduced opportunities for immigrant assimilation imply a social cost that compounds the economic costs resulting from partial immigrant incorporation into the German welfare state (against original intentions). Even if the problem derives not from the presence of the foreigners themselves but from an exclusivist, xenophobic political culture,[26] the past and present existence of this culture can be accepted as fact, no matter how distasteful it may be to American-style liberals. German policymakers, especially those concerned with questions broader than narrowly conceived economic performance, might have concluded on these grounds that it was in the country's interest at least to reduce the intake of foreign workers – again, *if* there had been an opportunity to learn that it would be impossible to send them home once their economic utility had declined. Some policymakers involved with the decision to expand the German guestworker program in the late 1960s and early 1970s reportedly came to believe that the decision was a mistake and that, with the benefit of hindsight, they would have tried a different method of dealing with labor supply problems.[27] The economic benefits of foreign labor were substantial, but they were not necessarily irreplaceable and there were also significant costs. But both of those latter points emerged too late for German policymakers to make any use of them. The same cannot be said, however, for the Japanese or the Israelis.

5
Labor Migration, Social Membership, and Race

In the preceding chapters we have discerned two distinct approaches to the problems of labor supply that arise when economic growth and rising living standards create citizens' expectations that clash with a persisting demand for low-wage, unskilled labor. One solution to the problem, illustrated here by the Israeli experience, is to expand the labor supply by drawing in labor from abroad. The main alternative (apart from sending some production processes abroad) is more complex and consists of restricting the available labor force to citizens; the restriction forces an increase in wages, particularly at the low end of the labor market, which then gives employers an incentive to invest in making that labor more productive. This path is embodied in the postwar Japanese experience, though more recently distortions in the Japanese economy have produced wage increases in some sectors even without significant advances in productivity.

To account for the different choices made in response to labor supply pressures, I have placed great emphasis on the structures of policymaking that create a bias towards certain types of solutions. The importation of labor in the form of guestworkers offers short-term benefits for certain private interests (especially employers) but carries significant long-term costs borne by the society as a whole. Recognition of this characteristic leads to the presumption that forward-thinking policymakers concerned about the general social welfare will shun the guestworker option and pursue alternative solutions to labor shortages. But choosing and implementing an alternative to foreign labor requires a state institutional structure that allows policymakers both to block employer preferences and to steer the economy in a way that departs from a path set by market signals alone. When the structure of the state does not foster these capabilities, importing foreign labor is likely to appear as the only viable choice, one which in any case is preferred by powerful domestic interests. This contrast is compatible with a core insight of the literature on state autonomy and capitalist development, which emphasizes the autonomy of the economic policy bureaucracy as an important condition for the implementation of positive development policies.

The empirical argument of the book is that this contrast informs an explanation for the different approaches of Israel and Japan to their own experiences with labor supply problems. Each country showed markedly different policymaking processes concerning foreign labor and labor supply. In Israel, a weak and divided bureaucracy was substantially ineffectual in its attempts to prevent adoption of a guestworker program; the real authority lay with the politicians, who were both beholden to private interests and more concerned about short-term political goals than long-term economic development. In contrast, the Japanese policymaking process, particularly in the earlier period, was more coherent, i.e., in *relative* terms. It would be easy to discern shortcomings or flaws in Japanese policymaking, even during the "golden era" of the developmental state: pollution and other quality of life problems were ignored in favor of growth, for example. But the relatively greater coherence of the state did make it possible for policymakers to avoid imported labor in significant measure. The concentration of authority in an autonomous bureaucracy – as well as supporting conditions such as long-term single party rule and a well-developed set of linkages between government and business – created the possibility of policies that speeded and directed investment toward the goal of increasing labor productivity. The authority of the bureaucrats also made it possible for the government to deny employers access to foreign labor, thus foreclosing the low-wage route to economic growth, while at the same time creating the conditions for the development of a high-wage alternative that kept Japanese workers employed in sectors staffed by foreigners elsewhere.

The comparison between Israel and Japan lays the foundation for a more general statement concerning the relationship between state structure, economic governance, and foreign labor. The theoretical leverage of the comparison exists not in spite of the many differences between the two countries but because of them. In particular, the fact that Japan's economy is more advanced and diversified would, on neoclassical grounds, lead us to expect that Japan would import *more* labor than Israel, not less. The gap between Japan's wealth and its neighbors' poverty is at least as large as the contrast between Israel and other countries in its region. Other obvious differences such as geographical location and size simply have no theoretical status: there is no reason to expect that

Japan's larger size and population, for example, would help explain the small presence of foreign labor. Just as importantly, the two countries are similar in ways that confound other popular theories of labor migration. Israel does not have a more dualist economy than Japan, nor is it more embedded in networks of trade or neocolonialism.[1] Finally, the undeniable cultural differences between Israel and Japan do not add up to the conclusion that Israeli culture is more welcoming to (non-Jewish) foreigners than Japanese culture. Comparative research involving two cases that differ on the dependent variable usually tries to control for differences that might interfere with the effort to analyze the effects of the independent variable of primary interest. That criterion is satisfied in this comparison as long as one takes into account the theoretical status of the secondary differences between Japan and Israel.

Toward a more general argument

This interpretation adds to our confidence that the contrasting modes of economic governance and state structure are factors that really matter in explaining the different approaches to resolving labor supply problems in each case. These factors mediate the effects of what appears to be a universal feature of advanced capitalist societies: as argued by dual labor market theorists, citizens shun insecure, poor-paying jobs in the secondary sector, leading employers to pressure their governments for access to foreign labor. What remains, of course, is to extend the analysis to other countries. The need to investigate other cases with small numbers of foreign workers seems especially compelling. The argument would be strengthened significantly if it turned out that the limited presence of low-wage foreign labor in Finland, Denmark, and Norway, for example, was attributable to a relatively coherent and long-term approach to economic governance, supported by an autonomous state that allowed only for relatively low levels of clientelism. Likewise, our confidence in the argument would increase if the growing numbers of foreign workers in, say, Italy and Spain derived from the existence of relatively weak and clientelized states. But these possibilities are offered here only as suggestions for further research.

In the introductory chapter, I emphasized that the theoretical argument concerning state structure, economic governance, and foreign labor policy was intended to apply only to a particular time period, roughly after 1970. The argument relies on the assumption that policymakers in potential receiving countries are aware of the serious economic and fiscal disadvantages associated with low-wage foreign labor: without such awareness, policymakers responsible for economic governance would have no particular reason to oppose employers' demands for importing labor. I argued that the drawbacks had become relatively clear in the European experience by the early 1970s, which enabled countries confronting labor supply problems in later years to gain some understanding of the long-term implications of a guestworker policy.

A more ambitious argument, however, would attempt to cover a greater variety of cases in an extended historical time frame, especially given that several important guestworker programs were initiated in the 1950s and 1960s (including those in France and West Germany). One potential way of constructing such an argument would be to theorize the interaction between state structure and the knowledge and beliefs of relevant policymakers. Briefly, in this version a developmentalist state will pursue alternatives to low-wage foreign labor only when it possesses information that leads to the conclusion that low-wage foreign labor is a losing proposition. Given employer pressure, a clientelist state is very likely to opt for guestworkers regardless of perceptions concerning costs to the larger society. But a non-clientelist state with limited or no access to information concerning such costs may also import labor, under the assumption that there are no significant long-term costs. An interactive model of this type holds some potential for explaining guestworker policies in West Germany, where the coherence of economic governance is generally held to be relatively high and the extent of clientelism relatively low.

Such an argument must still allow for the possibility, discussed briefly in Chapter 1, that even a developmentalist state (one which is able to resist pressure for guestworkers *and* aware of disadvantages) may still, under certain conditions, opt for such a program. Knowledge of disadvantages does not lead inevitably to a policy decision against guestworkers. Such knowledge must be interpreted in a particular context and balanced against other concerns and pressures. Foreign policy considerations, for example, might lead potential receiving country policymakers to determine that, even though importing foreign workers carries long-term social and economic costs, the constraints of international relations make it impossible to resist demands from potential sending countries for access to wealthier labor markets. Such considerations played a role in Japan's decision to expand its "trainee" program in the early 1990s (though that program still remained quite small).

Foreign labor and social membership

This discussion makes it clear that much depends on perceptions of the relative costs and benefits of low-wage foreign labor. This section therefore analyzes this issue in greater detail. There is a temptation in this type of analysis to reduce the question to whether the benefits are "greater than" the costs, as if we could calculate a single numerical value for each side of an equation and emerge with a definitive quantified conclusion. The assessment here will not pretend to such precision. Instead, I will introduce some considerations, not usually included in this type of discussion, that provide support for the contention that the costs are substantially greater than is commonly recognized.

It is sometimes considered that foreign workers are beneficial to the receiving country's economy insofar as they contribute to economic growth (in a situation where citizens are unwilling to supply labor for certain "necessary" tasks). We saw in Chapter 4 that numerous Japanese employers said they would have to reduce production levels or cancel planned expansions because they could not get enough workers. Employers in most European countries were not subject to the same constraint, and there is a clear consensus that the essentially unlimited supply of labor was a contributing factor to the European economic boom in the 1960s and early 1970s.[2] This boom led to significant mobility for some citizens of these countries, in terms of income gains and movement up the occupational status hierarchy. Likewise in Israel, the entry of non-citizen Palestinian workers is said to have facilitated mobility for Israeli citizens, just as the immigration of Sephardic Jews in the 1950s contributed to advances for the more established Ashkenazi population. Foreign and/or immigrant labor, then, might be understood as beneficial not just to German or French or Israeli employers but to ordinary citizens and workers in those countries as well.

This understanding of the effects of importing foreign labor is rather at odds with the position defended here, i.e., that the costs of foreign labor generally outweigh the benefits. Ordinary Germans and Israelis have in some respects benefited from the presence of foreign labor: the latter have performed labor considered undesirable but necessary (and have done so at low wages), and they have contributed to economic growth. On the other hand, as argued in earlier chapters, these benefits have come at a substantial and unforeseen cost, arising from the unplanned and unwanted settlement of many workers. The costs were substantial enough to cause some German policymakers to regret the choice to augment Germany's use of guestworkers in the late 1960s, as we saw in the previous chapter. Moreover, the perception that the disadvantages were very significant was a primary component of both Israeli and Japanese policymakers' reluctance to allow imported labor in more recent years.

But there is an additional consideration relating to the question of to what extent foreign labor is beneficial to the receiving society. The assessment in the first paragraph of this section rests in part on a definition of a "German" or an "Israeli" that excludes the foreign workers themselves. The question then arises: how appropriate is this restriction, given what we know about the strong tendency for foreign workers to settle more or less permanently in the receiving country? The grandchildren of Turkish foreign workers, born in Germany, speaking German but no Turkish, who have never set foot on Turkish soil, are avatars for the notion that there is something problematic here. Even in Israel, there are already foreign workers who consider themselves "Israeli," apparently unaware of how unfathomable that idea would be for most Israeli citizens.

There is no denying that labor migration also offers benefits to the foreign workers themselves. If there were none, there would be no migration: Thai workers on Israeli farms have chosen to put themselves there, though sometimes with imperfect information about what awaits them. Moreover, some workers do return permanently to their country of origin, and the savings from their employment in the receiving country often improve their circumstances substantially.

But if we ask how labor migration affects the receiving country society, it matters deeply how we think about the workers who settle. If we consider them "guests," then we need not think too hard about anything but the wages they receive for the work they perform during their "sojourn." But if we begin to think about them as members of the receiving society in important respects, then the notion that labor migration is essentially beneficial to the receiving society becomes less unequivocal. If labor migration brings clear benefits to Rumanian workers in Israel as Rumanians, it is less clear that it brings unambiguous benefits to Rumanian workers as Israelis. Poverty, political exclusion, substandard wages and working conditions, residential segregation into slums, vitiated legal protections, limited access to health and other social services – these typical byproducts of labor migration are problems not just for the individual foreign workers themselves but for the society, once it is accepted that the workers are somehow part of that society.

The argument here is not based on a simple change of names or labels. Referring to settled guestworkers as "Israelis" instead of "Rumanians" would not necessarily alter the calculus of cost and benefit for receiving country policymakers, who might appear to have no particular reason to care about the costs borne by the foreign workers themselves. But the real point is that eventually policymakers (at least in democratic countries) will likely come to perceive that they *must* pay attention to such costs. A government may disclaim responsibility for the welfare of foreigners (perhaps excepting basic issues such as safety and certain rights of legal due process), but a resident foreigner cannot remain "foreign" forever: as Tomas Hammar argues (1990), a "permanent foreigner" is an anomaly, according to current norms of democratic political culture. The problem is then compounded by the fact that guestworkers are usually ethnically or racially distinct from the rest of the population.

The real point is that yesterday's guestworker program typically becomes today's race problem. Foreign workers eventually achieve a significant degree of membership in the receiving society: they become denizens, in Hammar's term. In other words, they acquire a claim on the society's resources, including the attention of politicians. In part, this is because some social sectors among the native population are troubled by the presence of slums and deprivation in their midst. Membership has also come as a result of mobilization by the workers themselves (Miller 1981). Regardless of the form of its genesis, membership, even if partial, means that problems such as racially concentrated poverty are problems not just for the workers but for the native population as well. The receiving society may well be able to achieve some mobility for some of its citizens by importing labor, but at least some of the costs of doing so redound to the society itself and cannot be wholly externalized onto the workers.

It remains to be seen how Israel will contend with this particular pitfall. The Israeli state – its legal system, the constitution of its political parties, its general political culture – seems exceptionally ill-suited for consideration of the possibility that non-Jewish foreigners could come to have any meaningful membership in Israeli society. This is especially true at the national level and somewhat less true at the municipal level. Matters at the national level are illustrated by the government's response to the question of whether the children of foreign workers should be incorporated into Israeli schools. One official of the Ministry of Education asserted that it would be better for foreign children to stay at home and watch television than to learn the "Israeli heritage" by attending Israeli schools. The justification offered for this remark was that learning the country's heritage would give the children a sense that it was their heritage, that they belonged in Israel somehow, when in fact (in the eyes of this official) they did *not* belong and were present on a strictly temporary basis. Thus, there was to be no national budgetary support for accepting foreign children in Israeli schools (Rosenhek 1998), though this situation has been altered by legislation passed in 2000.

The transfer effect

This discussion leads to a further clarification of the argument made in Chapter 1 about rent-seeking and externalities. It might be imagined that the issue of whether foreign labor is beneficial for the receiving society hinges on whether there is a net economic gain. Benefits include additional profits for employers, more extensive use of existing capital and citizen labor, and lower prices and greater consumption of goods produced by foreign labor. Costs include the various externalities enumerated in previous chapters: extra budgetary expenditures to deal with social costs such as racial tensions, urban decay, and crime; additional infrastructural outlays; administration of the foreign worker program itself (including deportation of unauthorized workers); and the costs associated with the creation of a "race problem," as discussed in the previous section. If the former outweigh the latter, then it might appear that there is a net gain and that initiating a foreign labor program is a rational policy to pursue.

But the notion of a net economic gain obscures important aspects of this issue. In particular, it matters greatly who receives the benefits and who pays the costs. The argument here is not simply that there are rents and externalities associated with foreign labor, but that these two components together amount to a subsidy from tax-payers to employers. The idea that there is a net economic gain from foreign labor becomes rather less compelling if we consider that those enjoying the benefits are relatively wealthy construction contractors, while those paying the costs are middle-class tax-payers – not to mention unemployed citizens and low-level native workers who bear the opportunity cost associated with the failure to create more attractive jobs. Of course, matters would never be as simple as that formulation implies: if the middle class as tax-payers must bear an increased tax burden, the middle class as consumers may also enjoy greater purchasing power through restrained prices for consumer goods. But the more general point remains: a "net economic gain" is likely to be a less compelling argument in favor of foreign labor if it leads to enrichment for a few and to declining relative living standards for many, even if the latter effect is quantitatively smaller than the former.

Foreign labor and the labor process

There is one final feature of foreign labor as a component of capitalist development that needs discussion in this context. The core value that informs most discussions of development is rising living standards. In typical formulations, this value has to do mainly with increasing the population's ability to consume: the real meaning of wage increases, after all, is that individuals and families are able to buy more goods and services. Greater purchasing power leads to enhanced quality of life: even development cynics, suspicious of the way development leads to the adoption of Western "consumerist" values and to greater environmental degradation, cannot deny that individuals are better off when their increased earnings give them access to better health care and education.

It is less common, however, to focus on the impact development can have on the lives of individuals as *producers* rather than as consumers. Most people spend a very large portion of their lives working (whether for pay or not – it does not matter for present purposes), and one's quality of life is determined to a very significant extent by the work one does. Whether economic development improves the lives of workers as workers is of course a highly debatable proposition: quality of life is in many respects a subjective issue dependent on culturally and even individually specific factors such as values and preferences. While some observers might herald the end of the need to work the land with hand tools and animals, others might lament the decline of traditional agrarian societies or the depersonalization of service sector work (Head 2003). Even at a more advanced level, it is by no means obvious that, say, assembling electronic components is preferable as a way to spend one's day to peasant farming. In other words, there is no obvious relationship between the productivity of a certain type of labor and its contribution to one's quality of life.

But if we cannot make a general statement about the impact of development on workers' quality of life, the issue becomes somewhat less complicated when we focus more narrowly on the question as it relates to labor migration to particular receiving countries. Labor shortages arise not only because wages are too low to attract citizen workers, but also because the work itself is undesirable in the relevant social context. University professors accept low incomes relative to other professionals with advanced degrees because they generally find the work satisfying. There is no such tradeoff for those Israelis who refuse to work in the "wet" occupations in Israeli construction. Those who work in low-status, unpleasant jobs might appreciate a mode of development that allows them to escape back-breaking, mind-numbing labor (as long as there is something to escape *to*); it seems arguable that such development is at least as valuable as a form of development that simply augments purchasing power. Many observers will perhaps respond that it would be impossible to eliminate all unpleasant work. In Virginia Woolf's novel

To the Lighthouse, Mr. Ramsay, a scholar, asserts a sad but (in his view) incontrovertible truth: "The liftman in the Tube is an eternal necessity." The fact that he (or his creator) was unable to imagine the appearance of automatic elevators should perhaps cause us to wonder about what we ourselves are currently unable to imagine. On the other hand, the evolution of attitudes concerning types of labor is both culturally and temporally specific: work once considered desirable can later become widely detested. It is on this level that unpleasant work may be inescapable. But this possibility does not undermine the rationale for efforts to create better work; instead, it reinforces the imperative for such efforts.

There is no guarantee that development in the Japanese mode – without foreign labor, based on productivity increases and rising wages – will enhance the quality of work life for citizens. Again, more productive labor is not necessarily more satisfying labor. But it seems clearer that importing foreign labor *will* help guarantee the perpetuation of the undesirable work that currently exists – while at the same time concentrating such work among foreigners and racial/ethnic minorities. The scarcity of labor power can act as a powerful incentive for employers to devise methods of reducing or eliminating work that people do not want. Allowing employers to import labor, and so to continue employing workers at prevailing wage levels for undesirable work, reduces or removes that incentive.

The perspective of sending countries

Almost all of the analysis here has focused on processes and perspectives of the receiving countries. In part this is the result of a considered decision: the variation that matters for determining different labor migration outcomes exists primarily in receiving countries, not in sending countries. Pressures for emigration produce more potential foreign workers than receiving countries are willing to admit; receiving countries play the major role in determining to what extent migration takes place.[3]

The exclusive focus on receiving countries is less appropriate in a discussion of normative issues, however, and so I will end with a few words on this matter. So far I have defended the view that guestworker programs are harmful to the receiving society, despite the benefits they provide to certain private interests (mainly employers). I argued above that, when organized as a guestworker program, labor migration also involves significant drawbacks as well as benefits for the workers themselves. For the sending country as a whole, labor migration appears to offer mixed benefits as well. Some countries, such as the Philippines, perceive that the benefits are much greater than the costs and go to great lengths to encourage their citizens to find work abroad. In some cases, workers' remittances have become a significant source of foreign exchange earnings.

The great hopes that attended the initiation of guestworker programs in the early postwar period, however, have generally not been realized. Some planners believed workers would acquire the skills and capital that would make it possible for them to return home and invest in productive businesses, enhancing the development and employment prospects for the sending society. Importing labor was even touted as a form of development aid in some countries (including Japan). Many returning workers, however, did not invest their savings acquired abroad; instead, having earned enough to live quite comfortably according to the standards of their own society, they used the money for conspicuous consumption, including the building of lavish homes. The spin-off effects for the local economy were relatively modest (Martin 1991b; see also Massey *et al.* 1987).

Spin-off effects were naturally not very important to the workers themselves (even the ones who returned home). The ability to improve their standard of living constituted a sufficient return on the investment of time and effort made by those who worked abroad. The same point holds for those who did not go back: guestworker programs provided an opening for many individuals to become members of a wealthier society (though in some cases that membership has been significantly limited). Again, guestworker programs offered undeniable benefits to those who agreed to become guestworkers, although these benefits arguably became less compelling the longer the workers remained, as their frame of reference shifted, for example, from Turkey to Germany.

A thorough assessment of the normative dimensions of labor migration would have to look beyond the benefits accruing to a limited number of individuals. In its broadest expression, the "problem" of migration is inextricably linked with the problem of global economic inequality. It is by no means apparent that guestworker programs have had (or could have) any real positive effect in reducing this inequality. A limited number of individuals, with persistence and luck, have improved their circumstances, but the relative poverty of most sending countries has remained. The accident of being born in a particular place continues to act as a powerful determinant of an individual's poverty or prosperity.

Whether free immigration (as distinct from the restricted guestworker mode of entry) would have any effect in reducing inequality of opportunity is of course a highly debatable proposition. If it did so, it is possible that the reduction of inequality would take place via a downward leveling of income and wealth in the rich countries. Free immigration might simply result in the geographic redistribution of relative poverty, as established residents of rich countries maintain their advantage relative to new immigrants, perhaps even despite the extension of full political membership to the latter.

I will not take a stand here on the merits of such a scenario relative to the current configuration of global inequality. My point here is more modest. The guestworker mode of immigration implies that the restrictions on membership in the host society are a legitimate price to exact from foreigners in exchange for the latter's opportunity to improve their economic welfare. The premise is that this restriction is necessary to protect the interests of the host society. In fact, the restriction fails to protect those interests well: again, the guestworker mode of employing foreign labor entails significant costs for the host society as a whole. Moreover, even though some workers return with substantial savings, the guestworker mode of migration has only mixed benefits for the sending society as a whole. These points add to the perception that, in normative terms, guestworker programs are at best incoherent.

On the other hand, if my structuralist arguments are correct, these normative considerations can have little impact on policy outcomes. Some political leaders in receiving countries (such as Israel), well aware of the disadvantages, have made passionate arguments against importing labor, only to find that those arguments have little power in the face of powerful economic interests. The power of those interests is rooted in an institutional structure, which by definition is not easily altered through the efforts of individuals who might want something different. The point is meant not as dissuasion from the attempt to make a difference but as a means for appreciating the difficulties one might face.

Appendix
Newspaper and Interview codes

Newspapers

AM	Al HaMishmar
D	Davar (earlier Davar Rishon)
HA	HaAretz
M	Ma'ariv
YA	Yediot Ahronot

Interviews
(all interviews were conducted by the author)

Alexander	Dana Alexander, attorney for the Association for Civil Rights in Israel, 27 June 1995
Arbel	Yossi Arbel, Vice Director General, Contractors' Association, Tel Aviv, 4 May 1998.
Artum	Dani Artum, in charge of the budget, Labor Ministry, Jerusalem, 9 March 1998.
Barkan	Amir Barkan, Finance Ministry, liaison with the Agriculture Ministry, Jerusalem, 23 February 1998.
Bassi	Yonatan Bassi, formerly Director General of the Agriculture Ministry, Jerusalem, 29 March 1998.
Ben-Eliezer	Binyamin Ben-Eliezer, Member of Knesset (Parliament) and former Minister of Housing and Construction, Jerusalem, 4 November 1996.
Ben-Shalom	Avraham Ben-Shalom, formerly Director General of the Labor Ministry, Tel Aviv, 21 April 1998.
Brodet	David Brodet, formerly Director General of the Finance Ministry, Jerusalem, 2 June 1998.
Dar	Vered Dar, Deputy Director General, Finance Ministry, Jerusalem, 2 April 1998.
Eiges	Itai Eiges, Finance Ministry liaison to Construction Ministry, 1 July 1998.
Fefferman	Benny Fefferman, Head of the Manpower Planning Authority, Israeli Ministry of Labor, Jerusalem, 14 July 1996, 5 July 1998.
Fine	Liora Fine, in charge of Foreign Workers, Moshav Movement, Tel Aviv, 27 May 1996.
Fogel	Aharon Fogel, formerly Director General of the Finance Ministry, Tel Aviv, 29 June 1998.
Friedman	Ivan Friedman, construction contractor, Jerusalem, 6 July 1995.

Fruchtman	Ran Fruchtman, Director, Department for Industrial Management, Manufacturers' Association in Israel, Tel Aviv, 17 July 1995.
Gal-Yam	Tsippi Gal-Yam, Director, State Revenues Department, Finance Ministry, Jerusalem, 5 May 1998.
Geffen	Avie Geffen, formerly Finance Ministry liaison with the Labor Ministry, Jerusalem, 24 March 1998.
Hecht	Yaakov Hecht, formerly in charge of Occupational Training in Construction, Labor Ministry, Jerusalem, 26 March 1998.
Hikone	Shigeru Hikone, Principal, Arup Japan, Tokyo, 7 January 2002.
Himmelfarb	Micky Himmelfarb, Director of Contractors' Division, Contractors' Association, Tel Aviv, 29 June 1998.
Hollander	Rachel Hollander, Head of Informational Analysis Department, Construction Ministry, Jerusalem, 9 June 1998.
Kedmon	Mordechai Kedmon, Director of Planning Authority, Agricul-ture Ministry, Tel Aviv, 4 March 1998.
Maruya	Hiroaki Maruya, Director, Office for Construction Market Access, Policy Bureau, Ministry of Labour, Infrastructure, and Transport, Tokyo, 9 January 2002.
Michaelov	Natasha Michaelov, Finance Ministry Liaison to Labor Ministry, Jerusalem, 4 March 1998.
Mizrahi	Arieh Mizrahi, formerly Director General of the Construction Ministry, Rosh Ayin, 17 June 1998.
Nomoto	Nobuichi Nomoto, Chief Managing Advisor, Toko Engineer-ing Consultants Co., Ltd., Tokyo, 9 January 2002, Tokyo. (Formerly with the Ministry of Construction, in the 1960s and 1970s).
Paltiel	Ari Paltiel, Demographer, Central Bureau of Statistics, Jerusalem, 15 October 1996.
Pialkov	Haim Pialkov, Advisor to the Minister, Construction Ministry, Jerusalem, 25 March 1998.
Porshner	Hagai Porshner, *Davar Rishon* reporter, Tel Aviv, 14 April 1996.
Rubinstein	Amnon Rubinstein, formerly Minister of Education, Jerusalem, 13 January 1998.
Sanbar	Moshe Sanbar, formerly Governor of the Bank of Israel, and for-merly Director of the Budget, Finance Ministry, Tel Aviv, 2 November 1997.
Sela	Hanan Sela, in charge of foreign workers, Employment Service, Ministry of Labor, 21 May 1995.
Shabbat	Yossi Shabbat, Economist, Information Analysis Department, Construction Ministry, Jerusalem, 25 February 1998.
Shapira	Amit Shapira, in charge of foreign workers, Contractors' Association, Tel Aviv, 11 November 1996.
Shochat	Avraham Shochat, formerly Finance Minister, Jerusalem, 20 January 1998.
Shtern	David Shtern, Director General of the Fund for Encouragement and Development in the Construction Industry, Tel Aviv, 17 March 1998.
Smit	Hanoch Smit, formerly Head of the Manpower Planning Authority, Jerusalem, 20 November 1997.

Suzuki   Hajime Suzuki, Executive Director of Research Institution on
                Construction and Economy, Tokyo, 11 January 2002.
Yashiro   Tomo Yashiro, Professor of Construction Management and
                Economics at Institute for Industrial Science, University of
                Tokyo, 7 January 2002.
Zohar   Hanna Zohar, Workers' Hotline, Tel Aviv, 22 May 1995,
                28 June 1995.

Notes

1 Introduction

1. Orly Levy first drew my attention to this analogy.
2. In this respect my goals are similar to those of Eytan Meyers (2004), though my focus is limited to labor migration.
3. A number of studies address the relationship between migration and development in sending countries (e.g., Papademetriou and Martin 1991; Fischer *et al.* 1997; Díaz-Briquets and Weintraub 1991; Hermele 1997). The focus here is on labor migration as a component of development in receiving countries.
4. The American bracero program was the subject of a much more intense policy debate. See e.g., Hawley 1979.
5. See Miles & Satzewich (1990) for discussion of a similar argument with a different periodization.
6. Non-democratic countries such as Singapore and Libya have engaged in forced repatriations, although even they are not as successful in this regard as they would like (on Singapore, see Stahl 1986).
7. Hammar *et al.* (1997) address the question of immobility, i.e., why most people stay put. This is an important question in the study of migration, but it is different from the question guiding this book, i.e., why some wealthy countries receive only small numbers of immigrants.
8. On negative case methodology, see Emigh 1997; Lieberson (1992) also employs the term in the precise sense I intend here. See also Moore 1966.
9. Thus, as Massey has argued (1987, 1999), migration is caused not so much by the lack of economic development in poor regions but rather by development itself – a refutation of the basic neoclassical economic position. See also Martin and Taylor (2001).
10. We can also question the premise itself: Brubaker (1995) among others notes that this putative openness to immigration appears as something rather different from the perspective of those who would like to move to a wealthy country but are prevented from doing so by restrictive policies in wealthy countries.
11. See Hollifield (1986) for an analysis that has similar characteristics to the argument I am proposing. Hollifield's explanandum is rather different, however: he analyzes determinants of immigration policy in two countries (France and Germany) that already had large numbers of foreign workers.
12. The process of "offshoring" can happen in two ways: firms can relocate abroad, closing plants in one country and opening them in another, or firms in the high-wage country can simply die while others in a low-wage country take their market share. Foreign workers frequently work in sectors that produce non-tradable goods and services – hotels, restaurants, domestic services, etc. There is a common perception that construction is another sector where foreign workers are often employed because the product is

non-tradable (and local workers cannot be found). A more subtle understanding is required: as the Japanese case shows, it is possible (and economically feasible) to import prefabricated housing components. Erection must take place on site, but much of the production can take place abroad. The point is discussed in more detail in Chapter 4.

13. Why is the "low road" an ideal type, if many countries do in fact have large numbers of foreign workers? The best answer is that such countries also have plenty of high-paid, high-productivity jobs for citizens. Even concerning countries that have relatively large numbers of foreign workers, it is worth considering not only why there are so many but also why there are not more, given that employers would always prefer to substitute cheaper labor for more expensive labor of the same quality.

14. Conceptualizing profits based on migrant labor as rents is similar to Philip Martin's discussion (e.g., 1994) of an immigrant labor subsidy. Compare also Zolberg: "In good times the benefits of migrant labor flowed into the pockets of the manufacturers, but in bad times the costs were passed on to local authorities – and beyond them to the taxpayers" (1987: 63).

15. If governments address the social and economic problems associated with imported labor without increasing taxes, then budget allocations to other programs and services must decrease. When governments fail to address the social and economic problems associated with imported labor, many individuals (e.g., those living near foreign worker slums) suffer a welfare decline. In all of these scenarios, some individuals lose while others – especially employers – win.

16. For a dissenting view, i.e., that access to cheap foreign labor does not inhibit positive technological change, see Harris 1995.

17. Some scholars will likely object to this characterization of Japan. Cornelius, for example, notes that, while the foreign presence is still relatively small, "the trend since the late 1980s has been sharply upward" (Cornelius *et al.* 1994b: 382). Sassen (1993) also sees a major transformation in migration to Japan. And Mori (1997) speaks of the "massive entry" of migrants into some occupations. If these trends continue, then Japan might eventually become a significant receiving country (though the current recession in East Asia may reduce the demand). But at this point stocks are small, and formulating and testing theories should rely on data about what has happened rather than invoking future projections. Even if Japan eventually acquires a large foreign population, comparable to those of European countries, it will still possess a significant history of capitalist growth without extensive use of foreign labor. These points anticipate arguments made in Chapter 4.

18. This consensus is not universal. Papademetriou and Hamilton, for example, refer to "the other, less easily measured benefits of immigration, especially those associated with openness toward the outside world" (2000: 49). Significantly, however, they do not say any more about what those benefits are.

19. Non-citizen Palestinian workers in Israel are clearly "foreign workers" in many respects. Israel's occupation of the West Bank and Gaza, however, distinguishes these workers from foreign workers in other contexts and from other foreign workers in Israel. To introduce this distinction concisely, I refer separately to Palestinian and foreign workers here, and I will address the issue further in Chapter 3.

20. Johnson's "developmental state" is a much criticized characterization of the Japanese state. I use the term to introduce my main argument, and I will address the various debates over the appropriateness of the term in due course.

2 Labor Migration in the Postwar Period

1. I have no ability to know directly whether there are important theoretical contributions in, say, the Swedish or Dutch literatures on international migration. The idea that such contributions would not find their way into the mainstream English literature (via scholars whose linguistic competence is broader than mine) seems implausible, however.
2. In this regard it is noteworthy that relatively few EU nationals take advantage of the opportunity to work in other EU countries: in 1998, only 740,000 EU nationals worked outside their country of citizenship (Migration News, December 1998).
3. Workers usually provide for their families no matter where they are located (though their willingness to do so can decline over time); the point is that doing so is more expensive if the families are located in an expensive host country metropolis than if they are in a rural village in Turkey or Algeria. On the other hand, employers also want stable, productive workers, and some employers have pressed for family reunification because they find that their workers are more stable and productive if they have their families present (Castles 1986).
4. See Thomas (1985) for a discussion of how governments construct citizenship to maintain the exploitability of labor for employers' benefit.
5. Table 2.1, concerning foreign labor in 1964, provides only gross figures, because of data limitations. The last column of Table 2.2 already excludes workers from countries that are members of common labor market arrangements.
6. Again, however, workers from Spain and Portugal before 1993 did not enjoy freedom of mobility under EU arrangements. Only beginning in 1993 are these workers removed from the figures in the last column.
7. There are exceptions to this trend: Castles and Miller (1993) point out that some guestworkers originally from poor countries have achieved professional and well-paying positions in Germany. Such persons are exceptional, however.
8. For examples of such a claim, see Pessar 1988 and Rogers 1985.

3 Foreign Workers Policy in Israel

1. Non-Jewish foreigners are the real object of interest here. Non-citizen Jews present in Israel (e.g., for purposes of work or study) are not "really" foreign, though the position of Ethiopian Jews (even citizens) is somewhat problematic in this regard. Non-Jewish Russians and others who entered under the Law of Return (by virtue of having a Jewish parent, grandparent, or spouse) are citizens, but their presence is considered problematic as well (they number more than 200,000).

2. Note that this statement does not read: there are no structural differences between the Israeli and Japanese economies. The argument is that they do not differ in ways that obviously affect the demand for cheap/foreign labor.
3. Arab and Mizrachi workers in general never received the largesse and privilege afforded to the mostly Ashkenazi public sector workers.
4. Mintz cites data showing that "25% of the Israel's labor force is employed in the defense industries, and about half of all industrial workers are involved in defense-related projects" (1983: 111).
5. International factors are of course important influences on some types of economic policy, and the institutionalist literature sometimes takes this into account. It will become clear here that international factors were relevant to the question of foreign labor policy, but they were of secondary importance relative to the configuration of domestic interests – especially if our goal is to understand why the Israeli policy response to labor shortages was different from the Japanese.
6. Cf. Akzin (1966: 10): "It is a basic, though unwritten, rule of the coalition agreement that a department [ministry] allocated to a given political party should be conducted more or less as the minister and his party wish without much interference from the cabinet."
7. Nachmias and Rosenbloom's book is of course somewhat dated. In the process of my research, however, I saw little that would suggest a different assessment of current bureaucratic realities.
8. Even France/Algeria was distinguished by the fact that Algerians held French citizenship. Labor migration from former European colonies typically followed decolonization.
9. Plessner (1994) argues that the government's Employment Service, created in 1959, was designed specifically to shield Jews from Arab competition for jobs.
10. See Shalev 1990 and Shapiro (1988) for a discussion of how the Histadrut differs from most neo-corporatist labor federations. In particular, the Histadrut has long been part of the Israeli political establishment and is widely seen as a means for maintaining control over the labor movement rather than representing the latter's interests. See also Kleiman 1987 and Doron 1988.
11. Kadri and Macmillen argue that "the number and political type of [Palestinian] commuters allowed to work in Israel after 1993 have been chosen as part of a calculated policy of aggression against the occupied territories" (1998: 299). While it is not inconceivable that there may be some evidence for such a statement, they provide none.
12. A reasonable estimate of the total of illegal non-Palestinian foreign workers is 100,000 (see below). Bar-Tsuri (1998) estimates that half of such workers are employed in construction. In addition, it is likely that there are many undocumented Palestinian workers employed in construction as well.
13. This redistribution continued in more recent decades: in the early 1970s, labor's share was 72 percent; by the mid-1980s it had reached 88 percent (Rivlin 1992). See also Barkai 1984.
14. Israel's "Law of Return" permits unlimited immigration of Jews and grants them immediate citizenship on arrival; the state actively encourages such immigration. Substantial numbers of Jews emigrate every year, a source of shame for many Israelis and a perceived challenge to Israel's status as the "Jewish homeland," its primary raison d'être for many citizens.

15. Early Zionist ideology stress the concept of "Hebrew Labor," which advocated that Jews, accustomed to being merchants, bankers, and professionals in the Diaspora, learn to be farmers and production workers in Israel/Palestine and to take pride in this work. For some early Zionists, Hebrew labor also meant not exploiting non-Jews (especially the native Arab population), and Jews made a concerted effort during the pre-1948 period to create a separate Jewish economy (though not only for ideological reasons – see Kimmerling 1983; Shafir 1989). Some of those opposing imported labor still invoke the idea of Hebrew labor.
16. The contractors used the same tactic in 2000, with similar success (Asiskovitch 2004).
17. Or Jewish/Israeli terrorism, such as the massacre in Hebron in the spring of 1994; here the government closed the borders to prevent Palestinian retaliation, not because of an actual attack on Israelis.
18. Israel thus presents an instance of a gap between policy intended to reduce immigration and the reality of increasing inflows (Cornelius *et al.* 1994) – what Joppke analyzes as a "challenge to sovereignty" (1998).
19. In cultural terms, Israeli Jews sometimes say that no Jewish man would accept such work because no Jewish woman would consider a construction worker an acceptable mate. The status of this work is extremely low.
20. The phenomenon of high-technology construction methods has an interesting precedent in the pre-statehood period. A small number of German Jews fleeing National Socialism in the 1930s imported prefabricated houses made in German factories, under an arrangement that allowed the emigrants to bypass restrictions on exporting money by exporting German-made goods instead. Prefabricated houses also helped these immigrants to Palestine acquire housing in a period of labor shortages during a construction boom. The owners expressed satisfaction with them, and a few of the houses are still standing in Haifa (Herbert 1979). But any inclination to promote industrialized construction in Israel has long been rendered meaningless, given the large supply of cheap labor available to employers.
21. A plausible argument could be made that the government bears some responsibility for the slow pace of residential construction (and thus for the tightness of the housing market). The Israel Land Administration controls the release of land for development purposes, and some contractors assert that the process is difficult and slow (INT-Arbel). I do not know whether the high housing prices that result in part from restricted availability of land advance the interests of the contractors such that the contractors themselves exert pressure to maintain this status quo.
22. As in a case in 1999 where the court ordered the Ministry of Religion to seat two non-Orthodox Jews on the Jerusalem municipal religious council. The minister in question was not held in contempt or disciplined in any way for not doing so; instead, a representative from the Prime Minister's office, acting "on the former's behalf", signed the order as required by the court.
23. While Brodet and other opponents of foreign labor may have an interest in claiming more insight than they actually had several years previously, it is unlikely that their opposition to the idea itself was not real.
24. Shalev (1998) notes that the government took action against hyper-inflation not when it first emerged but only when it began to threaten the legitimacy of the government itself.

25. One Finance Ministry official (INT-anonymous) even claimed to have invoked a direct comparison with Japan, arguing to superiors that, yes, local services and other non-tradables in Japan were more expensive, but the long-term cost to the economy of importing labor is even higher.
26. A long-time Knesset member, Anat Maor (Meretz), wrote a graduate thesis for Tel Aviv University on foreign workers in Europe (Maor 1981).
27. I can think of no reason privately owned companies would be different in this respect. Data, however, were not available. In addition, the display of gross profits relates only to those companies for which I could get data; with more companies the absolute figures would be higher, though again there is no reason to think that the overall trend would look different.
28. A moshav is, or was, a cooperative farming village, differing from the more collectively oriented kibbutz in that the means of production are privately owned by individuals. Schwartz (1995) argues that the demise of most agricultural purchasing organizations in the 1990s has meant that moshavim have become little more than regular municipalities.
29. The objection might arise that foreign workers instead make possible an increase in economic activity by supplying labor that would otherwise not be available in particular sectors. This objection unreasonably discounts the possibility that employers would eventually adapt to the existing labor supply and find other means to make production go forward.

4 Alternatives to Foreign Labor in Japan

1. Before World War II, Japan forcibly imported millions of workers from countries in the region. After the war, however, most of these workers returned to their country of origin (Oka 1994).
2. A research assistant who explored the literature in Japanese supported this assertion, though I do not make a strong claim to the effect that we conducted an exhaustive survey of Japanese sources.
3. These sources refute a source quoted by Cornelius (1994) who asserted that the Japanese government simply never considered importing labor at this time.
4. Japanese labor unions are commonly described as enterprise unions without an influential voice in government policymaking (e.g., Pempel and Tsunekawa 1979). For a dissenting view, however, see Kume 1998.
5. Hiromi Mori, personal communication.
6. The precise term is employee compensation, which includes social insurance payments on behalf of workers. To reduce awkwardness, I will refer instead to wages.
7. Growth in the proportion of services employment to total employment has been quite slow in Norway, Finland, and Denmark as well, and from a substantially smaller base in 1970.
8. The category "services" in Table 4.4 covers a very diverse range, including wholesale and retail trade, transportation and communication, business services, and personal/community services. Sayer and Walker (1992) argue convincingly that the label "services" is misapplied to many of these

activities. For the other variables analyzed here, data from the OECD's ISDB allow disaggregation of this category, but this is not possible using the data available to me for sectoral consumer prices.

9. I will argue below that even in the construction sector there are real possibilities for international trade.

10. International trade in services has been increasing, in part because of advances in telecommunications technology, but, as Sassen notes (1991), one of the main mechanisms for trading services is precisely the migration of the service providers. We are focusing here on an important case in which this has not been a dominant mode of economic restructuring. On the increasing tradability of services, see also Petit 1986.

11. A certain number of prefabricated homes in Japan originate in Sweden, another prefab leader (Mathieu 1987). This fact illustrates that there are possibilities for international trade in construction "products": local labor is needed to erect and finish the house on site, but a substantial portion of the total value is added abroad.

12. The data from Finland, the country under consideration with the smallest percentage of foreign workers, are entirely consistent with the association.

13. A relatively minor but still quite telling example of this logic was reported on National Public Radio on 18 February 1999: a Japanese firm has created a mechanized way of putting detailed artistic designs on fingernails. This service, much in demand among Japanese teenage girls, takes an hour and a half and costs about $40 when done by hand; the mechanized version takes 15 minutes and costs about $12. By contrast, in New York nail salons are often staffed by Korean immigrant women. Again, it is possible to increase productivity in personal services in a way that is not entirely an artifact of increasing prices.

14. While the reverse may seem true as well, i.e., that other sectors (especially labor) would push for government policies helpful to themselves regardless of the impact on capital, there are compelling contrary arguments (Cohen and Rogers 1983; Przeworski 1985). When push comes to shove, labor leaders often understand that satisfying the interests of capital is a precondition to satisfying the interests of labor.

15. On the government's capacity for administrative guidance and its sway over private companies, see also Huber 1994.

16. Of course, not even American or British capitalism embodies all the elements of neoliberal economic philosophy. But the clear implication of the developmentalist state thesis is that Japan differs not only from the neoliberal model but also from American and British practice.

17. I am quoting the writer of the article here, not the words of the official.

18. There seems to be little substance to the idea that Japanese consumers disdain foreign goods (especially when prices of imports are much lower) (Katz 1998). But see also Dore 1990 for a slightly different view.

19. But see Haley (1990) for an argument to the effect that it is not collusion but fierce competition that keeps foreign firms out. However, Haley does not address the issue of high prices in Japan, an aspect of the problem that seems to undercut his argument.

20. Noland (1995) asserts that consumer prices in Japan would fall by as much as 41 percent if there were no barriers to imports and if the tight supplier–distributor relationships were broken up. See also Horioka 1998.

21. While Japanese elections are expensive for candidates, political contributions also contribute to a "lavish" lifestyle on the part of many politicians, especially from the LDP (Schlesinger 1997).
22. On both counts, Finland may be another suitable case: the share of foreign labor is smaller, and the coherence of economic governance is arguably more durable (see Vartiainen 1997).
23. Consolidation and the decline of small business could of course be undesirable according to other values.
24. Katzenstein (1985) analyzes two other labor importers, Austria and Switzerland, in similar terms.
25. Even if Finnish growth involved starting later from a lower base, the fact remains that it "caught up" without recourse to foreign labor. Germany as well had some catching up to do (see Dollar and Wolff 1993), as did Israel.
26. This formulation simplifies a complex reality and glosses over the fact that many Germans support full membership for long-term foreign residents. What matters in this discussion, however, is that the institutions of German political culture have long been exclusivist and are only beginning to show signs of opening.
27. Personal communications, Heinz Werner and John Bendix.

5 Labor Migration, Social Membership, and Race

1. While Israel's occupation of Palestinian territories was an important determinant of the use of non-citizen Palestinian labor, there is no parallel that helps explain the influx of workers from Romania or Thailand.
2. This point raises the question of whether Japan's economic growth in the same period would have been even more rapid if labor had been more freely available. One of the main arguments from the last chapter, however, was that Japan's technology-led growth was one of the main conditions that made it possible for the country to avoid importing labor.
3. As noted in earlier chapters, many countries fall into both categories. A more precise way of stating the point here is that Finland (for example) carries more weight in determining labor migration flows as a (potential) receiving country than as a sending country.

References

Abella, Manolo, and Hiromi Mori 1996. "Structural change and labour migration in East Asia," in *Development strategy, employment and migration: country experiences*, edited by David O'Connor. Paris: OECD.

Aharoni, Yair 1991. *The Israeli economy: dreams and realities*. New York: Routledge.

—— 1998. "The changing political economy of Israel." *Annals of the American Academy of Political and Social Scientists* 555: 127–46.

Akzin, Benjamin, and Yehezkel Dror 1966. *Israel: high-pressure planning*. Syracuse: Syracuse University Press.

Amir, Shmuel 1999. "Effects of the entry of foreign workers to the building sector," in *The new laborers: workers from foreign countries in Israel*, edited by Roby Natanson and Leah Achdut. Tel Aviv: HaKibbutz HaMeuchad (in Hebrew).

—— 2002. "Overseas foreign workers in Israel: policy aims and labor market outcomes." *International Migration Review* 36(1): 41–57.

Amsden, Alice H. 1989. *Asia's next giant: South Korea and late industrialization*. New York: Oxford University Press.

Angrist, Joshua D. 1994. *The demand for Palestinian labor*. Jerusalem: Falk Institute, Hebrew University of Jerusalem.

Aoki, Masahiko 1988. *Information, incentives, and bargaining in the Japanese economy*. Cambridge: Cambridge University Press.

——, Kevin Murdock, and Masahiro Okuno-Fujiwara 1997. "Beyond the East Asian miracle: introducing the market-enhancing view," in *The role of government in East Asian economic development*, edited by Masahiko Aoki, Hyung-Ki Kim, and Masahiro Okuno-Fujiwara. Oxford: Clarendon Press.

Aronson, Geoffrey 1987. *Creating facts: Israel, Palestinians, and the West Bank*. Washington, DC: Institute for Palestine Studies.

Asiskovitch, Sharon 2004. "The political economy of labor migration to Israel: immigration policies towards foreign workers in the 1990s." *Avoda, Hevra uMishpat (Labor, Society and Law)* 10: 79–113 (in Hebrew).

Awanohara, Susumu 1986. "Open the door some more?" *Far Eastern Economic Review*, 4 September 1986: 23–25.

Bank of Israel Research Department 1990. *Economic policy in a period of immigration*. Jerusalem: Bank of Israel (in Hebrew).

Barkai, Haim 1984. "The Israeli economy in the past decade." *Jerusalem Quarterly* 32: 3–15.

Bar-Natan, Moshe 1984. "Productivity and factors of production in the construction sector, 1960–1981." *Bank of Israel Survey* 58: 63–74.

Barnett, Michael N. ed. 1996. *Israel in comparative perspective: challenging the conventional wisdom*. Albany: State University of New York Press.

Bartram, David 1998. "Foreign workers in Israel: history and theory." *International Migration Review* 32: 303–25.

—— 2000. "Japan and labor migration: theoretical and methodological implications of negative cases." *International Migration Review* 34: 5–32.

177

Bar-Tsuri, Roni 1998. *Survey of illegal foreign workers in Israel.* Jerusalem: Ministry of Labor (in Hebrew).

Beaujot, R., K.G. Basavarajappa, and R.B.P. Verma 1981. *Current demographic analysis: income of immigrants to Canada: a census data analysis.* Ottawa: Statistics Canada.

Beck, Roy 1996. *The case against immigration: the moral, economic, social and environmental reasons for reducing U.S. immigration back to traditional levels.* New York: Norton.

Beham, Miriam and Ephraim Kleiman 1968. "The price of recession." *Banking Quarterly* 29: 31–42.

Bendix, John 1990. *Importing foreign workers: a comparison of German and American policy.* New York: Peter Lang.

Bennett, John 1993. "Japan's building industry: the new model." *Construction Management and Economics* 11: 3–17.

Bennett, John, Roger Flanagan, and George Norman 1987. *Capital & Counties Report: Japanese Construction Industry.* Reading: Centre for Strategic Studies in Construction (University of Reading).

Ben-Porath, Yoram 1982. "The revolution that wasn't: ideology and economic policies, 1977–1981." *Economic Quarterly* 115: 325–33 (in Hebrew).

Berger, Suzanne, and Ronald Dore, eds. 1996. *National diversity and global capitalism.* Ithaca: Cornell University Press.

Berger, Thomas U. 1998. "The perils and promise of pluralism: lessons from the German case for Japan," in *Temporary workers or foreign citizens? Japanese and U.S. migration policies,* edited by Myron Weiner and Tadashi Hanami. New York: New York University Press.

Bichler, Shimshon 1986. "The political economy of national security in Israel: some aspects of the activities of dominant capital groups." MA Thesis, Department of Political Science, Hebrew University of Jerusalem (in Hebrew).

Bilski, Raphaela *et al.* 1980. "National versus sub-national planning in Israel," in *Can planning replace politics? The Israeli experience,* edited by Raphaela Bilski *et al.* The Hague: Martinus Nijhoff Publishers.

Böhning, W.R. 1984. *Studies in international labor migration.* London: Macmillan.
—— 1991. "Integration and immigration pressures in Western Europe." *International Labour Review* 130: 445–9.

Boltho, Andrea 1975. *Japan: an economic survey, 1953–1973.* London: Oxford University Press.

Borowski, Allan, and Uri Yanai 1997. "Temporary and illegal labor migration: the Israeli experience." *International Migration* 35: 495–509.

Bourguignon, Francois, Bernard Fernet, and Georges Gallais-Hamonno 1977. *International labour migrations and economic choices: the European case.* Paris: Development Centre of the Organisation for Economic Co-operation and Development.

Briggs, Vernon J., Jr. 1996. *Mass immigration and the national interest.* Armonk, NY: M.E. Sharpe.

Brubaker, Rogers 1989. *Immigration and the politics of citizenship in Europe and North America.* Lanham, MD: University Press of America; German Marshall Fund of the United States.

Brubaker, Rogers 1992. *Citizenship and nationhood in France and Germany.* Cambridge, MA: Harvard University Press.

—— 1994. "Are immigration control efforts really failing?" in *Controlling immigration: a global approach*, edited by Wayne A. Cornelius, Philip L. Martin, and James F. Hollifield. Stanford: Stanford University Press.

—— 1995. "Comments on 'Modes of Immigration Politics in Liberal Democratic States'. " *International Migration Review* 29: 903–8.

Bruno, Michael 1993. *Crisis, stabilization, and economic reform: therapy by consensus.* Oxford: Oxford University Press.

Calavita, Kitty 1984. *U.S. immigration law and the control of labor, 1820–1924.* London; Orlando: Academic Press.

—— 1994. "Italy and the new immigration," in *Controlling immigration: a global perspective*, edited by Wayne A. Cornelius, Philip L. Martin, and James F. Hollifield. Cambridge: Cambridge University Press.

Calder, Kent E. 1988. *Crisis and compensation: public policy and political stability in Japan, 1949–1986.* Princeton, NJ: Princeton University Press.

Carens, Joseph H. 1988. "Immigration and the welfare state," in *Democracy and the welfare state*, edited by Amy Gutmann. Princeton: Princeton University Press.

Castles, Stephen 1986. "The guest-worker in Europe: an obituary." *International Migration Review* 20: 761–78.

—— 1992. "Migrants and minorities in post-Keynesian capitalism: the German case," in *Ethnic minorities and industrial change in Europe and North America*, edited by Malcolm Cross. Cambridge: Cambridge University Press.

—— Heather Booth, and Tina Wallace 1984. *Here for good: Western Europe's new ethnic minorities.* London: Pluto Press.

—— and Godula Kosack 1985. *Immigrant workers and class structure in Western Europe.* Oxford: Oxford University Press.

—— and Mark J. Miller 1993. *The age of migration: international population movements in the modern world.* London: Macmillan Press.

Central Bureau of Statistics 1994. *Statistical Abstract of Israel.* Jerusalem: Central Bureau of Statistics.

—— 2000. *Statistical Abstract of Israel.* Jerusalem: Central Bureau of Statistics.

Chamish, Barry 1992. *The fall of Israel.* Edinburgh: Canongate Publishers.

Cohen, Erik 1999. "Foreign Workers from Thailand in Israeli agriculture," in *The new laborers: workers from foreign countries in Israel*, edited by Leah Ahdut and Roby Natanson. Tel Aviv: HaKibbutz HaMeuhad (in Hebrew).

Cohen, Joshua, and Joel Rogers 1983. *On democracy: toward a transformation of American society.* New York: Penguin Books.

Cohen, Mitchell 1992. *Zion and state: nation, class, and the shaping of modern Israel.* New York: Columbia University Press.

Cohen, Robin 1987. *The new helots: migrants in the international division of labour.* Brookfield, VT: Gower Pub. Co.

Coleman, David A. 1997. "Europe under migration pressure: some facts on immigration," in *Immigration into Western societies: problems and policies*, edited by Emek M. Uçarer and Donald J. Puchala. London: Pinter.

Condor, Yaakov 1997. *Foreign workers in Israel.* Jerusalem: National Insurance Institute (in Hebrew).

Cook, Alice Hanson 1978. *The working mother: a survey of problems and programs in nine countries*. Ithaca: New York State School of Industrial and Labor Relations, Cornell University.

Cornelius, Wayne 1994. "Japan: the illusion of immigration control," in *Controlling immigration: a global perspective*, edited by Wayne A. Cornelius, Philip L. Martin, and James F. Hollifield. Cambridge: Cambridge University Press.

——, Philip L. Martin, and James F. Hollifield, eds. 1994. *Controlling immigration: a global perspective*. Cambridge: Cambridge University Press.

Crouch, Colin, and Wolfgang Streeck 1997. "Introduction: the future of capitalist diversity," in *The political economy of modern capitalism: mapping convergence and diversity*, edited by Colin Crouch and Wolfgang Streeck. London: Sage Publications.

Descloitres, R. 1967. *The foreign worker: adaptation to industrial work and urban life*. Paris: OECD.

Díaz-Briquets, Sergio, and Sidney Weintraub 1991. *The effects of receiving country policies on migration flows*. Boulder: Westview Press.

Dollar, David, and Edward N. Wolff 1993. *Competitiveness, convergence, and international specialization*. Cambridge: MIT Press.

Dore, Ronald P. 1986. *Flexible rigidities: industrial policy and structural adjustment in the Japanese economy, 1970–80*. Stanford, CA: Stanford University Press.

—— 1990. "An outsider's view," in *Japan's economic structure: should it change?*, edited by Kozo Yamamura. Seattle: Society for Japanese Studies.

Doron, Abraham 1988. "The Histadrut, social policy, and equality." *Jerusalem Quarterly* 47: 131–44.

Drori, I. and G. Kunda 1999. "The work cycle of foreign workers in Israel," Discussion paper #100, Golda Meir Institute for Social and Labor Studies, Tel Aviv University.

Emigh, Rebecca Jean 1997. "The power of negative thinking: the use of negative case methodology in the development of sociological theory." *Theory and Society* 26: 649–84.

Evans, Peter B. 1995. *Embedded autonomy: states and industrial transformation*. Princeton, NJ: Princeton University Press.

—— and John D. Stephens. 1988. "Studying development since the sixties: the emergence of a new comparative political economy." *Theory and Society* 17: 713–45.

Evans, Robert, Jr. 1971. *The labor economies of Japan and the United States*. New York: Praeger Publishers.

Fischer, Peter A., Reiner Martin, and Thomas Straubhaar 1997. "Interdependencies between development and migration," in *International migration, immobility, and development: multidisciplinary perspectives*, edited by Tomas Hammar, Grete Brochmann, Kristof Tamas, and Thomas Faist. New York: Berg.

Fischer, Peter A., and Thomas Straubhaar 1996. *Migration and economic integration in the Nordic Common Labor Market*. Copenhagen: Nordic Council of Ministers.

Fitzgerald, Keith 1996. *The face of the nation: immigration, the state, and the national identity*. Stanford, CA: Stanford University Press.

Foote, Daniel H. 1993. "Japan's 'foreign workers' policy: a view from the US." *Georgetown Immigration Law Journal* 7: 707–46.

Freeman, Gary P. 1979. *Immigrant labor and racial conflict in industrialized societies: the French and British experience, 1945–1975*. Princeton: Princeton University Press.

—— 1994. "Can liberal states control unwanted migration?" *Annals of the American Academy of Political and Social Science* 534: 17–30.

—— 1995. "Modes of immigration politics in liberal democratic states." *International Migration Review* 29: 881–902.

Friedman, David 1988. *The misunderstood miracle: industrial development and political change in Japan*. Ithaca: Cornell University Press.

Frisch, Max 1967. *Öffentlichkeit als Partner*. Frankfurt am Main: Suhrkamp.

Galenson, Walter, and K. Odaka 1976. "The Japanese labor market," in *Asia's new giant: how the Japanese economy works*, edited by Hugh T. Patrick and Henry Rosovsky. Washington: Brookings Institution.

Gann, David 1996. "Construction as a manufacturing process? Similarities and differences between industrialised housing and car production in Japan." *Construction Management and Economics* 14: 437–50.

Garcia y Griego, Manuel 1992. "Policymaking at the apex: international migration, state autonomy, and societal constraints," in *U.S.-Mexico relations: labor market interdependence*, edited by Jorge A. Bustamante, Winton Reynolds, and Raul Andres Hinojosa Ojeda. Stanford, CA: Stanford University Press.

Gerlach, Michael L. 1992. *Alliance capitalism: the social organization of Japanese business*. Berkeley: University of California Press.

Gerschenkron, Alexander 1962. *Economic backwardness in historical perspective, a book of essays*. Cambridge: Belknap Press of Harvard University Press.

Gharaybah, Fawzi 1985. *The economies of the West Bank and Gaza Strip*. Boulder, CO: Westview Press.

Ginzberg, Eli 1964. *Manpower surveys: fourth report on manpower in Israel*. Jerusalem: Labor Ministry, Manpower Planning Authority (in Hebrew).

Glytsos, Nicholas 1995. "Problems and policies regarding the socio-economic integration of returnees and foreign workers in Greece." *International Migration Review* 33: 155–76.

Gottlieb, Daniel 2002. "Effects of non-Israeli workers on employment, wages, and inequality: 1995–2000." *Economic Quarterly (Riv'on leKalkalah)* 49: 694–736 (in Hebrew).

Greenwald, Carol Schwartz 1973. *Recession as a policy instrument: Israel 1965–1969*. Rutherford: Fairleigh Dickinson University Press.

Grinberg, Lev Luis 1991. *Split corporatism in Israel*. Albany: State University of New York Press.

—— 1993a. *The Histadrut above all*. Jerusalem: Navo (in Hebrew).

—— 1993b. "The crisis of statehood: a weak state and strong political institutions in Israel." *Journal of Theoretical Politics* 5: 89–107.

Halevi, Nadav, and Ruth Klinov-Malul 1968. *The economic development of Israel*. New York: Frederick A. Praeger Publishers.

Haley, John O. 1990. "Weak law, strong competition, and trade barriers: competitiveness as a disincentive to foreign entry into Japanese markets," in *Japan's economic structure: should it change?*, edited by Kozo Yamamura. Seattle: Society for Japanese Studies.

Hall, Peter A. 1986. *Governing the economy: the politics of state intervention in Britain and France*. New York: Oxford University Press.

Hammar, Tomas 1985. *European immigration policy: a comparative study*. Cambridge: Cambridge University Press.

—— 1990. *Democracy and the nation state: aliens, denizens, and citizens in a world of international migration*. Aldershot: Avebury.

Hammar, Tomas, Grete Brochmann, Kristof Tamas, and Thomas Faist, eds. 1997. *International migration, immobility, and development: multidisciplinary perspectives.* New York: Berg.

Hansen, Bent 1993. "Immigration policies in Fortress Europe," in *Labor and an integrated Europe*, edited by Lloyd Ulman, Barry Eichengreen, and William Dickens. Washington, DC: Brookings Institution.

Harris, Nigel 1995. *The new untouchables: immigration and the new world worker.* London; New York: I.B. Tauris.

Hasegawa, Fumio 1988. *Built by Japan: Competitive Strategies of the Japanese construction industry.* New York: John Wiley and Sons.

Hart, Jeffrey A. 1992. *Rival capitalists: international competitiveness in the United States, Japan, and Western Europe.* Ithaca: Cornell University Press.

Hawley, Ellis W. 1979. "The politics of the Mexican labor issue, 1950–1965," in *Mexican workers in the United States: historical and political perspectives*, edited by George C. Kiser and Martha Woody Kiser. Albuquerque: University of New Mexico Press.

Head, Simon 2003. *The new ruthless economy: work and power in the digital age.* Oxford: Oxford University Press.

Herbert, Gilbert 1979. *The 'Palestine' prefabs of the 1930s.* Haifa: Center for Urban and Regional Studies, the Technion.

Herbert, Ulrich 1990. *A history of foreign labor in Germany, 1880–1980: seasonal workers, forced laborers, guest workers*, translated by William Templer. Ann Arbor: University of Michigan Press.

Hermele, Kenneth 1997. "The discourse on migration and development," in *International migration, immobility, and development: multidisciplinary perspectives*, edited by Tomas Hammar, Grete Brochmann, Kristof Tamas, and Thomas Faist. New York: Berg.

Hicks, George 1997. *Japan's hidden apartheid: The Korean minority and the Japanese.* Aldershot: Ashgate.

Hoffman-Nowotny, Hans-Joachim 1985. "Switzerland," in *European immigration policy: a comparative study*, edited by Tomas Hammar. Cambridge: Cambridge University Press.

Hollerman, Leon 1988. *Japan, disincorporated: the economic liberalization process.* Stanford: Hoover Institution Press.

Hollifield, James F. 1986. "Immigration policy in France and Germany: outputs versus outcomes." *Annals of the American Academy of Political and Social Science* 485.

—— 1992. *Immigrants, markets, and states: the political economy of postwar Europe.* Cambridge, MA: Harvard University Press.

—— 2000. "The politics of international migration: how can we 'bring the state back in?'," in *Migration theory: talking across disciplines*, edited by Caroline Brettell and James F. Hollifield. New York: Routledge.

Hollingsworth, J. Rogers, Philippe C. Schmitter, and Wolfgang Streeck 1994. *Governing capitalist economies: performance and control of economic sectors.* Oxford: Oxford University Press.

Hönekopp, Elmar 1997. "The new labor migration as an instrument of German foreign policy," in *Migrants, refugees, and foreign policy: U.S. and German policies towards countries of origin*, edited by Rainer Muenz and Myron Weiner. Providence: Berghahn Books.

Hopkinson, Nicholas 1992. *Migration into Western Europe*. London: HMSO.

Horioka, Charles Yuji 1998. "Do the Japanese live better than the Americans?" in *Japan: why it works, why it doesn't – economics in everyday life*, edited by James Mak, Shyam Sunder, Shigeyuki Abe, and Kazuhiro Igawa. Honolulu: University of Hawai'i Press.

Huber, Thomas M. 1994. *Strategic economy in Japan*. Boulder: Westview Press.

Huyssen, Andreas 1995. *Twighlight memories: marking time in a culture of amnesia*. New York: Routledge.

Iguchi, Yasushi 1998. "What we can learn from the German experiences with foreign labor," in *Temporary workers or foreign citizens? Japanese and U.S. migration policies*, edited by Myron Weiner and Tadashi Hanami. New York: New York University Press.

Imano, Koichiro 1997. "Internationalisation of the labour market: foreign workers and trainees," in *Japanese labour and management in transition*, edited by Mari Sako and Hiroki Sato. New York: Routledge.

Immigration Bureau, Japan 1990. *Japan and the development of international migration (Wagakuni wo meguru kokusai jinryu no hensen)*. Tokyo: Immigration Bureau, Study Group on Immigration Statistics.

International Labour Office 1989. "Report on the situation of workers of the occupied Arab territories," in *Report of the Director-General, Appendices*. Geneva: ILO.

Johnson, Chalmers A. 1982. *MITI and the Japanese miracle: the growth of industrial policy, 1925–1975*. Stanford, CA: Stanford University Press.

—— 1995. *Japan: who governs? the rise of the developmentalist state*. New York: Norton.

——, Laura D. Andrea Tyson, and John Zysman 1989. *Politics and productivity: the real story of why Japan works*. Cambridge, MA: Ballinger.

Joppke, Christian 1999. *Immigration and the nation-state; the United States, Germany, and Great Britain*. Oxford: Oxford University Press.

Kadri, Ali 1998. "A survey of commuting labor from the West Bank to Israel." *Middle East Journal* 52: 517–30.

—— and Malcolm Macmillen 1998. "The political economy of Israel's demand for Palestinian labour." *Third World Quarterly* 19: 297–311.

Kamerman, Sheila B. 1979. "Work and family in industrialized societies." *Signs* 4: 632–50.

Kanovsky, Eliyahu 1970. *The economic impact of the six-day war: Israel, the occupied territories, Egypt, Jordan*. New York: Praeger.

Katz, Richard 1998. *Japan, the system that soured: the rise and fall of the Japanese economic miracle*. Armonk NY: M.E. Sharpe.

Katzenstein, Peter J. 1978. *Between power and plenty: foreign economic policies of advanced industrial states*. Madison: University of Wisconsin Press.

—— 1985. *Small states in world markets: industrial policy in Europe*. Ithaca, NY: Cornell University Press.

Kawai, Masahiro, and Shujiro Urata 1998. "Foreign direct investment in Japan: empirical analyses of interactions between foreign direct investment flows and trade," in *Japanese economic policy reconsidered*, edited by Craig Friedman. Cheltenham: Edward Elgar Limited.

Kemp, Adriana, Rebecca Raijman, Julia Resnik, Silvina Schammah Gesser 2000. "Contesting the limits of political participation: Latinos and Black African migrant workers in Israel." *Ethnic and Racial Studies* 23: 94–119.

Kimmerling, Baruch 1983. *Zionism and economy*. Cambridge, MA: Schenkman Publishing.

—— 1989. *The Israeli state and society: boundaries and frontiers*. Albany, NY: State University of New York Press.

—— 1995. "Academic history caught in the cross-fire: the case of Israeli-Jewish historiography." *History and Memory* 7: 41–65.

Kindleberger, Charles P. 1967. *Europe's postwar growth; the role of labor supply*. Cambridge, MA: Harvard University Press.

Kleiman, Ephraim 1987. "The Histadrut economy of Israel: in search of criteria." *Jerusalem Quarterly* 41: 77–94.

—— 1996. *Does Israel need foreign workers?* Jerusalem: Falk Institute, Hebrew University of Jerusalem (in Hebrew).

—— 1997. "The waning of Israeli etatism." *Israel Studies* 2: 146–71.

Knoke, David 1996. *Comparing policy networks: labor politics in U.S., Germany, and Japan*. Cambridge: Cambridge University Press.

Kojima, K. 1983. "Japanese direct foreign investment in Asian developing countries," in *Japan's economy in a comparative perspective*, edited by Gianni Fodella. Tenterden, Kent: Paul Norbury Publications Ltd.

Komai, Hiroshi 1995. *Migrant workers in Japan*. London, New York: K. Paul.

Koshiro, Kazutoshi 1998. "Does Japan need immigrants?" in *Temporary workers or future citizens? Japanese and U.S. migration policies*, edited by Myron Weiner and Tadashi Hanami. New York: New York University Press.

Krauss, Ellis S., and Isobel Coles 1990. "Built-in impediments: the political economy of the U.S.-Japan construction dispute," in *Japan's economic structure: should it change?*, edited by Kozo Yamamura. Seattle: Society for Japanese Studies.

Kume, Ikuo 1998. *Disparaged success: labor politics in postwar Japan*. Ithaca: Cornell University Press.

Kuptsch, Christine, and Nana Oishi 1995. *German and Japanese schemes for workers from transition economies or developing countries*. Geneva: International Labour Office.

Lazin, Frederick A. 1994. *Politics and policy implementation: Project Renewal in Israel*. Albany: State University of New York Press.

Lee, Everett 1966. "A theory of migration." *Demography* 3: 47–57.

Levi-Faur, David 1998. "The developmental state: Israel, South Korea, and Taiwan compared." *Studies in Comparative International Development* 33: 65–93.

Lie, John 1997. "The 'problem' of foreign workers in contemporary Japan," in *The other Japan: conflict, compromise, and resistance since 1945*, edited by Joe Moore. London: M.E. Sharpe.

Lieberson, Stanley 1992. "Small Ns and big conclusions: an examination of the reasoning in comparative studies based on a small number of cases," in *What is a case? exploring the foundations of social inquiry*, edited by Charles C. Ragin and Howard S. Becker. Cambridge: Cambridge University Press.

Lim, Lin Lean 1992. "International labour movements: a perspective on economic exchanges and flows," in *International migration systems: a global approach*, edited by Mary M. Kritz, Lin Lean Lim, and Hania Zlotnik. Oxford: Clarendon Press.

Lustick, Ian 1980. *Arabs in the Jewish state: Israel's control of a national minority*. Austin: University of Texas Press.

McCormack, Gavan 1996. *The emptiness of Japanese affluence*. Armonk, NY: M.E. Sharpe.

Mahmood, Raisul Awal 1996. "Labor crunch, foreign workers, and policy responses: the experience of Japan." *International Migration* 34: 97–116.

Makhoul, Najwa 1982. "Changes in the employment structure of Arabs in Israel." *Journal of Palestine Studies* 11: 77–102.

Maman, Daniel 1997. "The power lies in the structure: economic policy forum networks in Israel." *British Journal of Sociology* 48: 267–85.

Maor, Anat 1981. "Aspects of the foreign labor process in western industrialized countries." MA Thesis, Dept. of Labor Studies, Tel Aviv University, Tel Aviv (in Hebrew).

March, James G., and Johan P. Olsen 1984. "The new institutionalism: organizational factors in political life." *American Political Science Review* 78: 734–49.

Martin, Philip L. 1991a. "Labor migration in Asia: a conference report." *International Migration Review* 25: 176–93.

—— 1991b. "Labor migration: theory and reality," in *The unsettled relationship: labor migration and economic development,* edited by Demetrios Papademetriou and Philip L. Martin. New York: Greenwood Press.

—— 1994. "Good intentions gone awry: IRCA and U.S. agriculture." *Annals of the American Academy of Political and Social Scientists* 534: 44–57.

—— 1997. "Guestworker policies for the twenty-first century." *New Community* 23: 483–94.

—— and Mark J. Miller 1980. "Guestworkers: lessons from Western Europe." *Industrial and Labor Relations Review* 33: 315–30.

—— and Edward Taylor 2001. "Managing migration: the role of economic policies," in *Global migrants, global refugees: problems and solutions,* edited by A. R. Zolberg and P. Benda. New York: Berghahn Books.

Massey, Douglas S. 1999. "International migration at the dawn of the twenty-first century: the role of the state." *Population and Development Review,* 25: 303–22.

—— Refael Alarcón, Jorge Durand, and Humberto González 1987. *Return to Aztlan: the social process of international migration from western Mexico.* Berkeley: University of California Press.

—— et al. 1998. *Worlds in motion: understanding international migration at the end of the millenium.* Oxford: Clarendon Press.

Mathieu, Renee 1987. "The prefabricated housing industries in the United States, Sweden, and Japan." *Construction Review* 33: 2–21.

Meissner, Doris, Roberto D. Hormats, Antonio Garrigues Walker, and Shijuro Ogata 1993. *International migration challenges in a new era: policy perspectives and priorities for Europe, Japan, North America, and the international community.* New York: The Trilateral Commission.

Meyers, Eytan 2004. *International immigration policies: a theoretical and comparative analysis.* New York: Palgrave Macmillan.

Miles, Robert 1987. *Capitalism and unfree labour: anomaly or necessity?* London: Tavistock Publications.

—— and Victor Satzewich 1990. "Migration, racism, and 'postmodern' capitalism." *Economy and Society* 19: 334–58.

Miller, Mark J. 1981. *Foreign workers in Western Europe: an emerging political force.* New York: Praeger

—— 1994. "Towards understanding state capacity to prevent unwanted migration: employer sanctions enforcement in France, 1975–1990," in *The politics of immigration in Western Europe*, edited by Martin Baldwin-Edwards and Martin A. Shain. Ilford: Frank Cass.

Miller, Mark J. 1997. "International migration and security: towards transatlantic convergence?" in *Immigration into western societies: problems and policies*, edited by Emek M. Uçarer and Donald J. Puchala. London: Pinter.

Minami, Ryoshin 1973. *The turning point in economic development; Japan's experience*. Tokyo: Kinokuniya Bookstore Co.

Ministry of Housing and Construction, Israel 1996. *Construction in Israel*. Jerusalem: Ministry of Housing and Construction (in Hebrew).

—— 1998. *The production function of the construction sector and the industrialization of construction*. Jerusalem: Ministry of Housing and Construction (in Hebrew).

Ministry of Labour, Japan 1993. "Foreign workers and the labour market in Japan." *International Migration* 31: 442–57.

Mintz, Alex 1983. "The military-industrial complex: the Israeli case." *Journal of Strategic Studies* 6: 103–27.

Miyazaki, Isamu 1970. "Economic planning in post-war Japan." *The Developing Economies* 8: 369–85.

Moon, Chung-in, and Rashemi Prasad 1998. "Networks, politics, and institutions." in *Beyond the developmental state: East Asia's political economies reconsidered*, edited by Steve Chan, Cal Clark, and Danny Lam. New York: St Martin's Press.

Moore, Barrington 1966. *Social origins of dictatorship and democracy; lord and peasant in the making of the modern world*. Boston: Beacon Press.

Mori, Hiromi 1997. *Immigration policy and foreign workers in Japan*. New York: St. Martin's Press.

Murumatsu, M., and E. S. Krauss 1987. "The conservative policy line and the development of patterned pluralism." in *The political economy of Japan, vol. 1: the domestic transformation*, edited by Kozo Yamamura and Yasukichi Yasuba. Stanford, CA: Stanford University Press.

Nachmias, David, and David H. Rosenblum 1978. *Bureaucratic culture: citizens and administrators in Israel*. New York: St. Martin's Press.

Nachmias, David, and Gila Menahem, eds. 2002. *Public policy in Israel*. London: Frank Cass.

Nagayama, Toshikazu 1992. "Clandestine migrant workers in Japan." *Asian and Pacific Migration Journal* 1: 623–36.

—— 1996. "Foreign workers recruiting policies in Japan." *Asian and Pacific Migration Journal* 5: 241–64.

Nakamura, Tadashi 1992. "Labor market and manpower policy 1945–1985." in *Employment security and labor market flexibility: an international perspective*, edited by Kazutoshi Koshiro. Detroit: Wayne State University Press.

Neuman, Shoshana 1994. "Ethnic occupational segregation in Israel." *Research on Economic Inequality* 5: 125–51.

Ng, C.Y., R. Hirono, and Narongchai Akrasanee 1987. *Industrial restructuring and adjustment for ASEAN-Japan investment and trade expansion*. Singapore: The ASEAN Secretariat and Japan Institute of International Affairs.

Nimura, Kazuo 1992. "The trade union response to migrant workers." in *The internationalization of Japan*, edited by Glenn D. Hook and Michael A. Weiner. New York: Routledge.

Nitzan, Jonathan, and Shimshon Bichler 1996. "From war profits to peace dividends: the new political economy of Israel." *Capital and Class* 60: 61–94.

Noland, Marcus 1995. "Why are prices in Japan so high?" *Japan and the World Economy* 7: 255–61.

Ochiai, Eishu 1974. *Ajiajin rodoryoko yunyu (The importation of Asian labor power)*. Tokyo: Gendai Hyoronsha.

OECD 1995. *SOPEMI: Continuous reporting system on migration.* Paris: OECD.

—— 2000. *SOPEMI: Trends in international migration.* Paris: OECD.

—— 2002. *Labor force statistics.* Paris: OECD.

—— 2002. *Economic outlook.* Paris: OECD.

Ofer, G., K. Flug, and N. Kassir 1991. "The absorption in employment of the immigrants from the Soviet Union: 1990 and beyond." *Economic Quarterly* 148: 135–79 (in Hebrew).

Oka, Takashi 1994. *Prying open the door: foreign workers in Japan.* Washington, DC: Carnegie Endowment for International Peace.

Okimoto, Daniel I. 1989. *Between MITI and the market: Japanese industrial policy for high technology.* Stanford: Stanford University Press.

Okunishi, Yoshio 1996. "Labor contracting in international migration: the Japanese case and implications for Asia." *Asian and Pacific Migration Journal* 5: 219–40.

Öncü, Ayse 1990. "International labour migration and class relations." *Current Sociology* 38: 175–201.

Pack, Howard 1971. *Structural change and economic policy in Israel.* New Haven: Yale University Press.

Papademetriou, Demetrios, and Kimberly Hamilton 2000. *Reinventing Japan: Immigration's role in shaping Japan's future.* Washington, DC: Carnegie Endowment for International Peace.

Papademetriou, Demetrios, and Philip L. Martin, eds. 1991. *The unsettled relationship: labor migration and economic development.* New York: Greenwood Press.

Pempel, T. J. 1978. "Japanese foreign economic policy: the domestic bases for international behavior," in *Between power and plenty: foreign economic policies of advanced industrial states*, edited by Peter J. Katzenstein. Madison: University of Wisconsin Press.

—— 1982. *Politics and polity in Japan: creative conservatism.* Philadelphia: Temple University Press.

——, ed. 1990. *Uncommon democracies: the one-party dominant regimes.* Ithaca: Cornell University Press.

—— 1998. *Regime shift: comparative dynamics of the Japanese political economy.* Ithaca: Cornell University Press.

—— and Keiichi Tsunekawa. 1979. "Corporatism without labor?" in *Trends towards corporatist intermediation*, edited by Philippe C. Schmitter and Gerhard Lembruch. London: Sage.

Pessar, Patricia R. 1988. *When borders don't divide: labor migration and refugee movements in the Americas.* New York: Center for Migration Studies.

Petit, Pascal 1986. *Slow growth and the service economy.* New York: St. Martin's Press.

Pilovsky, Leah 1999. " 'Present absentees': the functioning of manpower organizations in dealing with foreign workers in Israel, and their connections with government institutions," in *The new laborers: workers from foreign countries in Israel*, edited by Roby Natanson and Leah Achdut. Tel Aviv: HaKibbutz HaMeuchad (in Hebrew).

188   *References*

Piore, Michael J. 1979. *Birds of passage: migrant labor and industrial societies.* Cambridge: Cambridge University Press.

Plessner, Yakir 1994. *The political economy of Israel: from ideology to stagnation.* Albany: State University of New York Press.

Portes, Alejandro 1982. "International migration and national development," in *U.S. immigration and refugee policy: global and domestic issues*, edited by Mary M. Kritz. Lexington, MA: Lexington Books.

—— 1997. "Immigration theory for a new century: some problems and opportunities." *International Migration Review* 31: 799–825.

—— and Reuven Rumbaut 1996. *Immigrant America: a portrait.* Berkeley: University of California Press.

Portugali, Juval 1989. "Nomad labor: theory and practice in the Israeli-Palestinian case." *Transactions Institute of British Geography* 14: 207–20.

Przeworski, Adam 1985. *Capitalism and social democracy.* Cambridge: Cambridge University Press.

Ragin, Charles C. 1987. *The comparative method: moving beyond qualitiative and quantitative strategies.* Berkeley: University of California Press.

—— 2000. *Fuzzy-set social science.* Chicago: University of Chicago Press.

Raijman, Rebecca, Silvina Schammah-Gesser, and Adriana Kemp 2003. "International migration, domestic work, and care work: undocumented Latina migrants in Israel." *Gender & Society* 17: 727–49.

Ramseyer, J. Mark, and Frances McCall Rosenbluth 1993. *Japan's political marketplace.* Cambridge, MA: Harvard University Press.

Reubens, Edwin P. 1981. "Low-level work in Japan without foreign workers." *International Migration Review* 15: 749–57.

Richardson, Bradley M. 1997. *Japanese democracy: power, coordination, and performance.* New Haven, CT: Yale University Press.

Rist, Ray C. 1978. *Guestworkers in Germany: prospects for pluralism.* New York: Praeger Publishers.

Rivlin, Paul 1992. *The Israeli economy.* Boulder: Westview Press.

Rogers, Rosemary 1985. *Guests come to stay: the effects of European labor migration on sending and recieving countries.* Boulder: Westview Press.

Roniger, Luis 1994. "Images of clientelism and realities of patronage in Israel," in *Democracy, clientelism, and civil society*, edited by Luis Roniger and Ayse Günes-Ayata. Boulder: Lynne Rienner Publishers.

Rosenhek, Zeev 1998. "Migration regimes, intra-state conflicts and the politics of exclusion and inclusion: migrant workers in the Israeli welfare state", paper presented at the Third International Metropolis Conference, Zichron Yaacov, Israel, November/December.

—— 2000. "Migration regimes, intra-state conflicts and the politics of exclusion and inclusion: migrant workers in the Israeli welfare state." *Social Problems* 47: 49–67.

—— 2003. "The political dynamics of a segmented labour market – Palestinian citizens, Palestinians from the occupied territories and migrant workers in Israel." *Acta Sociologica* 46: 231–49.

Samuels, Richard J. 1987. *The business of the Japanese state: energy markets in comparative and historical perspective.* Ithaca: Cornell University Press.

Sassen, Saskia 1988. *The mobility of labor and capital: a study in international investment and labor flow.* Cambridge: Cambridge University Press.

—— 1991. *The global city: New York, London, Tokyo.* Princeton, NJ: Princeton University Press.

Sassen, Saskia 1993. "Economic internationalization: the new migration in Japan and the United States." *International Migration* 31: 73–99.

Sayer, Andrew, and Richard Walker 1992. *The new social economy: reworking the division of labor.* Cambridge: Blackwell Publishers.

Schain, Martin A. 1990. "Immigration and politics," in *Developments in French politics*, edited by Peter A. Hall, Jack Ernest Shalom Hayward, and Howard Machin. New York, NY: St Martin's Press.

Schecter, Steven B. 1972. "Israeli political and economic elites and some aspects of their relations." PhD Thesis, London School of Economics.

Schlesinger, Jacob M. 1997. *Shadow Shoguns: the rise and fall of Japan's post-war political machine.* New York: Simon & Schuster.

Schwartz, Moshe 1995. *Unlimited guarantees: history, political economy, and the crisis of cooperative agriculture in Israel.* Beer Sheva: Ben Gurion University of the Negev Press (in Hebrew).

Sekiguchi, Sueo 1991. "Japan: a plethora of programs," in *Pacific basin industries in distress: structural adjustment and trade policy in nine industrialized economies*, edited by Hugh Patrick. New York: Columbia University Press.

——, Munemichi Inoue, and Tadahisa Ooka 1979. *Japanese direct foreign investment.* Montclair, NJ: Allanheld Osmun.

Sellek, Yoko 1994. "Illegal foreign migrant workers in Japan: change and challenge in Japanese society," in *Migration: the Asian experience*, edited by Judith M. Brown and Rosemary Foot. New York: St. Martin's Press.

—— and Michael A. Weiner 1992. "Migrant workers: the Japanese case in international perspective," in *The internationalization of Japan*, edited by Glenn D. Hook and Michael Weiner. New York: Routledge.

Semyonov, Moshe, and Noah Lewin-Epstein 1987. *Hewers of wood and drawers of water: noncitizen Arabs in the Israeli labor market.* Ithaca, NY: ILR Press.

Shafir, Gershon 1989. *Land, labor, and the origins of the Israeli-Palestinian conflict, 1882–1914.* Cambridge: Cambridge University Press.

Shalev, Michael 1984. "Labor, state and crisis: an Israeli case study." *Industrial Relations* 23: 363–86.

—— 1989. "Israel's domestic policy regime: Zionism, dualism, and the rise of capital," in *The comparative history of public policy*, edited by F. G. Castles. Oxford: Polity Press.

—— 1990. "The political economy of Labor-Party dominance and decline in Israel," in *Uncommon democracies: the one-party dominant regimes*, edited by T. J. Pempel. Ithaca: Cornell University Press.

—— 1992. *Labour and the political economy in Israel.* Oxford: Oxford University Press.

—— 1998. "Zionism and liberalization: change and continuity in Israel's political economy." *Humboldt Journal of Social Relations* 23: 219–59.

Shapiro, Yonatan. 1988. *The full employment crisis, 1957–1965: a chapter in Israeli political economy.* Tel Aviv: Tel Aviv University, Golda Meir Institute (in Hebrew).

—— 1996. *Politicians as an hegemonic class: the case of Israel.* Tel Aviv: Sifriat Poalim Publishing House (in Hebrew).

Sheridan, Kyoko 1993. *Governing the Japanese economy.* Oxford: Polity Press.

Shimada, Haruo 1991. "Structural policies in Japan," in *Parallel politics: economic policymaking in the United States and Japan*, edited by Samuel Kernell. Tokyo: Japan Center for International Exchange.

—— 1994. *Japan's "guest workers": issues and public policies.* Translated by Roger Northridge. Tokyo: University of Tokyo Press.

Shimshoni, Daniel 1982. *Israeli democracy: the middle of the journey*. New York: Free Press.

Shirom, Arie 1984. "Employers associations in Israel," in *Employers' associations and industrial relations: a comparative study*, edited by John P. Windmuller and Alan Gladstone. Oxford: Clarendon Press.

Sidwell, A.C., W.A. Van Metzinger, and Richard L. Tucker 1998. *Japan, Korean, and U.S. Contruction Industries*. Austin: The Construction Industry Institute, University of Texas.

Simon, Julian Lincoln 1989. *The economic consequences of immigration*. Oxford: Basil Blackwell.

Soysal, Yasemin Nuhoglu 1994. *Limits of citizenship: migrants and postnational membership in Europe*. Chicago: University of Chicago.

Sprinzak, Ehud 1993. "Elite illegalism in Israel and the question of democracy," in *Israeli democracy under stress*, edited by Ehud Sprinzak and Larry Diamond. Boulder, CO: Lynne Rienner Publishers.

Stahl, C. W. 1986. *International labor migration: a study of the ASEAN countries*. New York: Center for Migration Studies.

State Comptroller, Israel 1996. *Annual Report*. Jerusalem: State Comptroller's Office (in Hebrew).

—— 1997. *Annual Report*. Jerusalem: State Comptroller's Office (in Hebrew).

Steinmo, Sven, Kathleen Ann Thelen, and Frank Longstreth 1992. *Structuring politics: historical institutionalism in comparative analysis*. Cambridge; New York: Cambridge University Press.

Thomas, Robert J. 1985. *Citizenship, gender, and work: social organization of industrial agriculture*. Berkeley: University of California Press.

Tilton, Mark 1996. *Restrained trade: cartels in Japan's basic materials industries*. Ithaca: Cornell University Press.

—— 1998. "Regulatory reform and market opening in Japan," in *Is Japan really changing its ways? Regulatory reform and the Japanese economy*, edited by Lonny E. Carlile and Mark C. Tilton. Washington, DC: Brookings Institution Press.

Todaro, Michael P. 1969. "A model of labor migration and urban unemployment in less developed countries." *American Economic Review* 59: 138–48.

Utsumi, Aiko 1988. "Will the Japanese Government Open the Legal Door?" *AMPO Japan-Asia Quarterly Review* 19(4): 12–21.

Vartiainen, Juhana 1997. "Understanding state-led industrialization," in *Government and growth*, edited by Villy Bergstrom. Oxford: Clarendon Press.

Wade, Robert 1990. *Governing the market: economic theory and the role of government in East Asian industrialization*. Princeton: Princeton University Press.

Walzer, Michael 1983. *Spheres of justice: a defense of pluralism and equality*. New York: Basic Books.

Warszawski, A., R. Becker, and Y. Rosenfeld 1999. *The industrialization of construction: obstacles and ways to cope with them*. Haifa: The Technion – National Building Research Institute (in Hebrew).

Weiner, Michael A. 1997. *Japan's minorities: the illusion of homogeneity*. London: Routledge.

Weiner, Myron 1993. *International migration and security*. Boulder: Westview Press.

—— 1995. *The global migration crisis: challenge to states and to human rights*. New York: HarperCollins College Publishers.

Weiner, Myron 1996. "Ethics, sovereignty, and the control of immigration." *International Migration Review* 30: 171–97.

Weir, Margaret, Ann Shola Orloff, and Theda Skocpol 1988. *The politics of social policy in the United States.* Princeton, NJ: Princeton University Press.

Weiss, Linda 1998. *The myth of the powerless state.* Ithaca: Cornell University Press.

Woodall, Brian 1996. *Japan under construction: corruption, politics, and public works.* Berkeley: University of California Press.

Wright, Erik Olin 1996. Review of Peter Evans' *Embedded Autonomy* (1995). *Contemporary Sociology* 25: 176–79.

Yamamura, Kozo 1982. "Success that soured: administrative guidance and cartels in Japan," in *Policy and trade issues of the Japanese economy: American and Japanese perspectives,* edited by Kozo Yamamura. Seattle: University of Washington Press.

Yamanaka, Keiko 1993. "New immigration policy and unskilled foreign workers in Japan." *Pacific Affairs* 66: 72–90.

—— 1994. "Commentary," in *Controlling immigration: a global perspective,* edited by Wayne A. Cornelius, Philip L. Martin, and James F. Hollifield. Cambridge: Cambridge University Press.

Zalmanovitch, Yair 1998. "Transitions in Israel's policymaking network." *Annals of the American Academy of Political and Social Scientists* 555: 193–208.

Zolberg, Aristide 1981. "International migrations in political perspective," in *Global trends in migration: theory and research on international population movements,* edited by Mary M. Kritz, Charles B. Keely, and Silvano M. Tomasi. Staten Island, NY: Center for Migration Studies.

—— 1987. "Wanted but not welcome: alien labor in Western development," in *Population in an interacting world,* edited by William Alonso. Cambridge, MA: Harvard University Press.

—— 1992. "Labour migration and international economic regimes: Bretton Woods and after," in *International migration systems: a global approach,* edited by Mary M. Kritz, Lin Lean Lim, and Hania Zlotnik. Oxford: Clarendon Press.

—— 1993. "The next waves: Migration theory for a changing world." *International Migration Review* 23: 403–30.

—— 1999. "Matters of state: theorizing immigration policy," in *The handbook of international migration: the american experience,* edited by Charles Hirschman, Josh DeWind, and Philip Kasinitz. New York: Russell Sage Foundation.

Zussman, Noam, and Dmitri Romanov 2003. "The substitution of Israeli workers for foreign workers in the construction sector: the current situation and implications for policy." *Economic Quarterly (Riv'on leKalkalah)* 50: 723–47 (in Hebrew).

Index